STATISTICS CORNER

Questions and answers about language testing statistics

James Dean Brown

University of Hawai'i at Mānoa

Testing and Evaluation Special Interest Group
of the Japan Association for Language Teaching

JALT Testing and Evaluation Special Interest Group

Chief Editor, book design and cover art: James Sick

Proofreaders: Jeff Durand, Jeff Hubbell, Trevor Holster, Takaaki Kumazawa, J. Lake, Bill Pellowe, Edward Schaefer, Tim Stoeckel, Miki Tokunaga

The original *Statistics Corner* articles that comprise the chapters of this book were edited and formatted for the world wide web by Tim Newfields (1999-2011), Aaron Batty and Jeff Stewart (2012-2014), and Trevor Holster and Bill Pellowe (2014 to present).

The sea water image incorporated in the cover art was designed by Bedneyimages - Freepik.com. It is used here under the Freepik terms "free license with attribution."

Copyright © 2016 by JALT Testing and Evaluation Special Interest Group
Urban Edge Bldg 5F, 1-37-9 Taito, Taito-ku, Tokyo 110-0016, Japan

Email: please use the contact form at **teval.jalt.org**

ISBN-13: 978-1537312866
ISBN-10: 1537312863

All rights reserved. No part of this publication may be reproduced or transmitted without express permission of the author and publisher.

TABLE OF CONTENTS

Forward v
序文 (Japanese Preface) vii
Background to This Book xiii

Part I: Second Language Testing

Section A: Testing Strategies 1
   1. Resources Available in Language Testing 3
   2. Solutions to Problems Teachers Have with Classroom Testing 9
   3. Differences in How Norm-Referenced and Criterion-Referenced Tests Are Developed and Validated 19
   4. What Is Construct Validity? 27
   5. What is Two-Stage Testing? 33
   6. Testing Intercultural Pragmatics Ability 37
   7. Test-Taker Motivations 45
   8. Extraneous Variables and the Washback Effect 49
   9. University Entrance Examinations: Strategies for Creating Positive Washback on English Language Teaching in Japan 55

Section B: Item Analyses 61
   10. Norm-Referenced Item Analysis: Item Facility and Item Discrimination 63
   11. Criterion-Referenced Item Analysis: The Difference Index and B-Index 69
   12. Point-Biserial Correlation Coefficients 75
   13. Distractor Efficiency Analysis in a Spreadsheet 83
   14. How Can We Calculate Item Statistics for Weighted Items? 91
   15. What Issues Affect Likert Item Questionnaire Formats? 95
   16. Likert Items and Scales of Measurement 99

Section C: Reliability Issues 105
   17. The Cronbach Alpha Reliability Estimate 107
   18. Cloze Tests and Optimum Test Length 111
   19. Standard Error Versus Standard Error of Measurement 117
   20. Can We Use the Spearman-Brown Prophecy Formula to Defend Low Reliability? 125

21. Generalizability and Decision Studies 131
22. How Do We Calculate Rater/Coder Agreement and Cohen's Kappa? 139
23. Reliability of Surveys 149

Part II: Second Language Research
    Section D: Planning Research 155
24. Characteristics of Sound Qualitative Research 157
25. Characteristics of Sound Quantitative Research 161
26. Characteristics of Sound Mixed Methods Research 167
    Section E: Interpreting Research 171
27. What Do Distributions, Assumptions, Significance vs. Meaningfulness,
    Multiple Statistical Tests, Causality, and Null Results Have in Common? 173
28. Generalizability from Second Language Research Samples 181
29. Sample Size and Power 187
30. Sample Size and Statistical Precision 195
31. Skewness and Kurtosis 199
32. Effect Size and Eta Squared 205
33. Confidence Intervals, Limits, and Levels 213
34. The Bonferroni Adjustment 221
    Section F: Research Analyses 229
35. The Coefficient of Determination 231
36. Principal Components Analysis and Exploratory Factor Analysis:
    Definitions, Differences, and Choices 237
37. Choosing the Right Number of Components or Factors in PCA and EFA 245
38. Choosing the Right Type of Rotation in PCA and EFA 255
39. How Are PCA and EFA Used in Language Research? 263
40. How Are PCA and EFA Used in Language Test and Questionnaire Development? ... 269
41. Chi Square and Related Statistics for 2 X 2 Contingency Tables 277

    Cross-Reference to Original Columns 287
    References 289
    Index 317

FORWARD

The JALT Testing and Evaluation Special Interest Group (TEVAL SIG) was formed in 1995 by a group of language teachers within the Japan Association for Language Teaching (JALT) who wished to research and promote scientific approaches to language testing. Then, as now, university admission in Japan was primarily determined by a single entrance examination, usually produced in-house by faculty at the admitting institution. Entrance examinations were intended to favor the most able and hardworking students, making university admission fair and meritocratic. Nevertheless, many JALT members at the time felt that a scientific approach to designing and validating these exams was lacking. In particular, there was concern about the impact entrance exams were having on curriculum and classroom practice in the emerging paradigm of communicative language teaching. TEVAL interests were not limited to Japanese entrance exams, however. Efforts to make language teaching more focused on communication demanded appropriate classroom assessments as well. How to assess listening, speaking, writing, and pragmatic competence in ways that were valid, reliable, and practical was a new frontier. TEVAL members hoped that through research and disseminating information, they could contribute to improving language testing and assessment throughout the profession.

One of the first TEVAL projects was to launch a regular newsletter called *Shiken: JALT Testing & Evaluation SIG Newsletter.* Early issues of *Shiken,* which first appeared in 1997, were photocopied and folded by hand, stuffed in envelopes, and mailed to TEVAL members by editor Paul Jaquith. Tim Newfields took over as editor in 1999 and served in that role until 2011. An early web pioneer, Tim also set up a TEVAL website and began to archive all *Shiken* articles so that they could be found by search engines and easily retrieved by interested readers around the world. This greatly increased the reach and impact of *Shiken* and helped to attract a wide range of quality submissions. When Tim decided to take a well-deserved break after serving as TEVAL publications chair for 12 years, the tradition of web access was carried on by the new editors, Aaron Batty and Jeff Stewart, followed by Trevor Holster and Bill Pellowe.

From its inception, the focus of *Shiken* was educational and practical. Articles helped clarify theoretical concepts underlying language assessment, reviewed books and other resources related to language testing, introduced readers to tools for designing and administering tests, and provided practical tips for implementing sound assessment in the classroom. For the launch, Professor JD Brown volunteered to contribute a regular column which would answer questions about testing and statistics in an informal and easy to understand format. Statistics Corner, based on questions submitted by readers in no particular order, thus became a regular feature of *Shiken*. In total, more than 40 Statistics Corner columns have appeared in *Shiken* since the first issue in 1997.

In 2015, TEVAL officers began discussing the possibility of organizing past Statistics Corner columns and publishing them in book format. Because the original columns had been responses to questions posed by readers, they did not appear in any coherent order. We believed arranging them thematically might enhance their readability and effectiveness. The original impetus was to create a single, convenient resource that would help bring new TEVAL members up to speed. However, we also believed that such a volume might attract interest beyond our SIG. We were aware that the columns, which are easily accessible on the web, were frequently cited. Nevertheless, it came as a surprise when a quick search in Google Scholar found more than 300 citations of Statistics Corner columns in published academic papers. It was even more of a surprise to find that citations were not limited to the field of language testing. Perhaps because of their straightforward explanations and easy accessibility, Statistics Corner columns on factor analysis, test and survey reliability, Likert scales, and other topics have been cited in fields as diverse as consumer satisfaction, organizational behavior, information technology, and medical science.

We were delighted that JD responded enthusiastically to our suggestion that we publish these columns as a book and immediately volunteered to update where necessary and to arrange columns thematically. Following a substantial round of organizing, formatting, and copy editing, it is with great pleasure that we present this printed edition of Statistics Corner. Although the original Statistics Corner columns are and will continue to be freely available on the web, we believe this consolidated volume has considerable value added. We hope it will be a useful and attractive addition to your bookshelf.

James Sick

TEVAL Coordinator

Tokyo, Japan

August, 2016

序　文

Kimi Kondo-Brown

教えたことを評価する。これは，第二言語・外国語（以下，言語）を教える者なら，だれもが常日頃行っていることだ。特に，クラスで使う到達度テストの作成とその採点には，殆どの言語教師が相当の時間を費やしていると思う。なぜ教師が年中テストを行うのかと言うと，学習者に定期的にフィードバックを与え，指導の効果を確かめる責任があるからだ。もちろん，言語教師の評価の仕事は，クラスで使う到達度テストの作成と採点だけではない。高校・大学入学試験，プレースメント・テスト，プログラム評価等の担当をしている教師も大勢いることだろう。さらには，大規模に実施される言語能力テストの開発に取り組んでいる教師も多くいるはずだ。このように，言語教師は現場で常に何らかの評価活動に従事している（もしくは追われている）と言っても，過言ではないだろう。

テスト評価は，学習者や教員等の関係者はもとより，社会全体にできるだけプラスの影響をもたらす方法で行われるべきだ。テストが学習や指導に与える影響は「波及効果（washback or backwash effect）」と呼ばれ，テスト開発において最も大切な概念の一つである。テストの波及効果は，プラスにもマイナスにもなりえる。従って「責任のあるテスト評価」とは，受験者をはじめその他の関係者になるべく多くのプラスの波及効果をもたらすことのできる評価と言える。逆に，学習に対するモチベーションの低下や学習成果の悪化を招く等，学習者にマイナスの影響を多く与えたテストは，「無責任なテスト」ということになる。

約二十年前に出版された著書で若林・根岸（1993）は，このような意味での「無責任なテスト」が日本の英語学習の「落ちこぼれ」や「英語ぎらい」をつくったと述べている（p. vii）。同様に，靜（2002）も日本の英語教育における大学入学試験の無責任さを指摘し，「従来のわが国の英語教育の成果が不十分だったとするならば，それは大学入試の波及効果であった部分が最も大きい」と断言している（p. 249）。今日に至ってはどうか。もし日本の英語教育に若林・根岸や靜が訴えるような「無責任なテスト」がまだまだ蔓延しているのであれば，この問題はもちろん個々の英語教員の責任を超えるものであり，組織や社会全体の言語教育に対するアカウンタビリティ（accountability）の問題として取り組んでいかなくてはならない。

靜（2002）は，上で引用した文献で，学習者にとって望ましいテストとは「まず何よりも，受験者がそのテストのための準備をすることが能力の伸長につながるような，学習者のためになるテストである」（p. iii）と述べている。心から共感できる一文だ。本書の読者も，そのようなテスト作りを望んでいるはずだ。そして，受験者も自分のためになるテストを受けられることをもちろん望んでいる。つまり，英語を必修科目あるいは入試科目として学習している学生でも，それだけのために英語を学んでいるのではなく，学ぶからにはその言語を使って何かができるようになりたいと望んでいると思う。私は長年海外での日本語教育に携わってきたが，教育現場で学習者の学びを支援するために，何をどうテストするかという問題は，日本国内外の日本語教育現場でも長年取り組まれてきた課題である（近藤ブラウン 2012）。

前置きが長くなったが，本書「Statistics Corner」を企画した The JALT Testing and Evaluation Special Interest Group (TEVAL SIG)は，日本の学校や大学における言語テストの向上を望む有志によって，1995年に立ち上げられたグループである。Forward で James Sick が述べているように，TEVAL SIG が 1997 年に始めた「Shiken」というニューズレターにて「Statistics Corner」というコラムが設けられた。そのコラムで，言語テストの専門家である JD Brown は，学生や同僚から受けた言語テスト開発や統計に関する数々の質問に，できるだけ「平たい」言葉で答えてきた。(ちなみに，JD は私の同僚でもあり，ライフ・パートナーでもある。)本書「Statistics Corner」は，過去約 20 年に渡って続けられた同コラムを編集したものである。言語テスト作成や研究に取り組んでいく過程で，私自身が JD に尋ねた質問の幾つかも (知らない間に) 引用されている。本書は「第二言語テスト（Second Language Testing）」と「第二言語研究（Second Language Research）」の二部で構成されている。第一部では，主にテスト評価ストラテジー，項目分析，信頼性に関する内容が取り上げられ，第二部では，研究の計画，解釈，そして分析に関する内容となっている。

以下，本書の各章で取り上げられた主な質問を概括する。

Part I. 第二言語テスト（Second Language Testing）

Section A. テスト評価ストラテジー（Testing Strategies）

- 言語テストについて学ぶには，どこからどのような情報を入手すればいいか。(Ch1, pp. 3 - 7)
- 言語テストをデザインする時に教師がよくするミスとは。どうすればそのようなミスを避けられるか。(Ch 2, pp. 9 - 18)
- 「集団基準準拠テスト（norm-referenced test）」と「目標規準準拠テスト（criterion-referenced test）」の違いは何か。(Ch 3, pp. 19 - 25)
- 「構成概念的妥当性（construct validity）」とは何か。他の種類の妥当性とどう違うのか。(Ch 4, pp. 27 - 31)
- 言語教師にとって，いわゆる「二段階テスト評価（two-stage testing）」は，実用的か。二段階テストを作成する時に留意すべき点は何か。(Ch 5, pp. 33 - 36)
- 「異文化語用論的能力（intercultural pragmatics ability）」を測定するためのどのようなテストが開発されているか。(Ch 6, pp. 37 - 43)
- ある英語プログラムでプレースメント・テストとして使ったテストを二年の学習後に再度実施したところ，平均得点が下がっていた。この結果をどう解釈すればいいか。(Ch 7, pp. 45 - 49)
- テスト結果や研究結果に影響を与える外的要因に「被験者期待（subject expectancy）」「ハロー効果（the halo effect）」「ホーソン効果（the Hawthorne effect）」等があるが，

これらの違いは何か。また，これらの概念はテストの波及効果と関係があるのか。(Ch 8, pp. 51 - 55)

- 日本の大学入学試験の波及効果を改善するには，どうすればよいか。(Ch 9, pp. 57 - 61)

Section B. 項目分析（Item Analyses）

- エクセル（表計算ソフト）を使って，テスト項目の分析（test item analysis）をどのようにするか。(Ch 10, pp. 65 - 69)

- 「異差指数（difference index）」と「B指数（B-index）」の違いは何か。これらの指数はどんなテストに使えるのか。(Ch 11, pp. 71 - 76)

- 「点双列相関係数（point-biserial correlation coefficient）」とは何か。言語テストで，同相関係数はどのように役立つのか。(Ch 12, pp. 77 - 83)

- テスト項目分析において，「錯乱肢有効度（distractor efficiency）」とは何か。エクセルを使ってどのように計算し，また解釈できるのか。(Ch 13, pp. 85 - 91)

- エクセルを使って，正誤法等の受容式応答テストの項目分析を行う際，通常，正答は「1」そして誤答は「0」に変換してデータ入力できる。文章完成法や短文応答法などの産出式応答テストの項目分析を行う場合は，どのようにデータ処理をすればよいか。(Ch 14, pp. 93 - 96)

- 「リッカート尺度（Likert-scale）」を使ったアンケート項目を作成する際に留意すべき点は何か。(Ch 15, pp. 97 - 100)

- リッカート尺度は，名義尺度（nominal scale），順位尺度（ordinal scale），間隔尺度（interval scale），比率尺度（ratio scale）のうち，どれと見なすべきか。(Ch 16, pp. 101 - 106)

Section C. 信頼性に関する問題（Reliability Issues）

- 「クロンバックのアルファ（信頼性）係数（Cronbach's alpha coefficient reliability）」はどんなテストに使用できるか。同係数は，どう解釈すべきか。(Ch 17, pp. 109 - 111)

- 入学試験でクローズ・テスト（cloze tests）等を使用する時，テスト項目が多ければ多い程，テスト結果の信頼性が高まることは理解できる。しかし同時に，テスト実施の効率も高めたい。どのようにしてテスト項目数を決定すべきか。(Ch 18, pp. 113 - 117)

- 「標準誤差（standard error）」と「測定の標準誤差（standard error of measurement）」の違いは何か。(Ch 19, pp. 119 - 125)

- テスト結果の信頼性係数が低かった場合に，同じ質のテスト項目を増やせば信頼性係数が改善されることを「スピアマン・ブラウン予言公式（Spearman-Brown prediction formula）」でどう証明できるか。(Ch 20, pp. 127 - 132)

- 「一般化可能性理論（G 理論）（generalizability theory）」そして「決定研究（D 研究）（decision study ["D-study"]）」とは何か。テスト開発にどのように役立つか。(Ch 21, pp. 133 - 139)

- 「評定者・コーダー間の一致度（rater/coder agreement）」そして「コーエンのカッパ係数（Cohen's Kappa）」とは何か。どのように計算できるのか。(Ch 22, pp. 141 - 149)

- クロンバックのアルファ係数を使用して，アンケート調査結果の「内部一貫性信頼性（internal consistency reliability）」をどのように計算し，また解釈すべきか。(Ch 23, pp. 151- 155)

Part 2. 第二言語研究（Second Language Research）

Section D. リサーチ計画（Planning Research）

- 質的研究（qualitative research）でいう「トライアンギュレーション（triangulation）」とは，何か。なぜ大切か。最も一般的な手順はどのようなものか。(Ch 24, pp. 159 - 162)

- 質的研究法や「混合研究法（mixed-methods research）」において，「credibility（信憑性）」「transferability（転用可能性）」「dependability（確実性）」「confirmability（確証性）」等が，なぜ大切か。(Ch 25 & Ch 26, pp. 163 - 172)

Section E. リサーチの解釈（Interpreting Research）

- 統計的分析には色々なアプローチがあるが，その結果を解釈する際に，どの統計的分析においても，共通して留意すべき事項とは何か。(Ch 27, pp. 175 - 181)

- 標本調査を行う際に，標本サイズ（sample size）が小さかった場合，研究結果の一般化（generalizability）にどのような注意を払うべきか。(Ch 28, pp. 183 - 187)

- 標本誤差（sampling error）は，どのように計算すべきか。また「統計の検定力（statistical power）」や「統計の精確さ（statistical precision）」とは何を意味し，どのように計算するのか。(Ch 29 & 30, pp. 189 - 200)

- データ分布を示す指標に「歪度（skewness）」や「尖度（kurtosis）」があるが，これらの統計はどう解釈するのか。(Ch 31, pp. 201 - 205)

- 「分散分析（analysis of variance [ANOVA]）」や「多変量分散分析（multivariate analysis of variance [MANOVA]）」を使った分析結果報告に，「偏イータ二乗（partial eta2）」が使用されていたが，これは何か。どう解釈すればいいのか。(Ch 32, pp. 207 - 213)

- 「信頼区間（confidence intervals）」「信頼限界（confidence limits）」また「信頼レベル（confidence levels）」とは何か。これらの概念は言語テストにどのように使われるのか。(Ch 33, pp. 215 - 222)
- 「ボンフェローニ補正法（Bonferroni adjustment）」とよばれる多重比較の調整法があるが、これは何か。いつ使用されるべきか。(Ch 34, pp. 223 - 229)

Section F. リサーチ分析（Research Analyses）

- クローズ・テストを扱った論文で、「決定係数（coefficients of determination）」という概念が使用されていたが、これは何か。どう計算するのか。(Ch 35, pp. 233 - 237)
- 「主成分分析（principal components analysis [PCA]）」とは何か。主成分分析は、「探索的因子分析（exploratory factor analysis [EFA]）」(もしくは「因子分析（factor analysis）」)と、どう違うのか。また、因子分析において「回転（rotation）」とは何を意味し、どのように使われるのか（例. バリマックス回転 [Varimax rotation]）。さらに、因子分析で「固有値（eigenvalue）」という統計がよく使用されているが、これは何か。(Ch 36 - 40, pp. 239 - 280)
- 色々な種類のカイ二乗検定（chi-square measure/test）があるが、違いは何か。例えば、「マンテル・ヘンツェルのカイ二乗検定（Mantel-Haenszel chi-square）」は、カイ二乗検定とどう違うのか。また、「ピアソンの補正 (Pearson correction)」と「イェーツの補正 (Yates' correction)」の違いは何か。(Ch 41, pp. 281 - 290)

このように、本書で取り上げられた質問は、その多くが、言語テスト評価や第二言語研究法の指導をする際に学生からよく問われるものである。従って、もしあなたが（特に英語で）言語テスト評価や第二言語研究法を教えている、もしくは教えたいと思っているのならば、本書は指導マニュアルの一つとして、本棚にぜひ備えておきたい一冊である。

近藤ブラウン妃美（Kimi Kondo-Brown）

ハワイ大学マノア校（University of Hawai'i at Mānoa）

引用文献

1. 近藤ブラウン妃美 (2012)『日本語教師のための評価入門』くろしお出版
2. 靜哲人 (2002)『英語テスト作成の達人マニュアル』大修館書店
3. 若林俊輔, 根岸雅史 (1993)『無責任なテストが「おちこぼれ」を作る』大修館書店

BACKGROUND TO THIS BOOK

James Dean Brown

I first visited Japan when I was invited in 1987 to teach a weekend course for Temple University Japan (TUJ) in Tokyo and Osaka. Over the ensuing years, I taught other such courses, regular semesters, and summer sessions that totaled about six years of teaching in Tokyo, Osaka, and Fukuoka across several decades. In the process, I found myself invited to do JALT chapter workshops as well as JACET, JALT, JALT N-SIG, and other conferences in places ranging from Miyazaki to Obihiro and many places in between. One thing I noticed consistently was that, no matter what I was talking about at these different venues, everywhere I went, Japanese and non-Japanese alike asked the same questions: What did I think of the university entrance examinations in Japan? Did I think they were fair? What can be done about the entrance examinations? And so forth.

Instinctively, I took the attitude that the Japanese entrance exam system was none of my business, that as an outsider it would be arrogant to even comment on the topic, and that it was an issue that *Japanese* teachers and policy makers needed to sort out. Nonetheless, everywhere I went these issues continued to come up. And when I would answer that the entrance examinations were none of my business and that they were a Japanese problem for Japanese people to solve, audience members would counter with something like: "You need to talk about the unfairness of the entrance examination system because you are a language tester and besides, the powers-that-be can't fire you because you can just go home to Hawai'i."

Eventually, they wore me down and curiosity drove me to look into the Japanese entrance examination system and learn as much as I possibly could, which in turn led me to consider the following:

1. The possibility of adding listening sections to the university English exams (Brown & Christensen, 1987)

2. The need for improving the assessment of false beginners on the university English exams (Brown, 1987)

3. Strategies for improving the ways tests fit into language programs (Brown, 1990a)

4. Ways that standardized tests like the TOEFL are sometimes misinterpreted in Japan (Brown, 1993a)

5. Examination hell and the appropriateness of the entrance examinations for testing English language skills in Japan (Brown, 1995a, 1995b; Brown & Kay, 1995; Brown & Gorsuch, 1995)

6. The actual content of the university English exams at ten private universities, ten public universities, and the center exam (Brown & Yamashita, 1995a, 1995c)

In all likelihood, it was these publications that led the organizers of the 1995 JALT Conference in Nagoya to invite me to do a plenary speech. In fact, the invitation specifically requested that my topic be the English language entrance examinations in Japan. During that speech (Brown, 1996c), I clearly remember that the audience was large and attentive and that most people responded enthusiastically to what I was saying, even though I was talking about esoteric topics like item analysis, test reliability, score validity, fairness, testing policy, and so forth. At the end of the speech, I was startled by the fact that many people rushed up to the stage to shake my hand and congratulate me, but also to let me know that there was going to be a meeting that I *really should attend* at such-and-such a time and such-and-such a place. That meeting turned out to be the very first meeting of what was to become the JALT Testing and Evaluation (TEVAL) special interest group (SIG). People talked excitedly about forming a SIG within JALT, JALT's rules for doing so, how it was necessary to have 50 members to get started, and so forth. With over 50 people willing to join on the spot, the group voted to form the SIG and also to make me honorary chair "for life." I must admit that that was one of the most interesting and exciting moments of my academic career.

Shortly thereafter, a TEVAL newsletter was born with the first issue appearing in 1997. For nearly twenty years, *Shiken: JALT Testing & Evaluation SIG Newsletter* and then *Shiken Research Bulletin* have regularly appeared year after year. From the very beginning, I volunteered to write a question-and-answer column for that newsletter called *Statistics Corner: Questions and answers about language testing statistics*. The first column appeared in Volume 1 Number 1 of what is sometimes just called *Shiken*.[1] It addressed the issues involved in calculating and interpreting *skewness* and *kurtosis* [Chapter 31].[2] From that point on, each of the 40-plus columns maintained the same question-and-answer format. Some of the questions were sent in by email, other questions were suggested to me in conversations or by the editors of the newsletters, and still others were raised by my students in Hawai'i, Japan, or elsewhere. Regardless of their source, all of the questions were raised by people other than me who were interested in testing, research, or statistics—and just plain curious about something.

Last year, some of the people holding leadership roles in the TEVAL SIG, contacted me by email to ask if I would be interested in publishing the columns in book form through the JALT TEVAL SIG. I thought that was a great idea, but since the columns were free online, I wanted to make sure that the book would provide added value. As a result, this book has the following features that the columns did not have:

1. The columns are now all in one place in this book as chapters.

2. The columns have been reorganized into chapters that fit together better into a convergent whole.

3. The book contains two parts with three subsections in each: Part I Second Language Testing (A. Testing Strategies, B. Item Analysis, & C. Reliability Issues) and Part II Second Language Research (D. Planning Research, E. Interpreting Research, & F. Research Analyses).

4. Two of the columns, Brown (2001b & 2004a), were not included in the book because they were redundant with material on e*igenvalues* and *Yates' correction*—material that is covered again in other more comprehensive chapters [Chapters 37 & 41].

5. All of the content has been carefully edited and updated in a number of places.

---

[1] For those not familiar with Japan or the Japanese language, *Shiken* is the Japanese word for "test" or "examination."

[2] Note that chapter references in brackets like this are always referring to chapters in this book.

6. Cross-references to other chapters have been added throughout the book.
7. The book has a Table of Contents to help readers find things and see how the chapters are organized.
8. The references have been carefully edited and put in one place at the end of the book.
9. Some of the references have been updated, though I stayed with the original references in most cases.
10. The book has an index to help readers to quickly locate information about specific topics.

I truly hope that all of those additions have led to a book that you will find interesting to read, as well as useful to keep on your bookshelf as a handy reference.

Part I: Second Language Testing

Section A: Testing Strategies

CHAPTER 1

RESOURCES AVAILABLE IN LANGUAGE TESTING

QUESTION: I'm new to language testing but have taken one language testing course and am very interested in learning more. Can you tell me where I can get more information so I can keep on learning about language testing?

ANSWER: In recent years, more and more people seem to share your interest in language testing, especially in Japan. I would suggest that you start with the following: (a) check out several Internet websites that I will give below, (b) subscribe to one or more language testing journals, (c) join a language testing organization, and (d) read some of the many books that have recently been published.

Check out several internet websites

A number of Internet websites specialize in language testing issues, but the single best source of information is the *Resources in Language Testing Page* maintained by Glenn Fulcher at **languagetesting.info**.[1] Fulcher's webpage includes videos, features, articles, links, podcasts, scenarios, statistics, bookstore, book search, and YouTube links. The links are particularly interesting because they will take you to other websites that he labels as language testing associations; test providers; specific tests; language tests for the aviation industry; personal pages; government websites; ERIC home; research associations, centers, and councils; models, frameworks, and scales; ethics and fairness in testing; statistics; tools online; tests online; computer based testing; private and commercial organizations; and search for a specific test.

---

[1] (Editor's note) To enhance legibility in this printed volume, we have deleted the initial http:// from all *urls* and formatted them in bold. Most modern web browsers will locate a webpage if you type in the *url* just as it is written here, without the initial http or https protocol.

Bob Godwin-Jones (2001) provides links to other websites on language testing (some of which are unfortunately out of date). His article covers the following topics with many links available within each: computerized testing; internet applications; authoring tools; outlook; and a resource list (including web-based testing resources; organizations and institutions; language tests; sample on-line practice tests; language placement tests on-line; test makers, tools, and templates).

A number of other generic testing and evaluation clearinghouses can also be found on the internet. Check out the following:

- Assessment and Evaluation on the Internet ERIC/AE Digest
  www.ericdigests.org/1996-1/evaluation.htm
- Assessment and Evaluation Resources on the NET
  www.misd.net/Assessment/webresources.htm
- Assessment and Evaluation: Resources on the Internet
  ericae.net/nintbod.htm
- Education Standards, Assessments, and Accountability
  www2.ed.gov/admins/lead/account/saa.html
- ERIC NET
  ericae.net

Subscribe to one or more language testing journals

At the moment, there are two primary language testing journals that serve as the gold standard for research in our sub-field (listed first below). You should definitely consider subscribing to some of the following journals at the following websites:

- *Language Assessment Quarterly*
  www.tandfonline.com/loi/hlaq20
- Language *Testing*
  ltj.sagepub.com
- Assessing *Writing*
  www.journals.elsevier.com/assessing-writing

- *Language Testing in Asia*
  www.springer.com/education+%26+language/journal/40468
- *Papers in* Language *Testing and Assessment*
  ltrc.unimelb.edu.au/resources/papers

And, don't forget to at least skim through them when they start to arrive.

Clearly, if you are reading this article, you already know about the JALT Testing and Evaluation SIG newsletter called *Shiken*, but you may not know that it is regularly available as a member of the JALT Testing and Evaluation SIG or that, after publication, the individual articles are available at **jalt.org/test/pub.htm** and more recently at **teval.jalt.org**.

Naturally, you should also keep an eye out for articles on language testing in other mainstream second language journals like: Applied Linguistics, JALT Journal, The Language Teacher, Language Learning, Language Teaching, Language Teaching Research, Modern Language Journal, RELC Journal, Studies in Second Language Acquisition (SSLA), TESOL Quarterly, and so forth.

If you find yourself getting pathologically serious about language testing, you will probably want to become conversant with one or more of the following measurement journals in education and psychology:

- *Applied Measurement in Education*
  www.tandfonline.com/loi/hame20/current
- *Applied Psychological Measurement*
  apm.sagepub.com
- *Educational and Psychological Measurement*
  epm.sagepub.com
- *Educational Measurement: Issues and practice*
  onlinelibrary.wiley.com/journal/10.1111/(ISSN)1745-3992
- *European Journal of Psychological Assessment*
  www.hogrefe.com/periodicals/european-journal-of-psychological-assessment

- *International Journal of Testing*
  www.tandfonline.com/toc/hijt20/current
- *Journal of Educational Measurement*
  onlinelibrary.wiley.com/journal/10.1111/(ISSN)1745-3984
- *NCME Newsletter*
  www.ncme.org/ncme/NCME/NCME/Publication/Newsletter.aspx
- *Psychometrika*
  link.springer.com/journal/11336

Join a language testing organization

One way to keep in touch with other language testers is to join a language testing organization. Some readers may be surprised to learn that there are a number of organizations that promote language testing. Premier among these is the International Language Testing Association (ILTA) **www.iltaonline.com**. However, other regional organizations may be of particular interest to those language testers who happen to live within those regions:

- Academic Committee for Research on Language Testing (ACROLT) in Israel
  info.smkb.ac.il/home/home.exe/11571
- Association of *Language* Testers in Europe (ALTE)
  www.alte.org
- European *Association* for Language Testing and Assessment (EALTA)
  www.ealta.eu.org
- JALT Testing and *Evaluation* SIG in Japan
  teval.jalt.org
- Japan Language *Testing* Association (JLTA)
  jlta.ac
- Midwest *Association* of Language Testers
  mwalt.msu.edu
- Southern California *Association* for Language Assessment Research (SCALAR)
  www.sites.google.com/site/scalaractivities

- The East Coast *Organization* of Language Testers (ECOLT)
  www.cal.org/ecolt

One of the primary benefits of joining these organizations is that they often sponsor conferences and workshops. Such events are a useful way to learn about language testing, but they can also help you begin establishing networks of friends and acquaintances in the field. Check the websites above for more on the various conferences and workshops that are going on near you.

Read some of the recently published books

Several websites offer selections of recently published books on language testing. For example:

- Fulcher's website has its own bookstore at
  languagetesting.info/book/store.html

- For a wider *selection* of books, check out Amazon.com at
  www.amazon.com/s/ref=nb_sb_noss_1?url=search-alias%3Daps&field-keywords=language+testing

- For a selection of my humble contributions to the field on language testing and other topics, go to my author page at Amazon.com at
  www.amazon.com/James-Dean-Brown/e/B001IU0K7E/ref=sr_ntt_srch_lnk_1?qid=1451090805&sr=8-1

Readers who prefer to read in Japanese on language testing might consider tracking down some or all of the references cited by Kondo-Brown in the Japanese Preface to this book.

New language testers might benefit from scanning through the lists above for titles or authors that interest them, order the book from the publisher or on Amazon.com, Amazon.co.jp, or elsewhere and start reading. More established language testers may want to scan through the lists to see if there is anything they have missed.

Conclusion

As you are checking out a few websites, subscribing to a couple of language testing journals, joining a language testing organization (and attending their conferences and workshops), and reading a half dozen books on language testing, you might also consider doing some actual nuts and bolts language testing. Such nuts and bolts involve getting your hands dirty by doing some actual language test development, which in turn involves writing test items, administering the items, item analyzing the results, revising the test on the basis of those results, validating the test, and doing research based on the test. Since doing language testing is the fun part, I recommend getting started with that as soon as possible. Once you take this hands on step, you'll truly be hooked. Enjoy!

(significantly updated and reprinted from Brown, 2006a)

Chapter 2

Solutions to Problems Teachers Have with Classroom Testing

QUESTION: I sometimes feel like I must be making lots of mistakes when I write tests for my students. What worries me most is that I may be wasting my time and theirs because I don't know what I am doing. Can you help me by explaining common mistakes that teachers make when they design tests and how to avoid them?

ANSWER: The problems that test designers have when writing and developing standardized tests (norm-referenced tests) are discussed in many language testing books. However, the problems that teachers have in implementing classroom tests (criterion-referenced tests) are rarely covered. Yet surely, testing occurs more often in language classrooms than in standardized language testing settings. So I will be happy to address the classroom testing problems that teachers face and offer solutions to those problems—at least to the best of my ability. I will do so in three sections about problems that teacher may have in test writing practices, test development practices, and test validation practices.

Test writing practices

In test writing practices, teachers sometimes have problems with: creating good quality test items, organizing those items in the test, and providing clear headings and directions.

Create good quality test items. The biggest single *problem* that most teachers have with tests is the tendency to treat tests as an afterthought, waiting until the last possible moment to write a test for the next day. This habit leaves teachers with too little time to create good quality items. In many cases, I suspect that this tendency is caused by lack of training in item writing that, if nothing else, would teach them that writing good test items takes time.

Clearly, the *solution* to this problem is to get a hold of a good book on language testing and read up on what good quality items are and how to write them (see e.g., Brown, 2005c, pp. 41-65; Brown & Hudson, 2002, pp. 56-100; or Carr, 2011, pp. 25-45, 63-101). Then when it is time to write a test, make sure to allot enough time for writing good quality test items by starting early. These strategies will pay off handsomely because a carefully written test will always be better than a shoddily written one.

Organize the items. The *problem* here is that tests sometimes seem like a disorganized hodge-podge. Any test will be clearer to the students and easier for them to negotiate if the items are clearly organized into sections that make up the whole test. Teachers naturally try to organize their tests, but this can always be done better.

The *solution* is to follow at least three basic principles: (a) group items that are testing the same language point together, (b) collect items of the same format (e.g., multiple-choice, true-false, matching, writing tasks, etc.) together, and (c) group items based on reading or listening passages together with the passages they are based on. Unfortunately, these three principles are sometimes in conflict. For instance, it would be reasonable to have a test with say three reading passages; each reading passage might have one multiple-choice main-idea item, one fact item, one vocabulary item, and one inference item, and each passage might be followed by an open-ended critical-thinking item that students must answer in writing. Clearly, such a test would be following principle (c) above but not (a) and (b). Another section on the same test might group multiple-choice questions together with five for articles, five for prepositions, five for copula, and so forth. That would be following principles (a) and (b) but not (c). I stand by these three principles, but they are not hard and fast rules, and they may not all apply at the same time. Common sense should guide which of the three need to be applied and in what combinations.

Provide clear headings and directions. The *problem* is that even when a test is well-organized, the students may not understand that organization, or worse yet, they may not realize exactly what they have to do on the test. Any test will be clearer to the students and easier for them to negotiate if it has clear headings and directions.

The *solutions* involve making sure the headings are distinct from the rest of the text (in the sense that they are italicized, made bold, or otherwise emphasized) and ensuring that they clearly indicate heading levels with different forms of placement and emphasis like those used in this book (left-justified and bold used for main headings and beginning of paragraph first letter cap with a period and bold italics for second-level headings).

In addition, given that the students taking these tests are usually second language speakers of the target language, the directions should probably be in the students' mother tongue, or if that is not possible, the directions should be simple and direct in the target language (with clear options for asking the teacher for further clarification). Two types of directions will often serve best: general and specific directions. General directions typically provide information about the overall test and apply to all sections of the test. Specific directions are particular to the section for which they are supplied. One thing to keep in mind: if the phrase or sentence appears in all of the specific directions, it probably belongs in a test-wide general directions.

Test development practices

In test development practices, teachers sometimes have problems with: proofreading the test, using a sufficient number of items, and examining student performances on the items.

Proofread the test. Another *problem* is that, even when a good deal of effort has gone into writing good quality items, clearly organizing those items, and providing clear headings and directions, other problems may still persist including typos, spelling errors, unclear formatting, and other problems that will make the test harder for the students to understand.

The *solution*, or at least a partial solution, is to carefully proofread the test several times even though you think you have finished it. I like to proofread my way through the test in different ways: reading from left to right on each line, then right to left; reading from top to bottom, and then bottom to top; I even throw the paper on the floor and look it over while standing above it (especially for logical formatting, e.g., making sure each item is on one page, ensuring that each reading passage is visible at the same time as the items associated with it, etc.). The trick is to look at the test from various perspectives because that will help in spotting typos and formatting issues before the tests are reproduced and handed out to students.

I also find that it helps to get others involved in the proofreading process because of the different and useful perspectives they may bring to the task. What I am suggesting is that you have a colleague, a former student, or even a spouse also proofread the test. You will be amazed at the sorts of problems they will uncover because their different perspectives on the test allow them to see things you are too close to the test to notice. Remember that, ultimately, when you administer the test to say 20 students, you will also have 20 people proofreading your test—people who are more than willing to point out a mistake that the teacher made in writing the test.

Use a sufficient number of items. The *problem* that some teachers create is that they try to test their course objectives with too few items. It stands to reason that more observations of a given phenomenon will be more accurate than fewer observations. This principle is well established in the sciences. However, even in language testing, common sense tells us that testing students with one multiple-choice item would not be reliable or accurate, indeed it simply wouldn't seem fair. Would two items be better? Or 3 items, or 10? So the principle that more items are generally better makes sense. The only real question is how many items are necessary to make the assessment of students reliable, accurate, and fair. The answer to that question depends on how good the items are. If the items are of good quality and suitable for the students in terms of their general proficiency level and what they are being taught, then fewer items will be necessary.

One *solution* is to make sure you have enough items to start with (say 50% more than you think you will need) so you can get rid of some items if they don't work very well. How many items should you have on your test? That will depend on common sense and thinking about the time constraints and the types of things you are asking your students to do on the items. The end number will be different for each situation, but this I know: more items will generally do a better job of measuring what your students can do, but you can get away with fewer items if they are good ones.

Examine students' performances on the items. Another *problem* that arises for teachers is that they do not analyze their students' performance on their test items, much less revise those items. As a result, such teachers continue to use the same items or same types of items over and over again even though those items do not work very well. You have probably found yourself in situations administering a test, when suddenly a student asks if there are two possible answers for number 11, and you realize she is right; then another student asks if any answer is correct for number 25, and you realize that there really isn't. So you tell the students to select the "best" answer, which essentially means that you recognize that there are problems with those items, and perhaps others. The next semester you are using the same test, when suddenly a student asks if there were two possible answers for number 11, and you instantly realize that you forgot to fix the items that had problems, even though students had helped you spot those problems.

One obvious *solution* is to carefully listen to students questions and comments about your test and take notes, then, after scoring the test, immediately take a few minutes to revise the test and save that version in such a way that you will remember to use it the next time you test the same material.

A more systematic solution would be to consider the first administration of any test a pilot run. You can then analyze the results statistically and revise on the basis of what you learn from the analysis. The actual item analyses that are probably most appropriate for classroom tests are called the *difference index*, which "shows the gain, or difference in performance, on each item between the pretest and posttest" (Brown, 2003c, p. 18 [Chapter 11]) and the *B-index*, which "shows how well each item is contributing to the pass/fail decisions that are often made with CRTs [criterion-referenced tests, also known as classroom tests]" (p. 20). These item analysis statistics are both based on the simple percentage of students who answered each item correctly at different times or in different groups. Using these statistics and common sense, you can select those items that are most closely related to what your students are learning in your course, replace any items that are not closely related, and make fairer decisions based on your test scores. For more about the steps in calculating and interpreting these classroom-test item statistics, see Brown (2003c [Chapter 11], 2005c). If you take the time to do item analysis every time you administer a test, your tests will continue to get better every time you use them.

Test validation practices

In test validation practices, teachers sometimes have problems with: reporting the scores as percentages, checking the reliability of the test, and thinking about the validity of the test.

Report the scores as percentages. The first validity-related *problem* is that some teachers report the number of items answered correctly to students along with information about the distribution of scores (e.g., the high and low scores, the number of students at each score, etc.). Teachers probably do this because they (and their students) are thinking in terms of the bell curve. This approach will lead students to think competitively in terms of how they did relative to other students, rather than in terms of how much learning they were able to demonstrate on the test.

The *solution* is a simple one. In order to encourage the students to think about how much they have learned, report their scores as percentages and explain to them that the scores reveal what proportion they learned of the material taught in the course. Your score report will be even more informative if you can give students their percentage scores for each section of the test or for each objective in the course. The important thing to keep in mind for yourself and your students is that your classroom tests are designed to measure their learning in the course (criterion-referenced testing), not to spread them out on a continuum (which is norm-referenced testing like that done on standardized tests).

Check the reliability of the test scores. The *problem* here is that some teachers fail to think about or check the degree to which they might be making decisions about their students (grading, passing/failing, etc.) based on unreliable information. What does reliability mean when it comes to test scores? Reliability can be defined as the degree to which a set of scores are consistent. This concept is important because teachers generally want to be fair and make decisions for all students in the same way. If the scores on a test are not consistent across time, across items, or especially across students, then the decision making may not be the same each time for all students. Thus reliability is really a question of fairness.

One *solution* to this reliability issue is for teachers to think about reliability in terms of *sufficiency of information*: "What teachers really need to know, from a reliability perspective, is, 'Do I have enough information here to make a reasonable decision about this student with regard to this domain of information?' The essential reliability issue is: Is there enough information here?" (Smith, 2003, p. 30). While Smith was pondering the idea of creating a reliability index for such an interpretation, teachers might simply ask themselves one question: do I have enough good quality information from these test items to make responsible decisions about my students?

Another *solution* to this reliability issue would be to directly address the question: To what degree are the scores on my test reliable? This could be addressed by calculating a reliability coefficient. These coefficients typically range from .00 to 1.00, which can be interpreted as a range from zero reliability to 100% reliability. Thus if a coefficient for a set of scores turns out to be .80, that means that the scores are 80% reliable (and by extension 20% unreliable). So generally, the higher this value is the more reliable the scores are. Most reliability estimates were designed for standardized tests and are not appropriate for classroom testing, but one such estimate, the Kuder-Richardson formula 21 (known affectionately as K-R21) is appropriate for classroom testing (as explained in Brown, 2005c, p. 209). Calculating this coefficient is relatively easy, requiring only that the teacher first calculate the mean (*M*), standard deviation (*SD*), and number of items (*k*) (all of which can be calculated fairly easily in the *Excel*® spreadsheet program), then enter these values into Walker's calculator for K-R21 at

www.cedu.niu.edu/~walker/calculators/kr.asp

The result will be a reliability coefficient that the teacher can interpret as an indication of the consistency of the test scores involved.

Think about common sense validity issues. Another *problem* that some teachers have is that they fail to consider the validity of their test scores. Validity has traditionally been defined as the degree to which a set of test scores is measuring what it was intended to measure. In recent years, language testers have expanded their thinking about validity to include issues related to the consequences and values implications of how those scores are used.

Classroom teachers who wish to address validity issues need not get involved in learning elaborate theories or statistical procedures. They can instead start by asking themselves the following relatively simple questions (adapted from and explained more fully in Brown, 2012c):

1. To what degree does the content of my test items match the objectives of the class and the material I covered?
2. To what degree do my course objectives meet the needs of the students?
3. To what degree do my test scores show that my students are learning something in my course?
4. Will my students think my test items match the material I am teaching them?
5. How do the values that underlie my test scores match my values? My students' values? Their parents' values? My boss' values? Etc.?
6. What are the consequences of the decisions I base on my test scores for my students, their parents, me, my boss, etc.?

Your answers to the above questions will probably be a matter of degree in each case, but those answers will nonetheless help you understand the degree to which your test scores are valid.

Conclusion

In this chapter, I have explored some of the problems that teachers may face in their classroom testing in terms of test writing practices, test development practices, and test validation practices. These notions are elaborated in Table 2.1 which shows the three general categories of testing practices (writing, development, and validation) and the general suggestions made in this column, but also summarizes the solutions offered for ways to implement those suggestions.

If even a few teachers begin to use some of these suggestions, I have no doubt that their testing and therefore their teaching will improve. As a result, they will be better serving their students, themselves, and their institutions.

Table 2.1. *Summary of Practices, Problems, and Solutions in Classroom Testing*

Practices	Problems	Solutions
Test Writing	Some teachers allow too little time for writing their test items (perhaps because they lack training in item writing)	*Create good quality items* by getting ahold of a good book on language testing & reading up on what good quality items are & how to write them; be sure to allot sufficient time by starting early.
Test Writing	Tests sometimes seem like a disorganized hodge-podge of items	*Organize the items* by keeping items that are testing the same language point together; grouping items of the same format (e.g., multiple-choice, true-false, etc.); &/or keeping reading or listening items together with their passages.
Test Writing	Students may find the organization of a test confusing, or worse, they may not understand what they need to do	*Provide clear headings & directions* by emphasizing headings (using bold, italics, etc.) & using them hierarchically; writing directions in students' mother tongue or in very simple/clear English; & using general & specific directions.
Development	Even with all of the above, other problems may remain (e.g., typos, spelling errors, etc.)	*Proofread the test* carefully yourself & get others to do so as well (including perhaps a colleague, former student, or even spouse) because another set of eyes can spot things you are too close to the test to see.
Development	Some teachers try to test their course objectives with too few items	*Use a sufficient number of items* by always writing 50% more good quality items than you think you will need; use common sense in deciding how many items to use while taking into account time constraints & the nature of the items.
Development	Some teachers fail to analyze & revise items even though they will use them again	*Examine the students' performances on the items* by listening to their questions/comments during the test & revising; by considering the first administration a pilot test & performing item analysis (i.e., the *difference index* & *B-index* & revising.
Validation	Some teachers report the number of items correct & explain scores in terms of the bell curve	*Report the scores as percentages* & explain to students that the scores reveal how much they learned of the material taught in the course, rather than how the scores spread them out.
Validation	Some teachers fail to consider & check if their score-based decisions are founded on unreliable information	*Check the reliability of the test items* in terms of sufficiency of information (the degree to which you have enough information to make consistent decisions) & calculate & interpret a K-R21 reliability coefficient.
Validation	Some teachers fail to consider & check the validity of the scores on their tests	*Think about common sense validity issues* in terms of the degree to which the scores are measuring what you intended & the implications & consequences of your score uses by answering the six validity questions posed above.

(updated and reprinted from Brown, 2013b)

CHAPTER 3

DIFFERENCES IN HOW NORM-REFERENCED AND CRITERION-REFERENCED TESTS ARE DEVELOPED AND VALIDATED

QUESTION: What are the major differences between norm-referenced and criterion-referenced tests? How can these two tests be best developed and validated? [Submitted by a participant in the Kuroshio (Aloha Friday) Seminar that Kimi Kondo-Brown and I conducted on May 23, 2014 at the Bunkyo Civic Center in Tokyo]

ANSWER: I have discussed the major differences between norm-referenced and criterion-referenced[1] tests in a number of places (most recently in Brown, 2012d). So I will only touch on those differences briefly here. I have also explained at length the different strategies that should be applied in developing and validating the two families of tests in a number of places. However, I have never summarized those different strategies side-by-side in one short and straightforward article. I will attempt to do just that here by addressing the following sub-questions: What are the differences between the norm-referenced and criterion-referenced families of tests? What strategies are used to develop and validate NRTs and CRTs? What are the differences in NRT and CRT development and validation strategies?

---

[1] Note that since the question addressed to this column was clearly written by a person interested in testing, but primarily a teacher, the types of CRTs I am referring to here are not the formal subcategory of CRTs known as domain-referenced tests (which tend to be large scale), but rather those CRTs used by teachers on a more focused classroom level.

Test writing practices

Norm-referenced tests (NRTs, sometimes referred to as *standardized tests*) and criterion-referenced tests (CRTs, also known as *classroom tests*) are two families of tests that are distinguished most clearly in terms of the ways scores are interpreted, the purposes of the tests, levels of specificity, the distributions of scores, the structures of the tests, and what we want the students to know in advance. In more detail, the two types of tests differ in:

- *The ways scores are interpreted* differ in that NRTs are designed to compare the performances of students to one another in relative terms, while CRTs are built to identify the amount or percentage of the material each examinee knows or can do in absolute terms.

- *The purposes of the tests* also differ with NRTs primarily designed to spread examinees out on a continuum of general abilities so examinees' performances can be compared to each other (usually with standardized scores), while CRTs are designed to assess the amount of material that the examinees know or can do (usually expressed in percentages).

- *Levels of specificity* are necessarily different with NRTs tending to measure very general language abilities (for proficiency or placement purposes), while CRTs usually focus on specific, well-defined (and usually objectives-based) language knowledges or skills (for diagnostic or achievement purposes).

- *The distributions of scores* also differ in that, ideally, NRT scores are normally distributed (indeed items are selected to ensure this is the case), while CRT scores ideally would produce quite different distributions at different times in the learning process: with students scoring very low in a positively skewed distribution (i.e., scrunched up toward the lower scores) at the beginning of a course on a diagnostic CRT (indicating that they needed to learn the material) and students scoring very high in a negatively skewed distribution (i.e., scrunched up toward the higher scores) at the end of the course on an achievement CRT (indicating that most of them mastered the material; indeed, in the unlikely event that all students master all the material, they should all score 100%).

- *The structures of the tests* also differ with NRTs tending to have many items with a few long subtests (e.g., listening, grammar, reading, etc.) each of which has diverse item content, while CRTs are typically built around numerous, short subtests that contain well-defined and similar items in each.

- *What we want the students to know in advance* of the test differs in that, for NRTs, security is usually an important issue because we do *not* want examinees to know the content of the test items, while for CRTs, we teach the content of the course and want the students to study that content, so we tell them what to study, and we test that content. If they know the content, they should succeed.

What strategies are used to develop and validate NRTs and CRTs?

Table 3.1 summarizes the strategies used to develop NRTs and CRTs in two separate columns. I hope that this table is clear without any direct explanation. Nonetheless, some discussion of the differences between NRT and CRT development strategies will be provided below.

Table 3.2 summarizes the strategies used to validate NRTs and CRTs in two separate columns. Again, this table should stand alone as a summary, but further discussion will be provided in the next section.

What are the differences in NRT and CRT development and validation strategies?

Careful examination of Table 3.1 will reveal key differences between NRT and CRT development strategies. In Step 1, the primary difference in *test planning* is that CRTs are more specific and objectives-based, while NRTs are more general. In Step 2, the difference in *creating items* is that a more general pool of items is developed for NRTs, but smaller, more specific item pools are created for each objective/subtest in CRTs. In Step 3, *editing items* includes using item guidelines for both types of tests, but item congruence and applicability analyses are key to CRT development. In Step 4, the key difference in *piloting items* is that NRTs can be piloted in one shot and must include the whole range of abilities being tested, while CRTs are best piloted at the beginning and end of appropriate instruction and should focus only on what is being taught. In Step 5, the key difference is that *analyzing items* for NRTs is based on *ID* and *IF* (in that order), while ideally, CRT item analysis is based on *DI*, but in a pinch can be based on *BI*. In Step 6, the key difference in *selecting items* is that, for NRTs, it is based on the highest *ID*s, and then on *IF* (to adjust test difficulty), while ideally CRT item selection is based on the highest *DI*s, but in a pinch on the highest *BI* values. In Step 7, the prime difference

Table 3.1. *Strategies Used to Develop NRTs and CRTs*

Steps	NRT (Standardized)	CRT (Classroom)
1. Plan test	Plan based on test specification / blueprint and general item specifications.	Plan with course objectives developed and in hand; when possible, using item specifications may help.
2. Create items	Create a large pool of items at about the right level of difficulty in the general area being tested (e.g., reading comprehension).	Create about 10 items that measure what the students should be able to do on each of the course objectives (say objectives 1-9) at the end of the course; divide the items into two forms of the test, say forms A and B such that there are about 5 items on each test for each of the 9 objectives/subtests.
3. Edit items	Use item writing guidelines like those found in the third chapter of Brown (2005c) to carefully proofread and improve all items.	Use item writing guidelines like those found in the third chapter of Brown & Hudson (2002) to proofread and improve all items. Perform item congruence and applicability analysis (as described in Brown & Hudson, 2002, pp. 98-100) to make sure items match the course objectives.
4. Pilot items	Pilot the items *with a single large group of examinees* that has the same characteristics and range of abilities as the examinees in the ultimate test group (e.g., if the test is being developed for proficiency purposes, pilot it with a large group of students ranging from near-zero English to near-native; if the test is for placement purposes at a specific institution, the test should be piloted with examinees in the narrower range of abilities found there).	Ideally, pilot the two forms *at the beginning of the course* as diagnostics tests (with half of the students randomly selected to take each form); score and give the students diagnostic feedback objective-by-objective based on the subtests. Then, administer the same tests *at the end of the course* as achievement tests such that students who took Form A at the beginning take Form B at the end, and vice versa; include the scores in the students' grades, but keep the tests and results for further analysis.
5. Analyze items	Calculate *item facility* (IF = the proportion of examinees who answered each item correctly) and *item discrimination* indexes (ID = the proportion of examinees in the upper third on the whole test who answered each item correctly minus the proportion in the lower third) (see Brown, 2005c, pp. 66-76).	Calculate *difference indexes* (DI = the proportion of students who answered each item correctly at the end of the course minus the proportion at the beginning) and/or *B-indexes* (BI = the proportion of examinees who passed the whole test that answered each item correctly minus the proportion for those students who failed) (see Brown, 2005c, pp. 76-84, or Brown & Hudson, 2002, pp. 118-148).
6. Select items	Revise the test by selecting those items with the highest *ID* values while keeping an eye on the *IF* values to adjust the difficulty of the test up or down as necessary.	Revise the test by selecting those items with the highest *DI* values within each objective/subtest (perhaps the best 3 out of 5). If *DI* values are not available, select the highest *BI* values in each objective/subtest (again, perhaps the best 3 out of 5).
7. Revise test	Create a new, shorter, more efficient revised test based on the item analyses and selection in Steps 5 and 6 for future proficiency or placement purposes.	Create new, shorter, more efficient, revised Forms A and B based on the item analyses and selection in Steps 5 and 6 for future use as diagnostic and achievement tests.

Table 3.2. *Strategies Used to Validate NRTs and CRTs*

Steps	NRT (Standardized)	CRT (Classroom)
8. Examine consistency	Study the *reliability* of scores by using test-retest, parallel forms, or internal consistency strategies. The most commonly applied internal consistency estimates are Cronbach alpha or K-R21 (for full explanations of all these reliability strategies, see Bachman, 2004, pp. 153-191; Brown, 2005c, pp. 169-198; Brown, 2013c)., K-R20,	Study the *dependability* of scores by using threshold loss agreement (agreement or kappa), squared error loss (Φ_λ), or domain score dependability (Φ) strategies. If resources are limited as in most classroom settings, teachers can use the K-R21 reliability statistic as a conservative estimate of Φ mentioned above (for full explanations of these dependability strategies, see Bachman, 2004, pp. 192-205; Brown, 2005c, pp. 199-219; Brown, 2013d).
9. Examine validity	Use evidential strategies, which include the traditional content, construct, and criterion-related validity strategies. Also use the more recently developed consequential strategies have been employed including examination of the values implications and social consequences of score interpretations and uses (see Bachman, 2004, pp. 257-293; Brown, 2005c, pp. 220-248).	Use the only evidential strategy that typically makes sense for CRTs, which is the traditional content validity approach. Teachers may also want to use the more recently developed consequential strategies that take into the account values implications that they are expressing by the choices they make in test design as well as the social consequences of their score interpretations and uses (see Brown, 2012c; Brown & Hudson, 2002, pp. 212-268).

when *test revising* is that the ultimate product for NRTs is typically one large general test (or sometimes large subtests like grammar, listening, reading, etc.), but for CRTs, the resulting product is usually a collection of small, focused, objectives-based subtests, ideally in two forms.

Table 3.2 reveals key differences between NRT and CRT validation strategies. In Step 8, the NRT *reliability* practices listed in the table are those laid out and explained for NRTs in most language testing (or more general testing) books. For CRTs, the *dependability* procedures shown in the table can clearly become quite elaborate. However, teachers need only address the common-sense questions of whether the scores on their tests are consistent, fair, and consistently represent the knowledge and abilities of all students. If resources are limited as is the case in most classroom settings, teachers can use the K-R21 reliability estimate as a conservative estimate of domain-score dependability (Φ) referred to in the table (see argument for this strategy in Brown, 2005c, p. 209).

In Step 9, the *validity practices* for NRTs listed here are also those laid out and explained for NRTs in most language testing (or more general testing) books including evidential strategies like content, construct, and criterion-related validity strategies and consequential strategies examining values implications and social consequences. For CRTs, the content validity approach listed in the table is the only one that always makes sense; it involves systematically analyzing and assessing the degree to which test items are measuring what the teacher is claiming to test, often by laying out the test items side-by-side with the course objectives (and with the teaching materials nearby for reference) and systematically comparing items to objectives. There are three key questions that teachers may want to consider in this regard (note that these questions and those in the next paragraph are adapted from and explained more fully in Brown, 2012c, 2013b [Chapter 2]):

1. To what degree does the content of my test match the objectives of the class and the material covered?
2. To what degree do my course objectives meet the needs of the students?
3. To what degree do my tests show that my students are learning something in my course?

Teachers may also want to consider the *values implications* of their testing, scoring, and decision making by addressing some or all of the following questions: How do the learning/teaching values that underlie my test design, the resulting scores, and the decisions based on them match my beliefs and values? The beliefs and values of my students? Their parents? My colleagues? My boss? Etc.? Teachers may also want to think about the *social* consequences of their scores and consequences for students by addressing the following questions: What will happen to my students as a consequence of the decisions I make based on these test scores? Is this a small-stakes decision that is only a small part of a course grade, or will this test have larger consequences for students (e.g., determine whether or not the student passes the course, graduates with a diploma, etc.)?

Conclusion

In answering the question posed at the top of this column, length restrictions limited me to summarizing the differences in characteristics, development steps, and validation strategies used for NRTs and CRTs. I hope that this overview will nonetheless prove useful to readers and that anyone who wants more in-depth coverage of any aspect of these differences will be able to use the citations and references provided here to continue exploring these and related topics. I especially hope that this explanation will help practicing language teachers realize that most of the testing they do in the classroom ought to be CRT and that this column ought to be read along with Brown, 2013b [Chapter 2], which discusses solutions to problems that teachers often have with their classroom assessment.

(updated and reprinted from Brown, 2014a)

CHAPTER 4

WHAT IS CONSTRUCT VALIDITY?

QUESTION: Recently I came across an article mentioning that a test had poor construct validity. What exactly is construct validity? How well accepted is the concept of construct validity? How does it differ from other forms of validity? What is the best way of measuring construct validity? And finally, what are the most common threats to construct validity?

ANSWER: The general concept of validity was traditionally defined as "the degree to which a test measures what it claims, or purports, to be measuring" (Brown, 1996a, p. 231). However, as your questions indicate, the issues involved in validity are not that simple. To address these issues head on, I will use your questions as headings and take the liberty of rearranging them a bit.

How does construct validity differ from other forms of validity?

Validity was traditionally subdivided into three categories: content, criterion-related, and construct validity (see Brown 1996a, pp. 231-249). *Content validity* includes any validity strategies that focus on the content of the test. To demonstrate content validity, testers investigate the degree to which a test is a representative sample of the content of whatever objectives or specifications the test was originally designed to measure. To investigate the degree of match, test developers often enlist well-trained colleagues to make judgments about the degree to which the test items matched the test objectives or specifications.

Criterion-related validity usually includes any validity strategies that focus on the correlation of the test being validated with some well-respected outside measure(s) of the same objectives or specifications. For instance, if a group of testers were trying to develop a test for business English to be administered primarily in Japan and Korea, they might decide to administer their new test and the TOEIC to a fairly large group of students and then calculate the degree of correlation between the two tests. If the correlation coefficient between the new test and the TOEIC turned out to be high, that would indicate that the new test was arranging the students along a continuum of proficiency levels very much like the TOEIC does—a result that could, in turn, be used to support the validity of the new test. Criterion-related validity of this sort is sometimes called concurrent validity (because both tests are administered at about the same time).

Another version of criterion-related validity is called *predictive validity*. Predictive validity is the degree of correlation between the scores on a test and some other measure that the test is designed to predict. For example, a number of studies have been conducted to examine the degree of relationship between students' Graduate Record Examination (GRE) scores and their grade point averages (GPA) after two years of graduate study. The correlation between these two variables represents the degree to which the GRE predicts academic achievement as measured by two years of GPA in graduate school.

What exactly is construct validity?

To understand the traditional definition of construct validity, it is first necessary to understand what a construct is. A construct, or psychological construct as it is also called, is an attribute, proficiency, ability, or skill that happens in the human brain and is defined by established theories. For example, *overall English language proficiency* is a construct. It exists in theory and has been observed to exist in practice.

Construct validity has traditionally been defined as the experimental demonstration that a test is measuring the construct it claims to be measuring. Such an experiment could take the form of a differential-groups study, wherein the performances on the test are compared for two groups: one that has the construct and one that does not have the construct. If the group with the construct performs better than the group without the construct, that result is said to provide evidence of the construct validity of the test. An alternative strategy is called an intervention study, wherein a group that is weak in the construct is measured using the test, then taught the construct, and measured again. If a non-trivial difference is found between the pretest and posttest, the difference can be said to support the construct validity of the test scores. Numerous other strategies can be used to study the construct validity of a test, but more about that later.

How well accepted is the concept of construct validity?

The concept of construct validity is very well accepted. Indeed, in educational measurement circles, all three types of validity discussed above (content, criterion-related, and construct validity) are now taken to be different facets of a single unified concept of construct validity. This unified view of construct validity is considered a new development by many of the language testers around the world. However, it can hardly be new given that I remember discussing it in courses I took with Richard Shavelson at UCLA in the late 1970s.

Coming back to your question, either the traditional view of construct validity or the unified view is held by virtually all psychometricians inside or outside of language testing. Thus, construct validity can be said to be well-accepted, one way or the other.

What is the best way of measuring construct validity?

Regardless of how construct validity is defined, there is no single best way to study it. In most cases, construct validity should be demonstrated from a number of perspectives. Hence, the more strategies used to demonstrate the validity of the scores on a test, the more confidence test users can have in the construct validity of those test scores, but only if the evidence provided by those strategies is convincing.

In short, the construct validity of the scores on a test should be demonstrated by an accumulation of evidence. For example, taking the unified definition of construct validity, we could demonstrate it using content analysis, correlation coefficients, factor analysis, ANOVA studies demonstrating differences between differential groups or pretest-posttest intervention studies, multi-trait/multi-method studies and so on. Naturally, doing all of the above would be a tremendous amount of work, so the amount of work a group of test developers is willing to put into demonstrating the construct validity of their test scores is directly related to the number of such demonstrations they can provide. Smart test developers will stop when they feel they have provided a convincing set of validity arguments.

What are the most common threats to construct validity?

Any threats to the reliability (or consistency) of a set of test scores will also pose threats to its validity because the scores on a test cannot be more systematically *valid* than they are *systematic* (or consistent). Put another way, the portion of the test score variance which is not reliable (the error variance), cannot be said to be validly measuring any construct and so puts a limit on the systematic validity of the test scores. Thirty-six such threats to reliability are discussed in detail in Brown (1996a, pp. 188-192) in five different categories of problems due to the: environment of the test administration, administration procedures, examinees, scoring procedures, and test construction (or quality of test items).

In my view, the validity problems I have most often observed in Japan are an inadequate number of items, poor item writing, lack of pilot testing, lack of item analysis procedures, lack of reliability studies, and lack of validity analysis. These are all problems that could be rectified by using the well-developed psychometric procedures used in many countries around the world.

Conclusion

In discussing language testing validity at this point in time, I would be remiss to not at least mention Messick's (1988, 1989, 1996) thinking about validity. Messick presented a unified and expanded theory of validity, which included the evidential and consequential bases of test score interpretation and use. Table 4.1 shows how this theory works. Notice that the evidential basis for validity includes both test score interpretation and test score use. The evidential basis for interpreting test scores involves the empirical study of construct validity, which is defined by Messick as the theoretical context of implied relationships to other constructs. The evidential basis for using test scores involves the empirical investigation of both construct validity and relevance/utility, which are defined as the theoretical contexts of implied applicability and usefulness.

Table 4.1. *Facets of test validity according to Messick (1988, p. 42)*

	Test Interpretation	Test Use
Evidential Basis	Construct Validity	Construct Validity + Relevance and Utility
Consequential Basis	Value Implications	Social Consequences

The consequential basis of validity involves both test score interpretation and test score use. The consequential basis for interpreting test scores requires making judgments of the value implications, which are defined as the contexts of implied relationships to good/bad, desirable/undesirable, etc. score interpretations. The consequential basis for using test scores involves making judgments of social consequences, which are defined as the value contexts of implied consequences of test score use and the tangible effects of actually applying that test. The value implications and social consequences issues have special importance in Japan, where the values underlying creation and use of tests like the university entrance exams and the social consequences of their use are so omnipresent in educators' minds. (For more information on this model of validity, see Messick, 1988, 1989; for some interesting discussions of the consequential aspects of validity, see Green, 1998; Linn, 1998; Lune, Parke, & Stone, 1998; Moss, 1998; Reckase, 1998; Taleporos, 1998; and Yen, 1998.)

Clearly then, while construct validity is still an important concept, our responsibilities as language testers appear to have expanded considerably with Messick's call for test developers to pay attention to the evidential and consequential bases for the use and interpretation of test scores.

(updated and reprinted from Brown, 2000d)

CHAPTER 5

WHAT IS TWO-STAGE TESTING?

QUESTION: Recently I came across an article comparing two-stage testing to traditional multiple-choice testing. Who first developed the concept of two-stage testing? Does two-stage testing have any practical applications for language teachers? In what situations would it be appropriate to develop a two-stage language proficiency test? Are there any things teachers need to be especially careful of when developing two-stage tests?

ANSWER: Let me answer your questions one at a time. I'll use the questions themselves as headings to help organize the discussion.

Who first developed the concept of two-stage testing?

I've spent considerable time looking for an answer to your first question, but in the end, I have to admit that I still do not know who first developed two-stage testing. The first references I find in the literature are Cleary, Linn, and Rock (1968a and b) and Lord (1971). Personally, Earl Rand at UCLA first introduced me to two-stage testing in 1977. I used it shortly thereafter (in conjunction with item response theory) to develop two different sets of placement tests for two textbook series (Cornelius & Brown, 1981; Sheeler & Brown, 1980a).

What is two-stage testing?

Essentially, the label two-stage testing can be applied to any examination in which the students begin by taking a short routing test (using 5-10 items with a wide range of difficulty levels), the scores on which are used to decide which of the longer measurement tests (say three alternatives at relatively low, middle, and high difficulty levels) they should take (see Figure 5.1). Their final score is typically based on standardized scores that are equated across the three measurement tests.

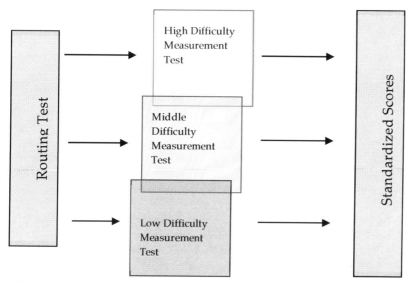

Figure 5.1. Two-Stage Testing

Does two-stage testing have any practical applications for language teachers?

Two-stage testing is probably more applicable for norm-referenced purposes like general proficiency testing (for say admissions decisions) or placement testing than it is for criterion-referenced classroom purposes like diagnostic, progress, and achievement testing. That, I suppose, is why I used two-stage testing to develop the placement tests for two ESL textbook series (Cornelius & Brown, 1981; Sheeler & Brown, 1980a), but not for the progress and achievement tests (Cornelius & Brown, 1982; Sheeler & Brown, 1980b) associated with those same series. Four reasons why two-stage testing is more appropriate for norm-referenced testing are that two-stage testing is:

1. best based on relatively wide ranges of ability,
2. best developed to produce standardized scores,
3. labor intensive to develop, validate, and maintain, and
4. based on fairly sophisticated statistical analyses.

In what situations would it be appropriate to develop a two-stage language proficiency test?

As a consequence, two-stage testing will prove most useful for norm-referenced testing, which means that it will probably work best for language proficiency or placement testing. In such testing projects, two-stage testing has at least two distinct advantages:

1. It allows developing tests in which students only have to answer items that are at about their level of ability without having to answer many items that are either too easy or too difficult for them.
2. It allows for accurate scores with far fewer items on average than traditional one-test-fits-all strategies.

Consequently, if you want to develop a proficiency or placement test that saves the students time and avoids presenting them with many items that are too easy (boring) or two difficult (depressing), then two-stage testing may be for you.

Are there any things teachers need to be especially careful of when developing two-stage tests?

Like all tests, the items on a two-stage test should be of the highest quality (for guidelines on item quality, see the third chapter of Brown, 1996a). It is especially important that superior items be used on the routing test, which means the items must be well written, must vary considerably in difficulty, and must discriminate very well. If the items in the routing test are not working particularly well, then their ineffectiveness in channeling students into the measurement tests could create considerable unreliability in the resulting scores. Given that even the best routing test cannot be perfectly reliable, it is a good idea to make sure the difficulty levels of the items in the measurement tests overlap to some degree (as shown in Figure 5.1) in order to account for any errors near the decision points for putting the students into the measurement tests. In addition, some form of equating will be necessary so the scores from the measurement tests can all be expressed on the same standardized scale. This equating process will probably involve item analysis (either classical theory or item response theory) and regression analysis, or both (all of which is beyond the scope of this article).

Conclusion

In short, two-stage testing can be very useful in norm-referenced testing situations (typically for proficiency or placement purposes) for saving the students time and avoiding making them answer many items that are too easy or two difficult for them. However, before deciding to develop a two-stage test, remember that it works best for students from a wide range of abilities, it will typically result in standardized scores, it is labor intensive to develop, and it requires considerable statistical sophistication to do two-stage testing well.

Computer adaptive testing (CAT) further improves on the concepts first developed for two-stage testing. In CAT, the students are channeled by a routing test into items exactly at their ability levels. In essence, the computer uses the information it gets from the routing test to select items specifically for each student's level of ability. Each student essentially takes a different test, a test that is even shorter and more precise than a two-stage measurement test. However, unlike two-stage testing, CAT requires that a large item bank be piloted and analyzed. It further requires that test developers have some background in item-response theory statistics, as well as considerable knowledge of computer programming (Basic, C, Pascal, etc.) or internet browser programming (HTML and/or Java) in order to design and implement the test.

(updated and reprinted from Brown, 2001c)

CHAPTER 6

TESTING INTERCULTURAL PRAGMATICS ABILITY

QUESTION: What sorts of tests have been developed and used for testing intercultural pragmatics ability? What do we know about such testing? And, how have those tests been analyzed statistically?

ANSWER: The literature on developing intercultural pragmatics tests has (a) found that different testing formats vary in their effectiveness for testing pragmatics, (b) discovered that certain variables are particularly important in testing pragmatics tests, and (c) relied on increasingly sophisticated statistical analyses in studying pragmatics testing over the years. I will address each of these three issues in turn.

Different testing formats vary in their effectiveness for testing pragmatics

Starting with Hudson, Detmer, and Brown (1992, 1995), six testing methods have been prominent to varying degrees in the literature to date (as shown in Table 6.1):

- *Multiple-Choice Discourse Completion Task* (MDCT) – requires examinees to read a situation description and choose what they would say next.

- *Oral Discourse Completion Task* (ODCT) – expects examinees to listen to an orally described situation and record what they would say next.

- *Discourse Role-Play Task* (DRPT) – directs examinees to read a situation description and then play a particular role with an examiner in the situation.

- *Discourse Self-Assessment Task* (DSAT) – asks examinees to read a written description of a situation and then rate their own pragmatic ability to respond correctly in the situation.

- *Role-Play Self-Assessment* (RPSA) – instructs examinees to rate their own performance in the recording of the role play in the DRPT.

Hudson et al. (1992, 1995) created initial prototype tests and validated them for EFL students at a US university. They noted that the MDCT did not work particularly well for them. Yamashita (1996) then created Japanese versions of those same tests and verified that all but MDCT worked reasonably well for Japanese as a second language (SL). Yoshitake (1997) and Enochs and Yoshitake-Strain (1999) verified that the six assessments worked well for Japanese university EFL students. Ahn (2005) created Korean versions for all but the MDCT and verified that they worked reasonably well for Korean as a FL. Liu (2007) reported on developing a MDCT that worked, which he accomplished by having students generate the speech acts and situations that were used.

Hudson et al. (1992, 1995) and Brown (2001g), as well as a majority of the other researchers have used paper-and-pencil testing formats. However, other formats have also been used. Tada (2005) was the first to create computer-delivered tests with video prompts. Roever (2005, 2006, 2007, 2008) was the first to develop and use web-based testing, followed by Itomitsu (2009). Rylander, Clark, and Derrah (2013) focused on the importance of video formats, and Timpe (2013) was the first to use *Skype* role-play tasks.

Certain variables are particularly important in testing pragmatics

In creating their first prototype tests, Hudson et al. (1992, 1995) identified a number of variables that have proven important across many of the subsequent studies, but to varying degrees. These variables are labeled across the top of Table 6.1. The first was the six **testing methods** discussed in the previous section. The second variable was **speech acts**, which initially included three key ones: (a) *requesting* (i.e., asking another person to do something or for something), (b) *refusing* (i.e., rejecting another person's request), and (c) *apologizing* (i.e., acknowledging fault and showing regret for doing or saying something). The third variable was **contextual conditions**, which initially included three key conditions: (a) *imposition* (i.e., the degree of inconvenience to the listener of the request, refusal, or apology), (b) *power difference* (i.e., the degree and direction of differences in power or position between the speaker and listener), and (c) *social distance* (i.e., the degree of shared social familiarity or solidarity between the speaker and listener).

Other variables were added as research continued. For example, Roever (2005, 2006, 2007, 2008) added the assessment of idiosyncratic and formulaic implicatures, as well as situational routines in addition to speech acts. He also added rejoinders after the response slot in designing his items. Tada (2005) specifically examined perception versus production of pragmatics in his study. Liu (2006, 2007) innovatively used speech acts and situations generated by students. Grabowski (2009, 2013) examined the relationship between grammar and pragmatic knowledge (which he further subdivided into sociolinguistic, sociocultural, & psychological knowledges). Itomitsu (2009) also studied grammar and three aspects of pragmatics (appropriate speech acts, routines, & speech styles) and used request speech acts, but also added offers and suggestions. Roever (2013) focused on implicature, but also considered vocabulary, collocations, idiomatic word meanings, and morphology. Rylander et al. (2013) added a number of speech acts using refusals and apologies, but also compliments, farewells, greetings, introductions, invitations, suggestions, offers, and complaints. In addition to requests, Timpe (2013) included new speech acts; she used offers, and also examined routine phrases, and phrases/idioms. Youn (2013) added the speech acts of expressing opinion and giving feedback on email and compared role-plays with monologic speaking and pragmatics tasks. And finally, Youn and Brown (2013) compared heritage and non-heritage KFL students' performances on such tests. Increasingly sophisticated statistical analyses have been used to study pragmatics tests.

A quick glance at the second to last column in Table 6.1 will reveal that all of the studies have used classical testing theory (CTT), which involves traditional descriptive statistics, reliability estimates, correlation coefficients, and in some cases, item analyses. However, as time went by, researchers increasingly used more sophisticated analyses, including:

- *Rasch analysis* allows researchers to put items and examinees on the same logit scales.

- *FACETS analysis* is a variation of Rasch analysis that allows researchers to put a variety of different facets (e.g., items, raters, rating categories, etc.) on the same logit scale and, among other things, allows simultaneous display of whatever facets are selected so they can be compared to examinee performances (for instance, examinees can be represented on the same scale as raters and rating categories, as in Brown, 2008c).

- *Generalizability theory* (G theory) allows researchers to study and minimize multiple sources of error in two stages. First, a *Generalizability study* is used to estimate variance components for whatever facets the researcher wishes to study, enabling the researcher to better understand the relative proportions of variance accounted for by the object of measurement. This is usually variance due to examinees, plus other facets that are sources of variance, such as raters and rating categories. Note that this can be done for either norm-referenced or criterion-referenced tests by using different procedures. The second stage is a *Decision study*, which is used to estimate the appropriate generalizability coefficients (analogous to reliability estimates) for different numbers of levels in each facet. For example, generalizability estimates can be provided for 2 raters versus 3, 4, or 5, etc. The researcher can simultaneously examine what happens if 2 or more rating categories are used in conjunction with different numbers of raters, ultimately identifying the most cost effective design for the test. For an example of this entire process, see Brown and Ahn (2013).

These analyses and others have been applied in various ways with generally increasing levels of sophistication in the pragmatics testing literature. Hudson et al. (1992, 1995) created the initial tests and validated all but the MDCT for EFL students at a US university using CTT. Yoshitake (1997) and Enochs and Yoshitake (1999) verified that the six assessments worked reasonably well for Japanese university EFL students using CTT. Those scores were also compared to the three sets of TOEFL subtest scores available at that time. Yamashita (1996) created Japanese versions and verified that all but MDCT worked reasonably well using CTT. Ahn (2005), Brown (2008c), and Brown and Ahn (2011) used FACETS and G Theory analyses to examine the effects of numbers of raters, functions, item types, and item characteristics on reliability and difficulty/severity in various combinations. Roever (2005, 2006, 2007) used FACETS and differential item functioning analyses. Liu (2006) used Rasch analysis to study the effectiveness of speech acts and situations that had been generated by students. Liu (2007) also used Rasch analysis but focused on developing a MDCT that worked. Roever (2008) applied FACETS analysis to study the effects of raters and items. Youn (2008) used FACETS analysis to examine the effects of test types and speech acts on raters' assessments. Grabowski (2009, 2013) used both G theory and FACETS analysis in the process of examining speaking tests similar to a DRPT with a focus on the relationship between grammar and pragmatic knowledge. Roever (2013) used FACETS analysis in his study of implicature. Rylander et al. (2013) used Rasch analysis in their study testing many different speech acts while using video formats. Timpe (2013) also used Rasch analysis in her study of American English self-assessment, a sociopragmatic comprehension test, and *Skype* role-play tasks. Youn (2013) relied on Rasch analysis in her elaborate validity study, based on Kane's (2006) argument-based approach, of role-plays with monologic speaking and pragmatics tasks. And finally, Youn and

Brown (2013) used FACETS analysis in their comparison of heritage and non-heritage KFL students' performances.

Conclusion

Different testing formats (including the original WDCT, MDCT, ODCT, DRPT, DSAT, RPSA, and a number of variations on those themes) have been shown to vary in their effectiveness for testing pragmatics, depending on the context and the variables involved. In the process, a wide range of variables have been studied in the literature to date (especially testing methods, speech acts, and various conditions). In addition, CTT, Rasch, FACETS, and G theory have been the major forms of analysis in the increasingly sophisticated pragmatics testing literature in a variety of different ways.

In all probability, pragmatics testing will continue to grow in the future. No doubt additional tests will be developed (a) to assess pragmatics in additional languages, (b) to accommodate new additional variables as the subfield of intercultural pragmatics continues to expand, and finally, (c) to adjust to refinements in pragmatics constructs and testing formats. It will be interesting to see what impacts all this activity will have on the teaching and testing of English and other languages around the world—and of course in Japan.

(updated and reprinted from Brown, 2015a)

Table 6.1. *Pragmatics Testing Projects (Quantitative) Described in Terms of Testing Methods, Speech Acts, Contextual Conditions and Value Added to the Knowledge of Pragmatics Assessment*

Testing Project; L2 involved & where	Testing Method[1]						Speech Acts				Cond[2]			Test Type[3]	Statistical Analyses[4]	Value Added to Knowledge of Pragmatics Assessment
	WDCT	MDCT	ODCT	DRPT	DSAT	RPSA	Request	Refusal	Apology	Other	Imposition	Power	Social Dis.			
Hudson et al., 1992, 1995; ESL in US	X	X	X	X	X	X	X	X	X		2	2	2	P&P	CTT	Created the initial tests & validated all but the MDCT for EFL students at a US university.
Enochs & Yoshitake-Strain, 1999; Yoshitake, 1997; EFL in Japan	X	X	X	X	X	X	X	X	X		2	2	2	P&P	CTT	Verified that six assessments worked reasonably well for Japanese university EFL students; scores also compared to 3 TOEFL subtests.
Yamashita, 1996; JSL in Japan	X	X	X	X	X	X	X	X	X		2	2	2	P&P	CTT	Created Japanese versions & verified that all but MDCT worked reasonably well for Japanese as a SL.
Ahn, 2005; Brown, 2008a; Brown & Ahn, 2011; All KFL in US	X		X	X	X	X	X	X	X		2	2	2	P&P	CTT, G-theory, FACETS	Examined the effects of varying the numbers of raters, functions, item types, & item characteristics on reliability & difficulty/severity.
Roever, 2005, 2006, 2007; ESL/EFL in US/Germany/Japan		S					X	X	X		2	1	1	WBT	CTT, FACETS, DIF	Assessed idiosyncratic & formulaic implicatures, situational routines, & speech acts; formats similar to MDCT, but speech acts added rejoinders after the response slot.
Tada, 2005; EFL in Japan		S	S				X	X	X		2	2	1	CLT, Video	CTT	1st to be computer delivered with video prompts for tests similar to MDCT & OPDCT (specifically examined perception vs. production of pragmatics).
Liu, 2006; EFL in PRC	S	S		S							2	2	2	P&P	CTT, Rasch	Speech acts & situations were generated by students.
Liu 2007; EFL in PRC	S										2	2	2	P&P	CTT, Rasch	Focused on developing a MDCT that worked; Speech acts & situations were generated by students.
Roever, 2008; ESL/EFL in US/Germany/Japan		S					X	X	X		2	1	1	WBT	CTT, FACETS	Speech acts section only; rejoinders after response slots; examined effects of raters & items.
Youn, 2008; KFL in US	X		X	X			X	X	X		2	2	2	P&P	CTT, FACETS	Examined the effects of test types & speech acts on raters' assessments.

Testing Intercultural Pragmatics Ability

Testing Project; L2 involved & where	Testing Method[1] WDCT	MDCT	ODCT	DRPT	DSAT	RPSA	Speech Acts Request	Refusal	Apology	Other	Cond[2] Imposition	Power	Social Dis.	Test Type[3]	Statistical Analyses[4]	Value Added to Knowledge of Pragmatics Assessment
Grabowski, 2009, 2013; ESL in US				S								1	2	P&P	CTT, G theory, FACETS	Speaking tests similar to DRPT; rated & examined the relationship between grammar & pragmatic knowledge (further subdivided into sociolinguistic, sociocultural, psychological knowledges).
Itomitsu, 2009; JFL in US	S						X		X					WBT	CTT	Grammar & three aspects of pragmatics (appropriate speech acts, routines, & speech styles); only total scores validated; speech acts included requests, offers, suggestions.
Roever, 2013; NS & ESL in Australia	S													P&P	CTT, FACETS	Focused on implicature (along with subtests on vocabulary, collocations, idiomatic word meanings, & morphology).
Rylander, Clark, & Derrah, 2013; EFL in Japan							X	X	X					P&P, Video	CTT, Rasch	Focused on importance of video: added speech acts (refusals & apologies, but also compliments, farewells, greetings, introductions, invitations, suggestions, offers, & complaints).
Timpe, 2013; EFL in Germany	S			S			X		X			2	2	WBT	CTT, Rasch	American English self-assessment, a sociopragmatic comprehension test, & Skype role-play tasks. Sociopragmatics test included speech acts, routine phrases, & phrases/idioms.
Youn, 2013; KFL in US				S			X		X			2		P&P	CTT, FACETS	(a) based on needs analysis, developed open role-play tasks similar to DRPT but more interactive; (b) added speech acts of expressing opinion & giving feedback on email; (c) compared role-play with monologic speaking & pragmatics tasks; & (d) exceptionally thorough reliability & validity study based on Kane's (2006) argument-based approach.
Youn & Brown, 2013; KFL in US	X	X	X				X	X	X		2	2	2	P&P	CTT, FACETS	Focused on comparison of heritage & non-heritage KFL students.

[1] X = adapted same test; S = Similar test. [2] Number of levels (1 or 2) of each condition, e.g., Imposition high or low would be 2 levels. [3] P&P = Paper & Pencil test; CLT = Computerized Language Testing; WBT = Web-based Language Testing. [4] CTT = Classical Test Theory; G Theory = Generalizability theory; Rasch = Rasch analysis; FACETS = Multifaceted Rasch analyses; DIF Differential Item Functioning

CHAPTER 7

TEST-TAKER MOTIVATIONS

QUESTION: This isn't exactly a statistical question, but it does have to do with gathering test data for statistical analyses. At my university, we just did a study comparing the scores of students on our English language placement test with their scores two years later on the same test. Their average scores went down nearly a standard deviation after two years of studying English. Do you think they unlearned English somehow over the years, or is it possible they weren't as motivated to do well in the second test?

ANSWER: Both of your ideas provide plausible explanations for your results: the average English level of your students may indeed have declined over two years, but it seems more likely to me that their motivations for taking the test may have changed. I have seen a number of instances over the years of students who have either had good reasons to score poorly on a test or have simply not been motivated to do well on a test. In either case, such factors can cause students to score lower than their actual abilities. In this column, I will address three sub-questions related to what you are asking: Why would some students purposely perform poorly on a test? What factors can muddy the interpretation of gain scores? And finally, what strategies can we use to counter such factors?

Why would some students purposely perform poorly on a test?

Quite reasonably, when taking a test, students will do whatever they feel is in their best interests, and sometimes, it is not in their best interests (at least from their points of view) to perform well on a test. For example, when I was an undergraduate, I once took a French pronunciation course. On the first day of class, my teacher took us to the language lab and asked us to read a French poem into a tape recorder. Before starting, she told us that she was going to compare our pronunciation at the beginning and end of the course and count improvement as part of our grade. As a consequence, during the pretest, I consciously decided to read the poem with my best American accent (it must have hurt her ears). However, when it came time for the posttest, I put real effort into getting the pronunciation right. The story ends happily, at least from my point of view: I improved a great deal in my pronunciation and got an "A". *Note:* it's possible that I could have improved equally well minutes later by simply doing a serious reading of the poem, without ever taking the course. Was I an evil student trying to mess up my teacher's test results? No, I was a cynical undergraduate (much like undergraduates everywhere) doing what I perceived to be in my best interests.

Another example, again taken from my family, is that of my son who took the Japanese language placement test at the University of Hawai'i at Mānoa (UHM). He had lived in Japan for several years and studied Japanese for a number of years. Yet, he performed very poorly (below chance as I recall) on the UHM Japanese Placement Test. Why? His explanation was that he had to take two years of Japanese one way or another, and it would be easier for him if he took the lowest levels possible. Sure enough, he took four semesters of Japanese 101, 102, 201, and 202 during which he really didn't need to study at all.

What factors can muddy the interpretation of gain scores?

The case that you bring up in your question at the top of this article may be an example of how students' motivations can change between two different administrations of a test. If the students at your school would benefit from scoring well on the placement examination at the beginning of their studies, say by needing to study fewer years of English, they might well do their best on the placement test. However, when they take the test two years later, the purpose (to determine how much they had learned) may not be important to them. As a result they might have no personal reason to care if they do well on the test, or alternatively, at that point, they might simply be distracted by their busy lives, family problems, or their other course work. Any of the above factors could noticeably affect the average scores on that second administration, even if those factors only applied to some of the students.

Another possible explanation for your results is that you may not have had exactly the same students taking the pretest and posttest. Say, for instance, that the students who performed well on your placement test by scoring 90% or higher were exempted from further English study and thus did not ever take the posttest. When comparing the pretest scores with the posttest scores, it would be important to eliminate the data from those students who were exempted on the basis of their high pretest scores so that the pretest/posttest comparison would be comparing the same people. If these exempted students were inadvertently left in the analysis, the effect might be to minimize the pretest/posttest gains or even to create losses on average.

What strategies can we use to counter such factors?

The bottom line is that student motivations need to be taken into consideration when planning studies involving tests, and indeed in interpreting the scores of any test, especially in light of the observation that many students will act in what they consider to be their best interests. To avoid such effects, we must, in one way or another, ensure that students are motivated to do well on each and every test they take. Otherwise the resulting scores may be a meaningless waste of everybody's time.

Consider the following example of one way to motivate students to perform to the best of their abilities. In one situation where I was teaching, if students did very well (defined as 80% or better) on the diagnostic test at the beginning of the course, I would move them out of my class to a higher level. Importantly, in order to motivate them to do their best, I told the students about this before they took the test. Since these were students who were eager to finish their English language training and get on with their educations, I believe they did their very best on the pretest. Then, when those remaining in the course took the final examination, they knew that a good portion of their grades depended on their scores, so I am sure they did their best on the posttest as well. Only under such conditions, where it is in the best interest of students (from their point of view) to perform well, will comparisons between pretest and posttest scores be meaningful. Note also that only the scores of students who took both tests were compared in this situation.

In the case that you bring up in your question at the top of this article, it seems to be in the best interests of the students to perform well on the placement test, but they seem to have no reason to perform well on the posttest. You need to figure out a way to get the students motivated to do well on that posttest as well. To that end, you will need to change your school's policies if that is possible. Perhaps you could tell the students that their performances on the posttest will be included as a component of their grades in their final course, or that a certain score (or score gain) must be achieved in order to finally be exempted from English training, or that the scores will be reported to their parents, etc. In short, if you want the results of that pretest/posttest comparison to have any meaning, you probably need to make some policy change that will ensure that performing well on the posttest is in the best interests of the students. [For more on other testing policy issues, see Brown, 2004c].

Consider another example, that of my son who purposely performed poorly on the Japanese language placement test. To address that and other language policy problems at UHM, we formed a committee that ultimately changed the policies such that it was in the best interest of students to perform well on the placement test. Now instead of having to take two years of a language starting from whatever level the students place into, they must reach a certain level (at least the equivalent of four semesters), while taking at least one course. In addition, they get credit for all courses in the sequence that they did not have to take. Thus, it would now be to my son's advantage to place high in the sequence. If for instance he had placed into the fourth course (Japanese 202), he could have received credit for four courses by taking only one. My guess is that, under these new policies, my son and other students like him would do their absolute best on the test because that behavior would be in their best interests.

I once was asked about a similar situation at a university in Taiwan. The teachers complained that their students were purposely doing poorly on the placement test. Those students had to take two years of English classes starting from whatever level they placed into. So students were purposely performing poorly. The solution that I suggested was that the students be required to finish two years of English, and if they placed high in that training or placed out of the training so much the better. Under such conditions, it would be in the best interests of most students to perform at their highest levels of ability.

Conclusion

Clearly then, researchers and other test score users must put themselves in the students' shoes and think about what possible motivations the students might have during a test administration as well as how those motivations might affect the test results. These issues clearly seem to me to be part of what Messick called *consequential validity* (Messick, 1988, 1989, 1996; also see Brown, 1996a, Brown & Hudson, 2002). Since addressing changes in student proficiency before and after two years of instruction, as you are doing, has important potential policy consequences, you will want to do the comparison as well as you can. At minimum, doing so probably means adopting policies that will create conditions under which students will be motivated to score well on both administrations of the test and insuring that the comparison only includes students who took both administrations.

(updated and reprinted from Brown, 2004b)

CHAPTER 8

EXTRANEOUS VARIABLES AND THE WASHBACK EFFECT

QUESTION: In your 1988 book *Understanding Research in Second Language Learning* you mention different types of extraneous variables such as subject expectancy, the halo effect, and the Hawthorne effect. Can you explain the difference between these terms? Also, what is the relation of these terms with washback? Finally, can you explain why some language researchers prefer to avoid the term "washback"?

ANSWER: Let me rephrase these questions and address them in the following order: (a) What are the different extraneous variables that researchers must guard against? (b) What is "washback", and why do some language researchers avoid the term? (c) What is the relationship between extraneous variables and washback?

What are the extraneous variables that researchers must guard against?

In Brown (1988), I described a whole set of extraneous variables that might affect the correct interpretation of a statistical study. I categorized these into four main categories: environment issues, grouping issues, people issues, and measurement issues.

Environment issues. Environment issues include naturally occurring variables (i.e., those which occur naturally in the research setting, like noise, temperature, adequacy of light, time of day, seating arrangements, etc.) and artificiality (unnatural arrangements within the study, e.g., the effects of students performing in front of a video camera, or under other artificial conditions).

Grouping issues. Grouping issues are related to the initial make-up of the groups or changes in their composition over the course of the study. These include self-selection (the practice of letting research participants choose to enter a study or decide which group to join, e.g., volunteerism), mortality (the effects of participants dropping out of the study), and maturation (the effects of different experiences on various participants, e.g., other simultaneous learning, puberty, family catastrophes, etc.).

People issues. People issues include the Hawthorne effect (the fact of being included in a study may affect the behavior of the participants in a study, and therefore affect the results), halo effect (the human tendency to respond positively to a person, e.g., the researcher, treatment, teacher, etc., may affect the results of the study), subject expectancy (the participants may guess what a study is about and then consciously or subconsciously "help" or resist the objectives of the research), and researcher expectancy (instances where the attitudes and motivations of the researchers themselves affect or color the results of a study).

Measurement issues. Because the results of a study are only as good as the data upon which they are based, it is crucial to ensure that the measures themselves are not introducing extraneous variables such as the *practice effect* (the potential influence over time of the measures in a study on each other, e.g., the effect of a pretest on a subsequent similar posttest), *reactivity effect* (the influence of parts of a measure on subsequent performance on other parts of the measure, e.g., answering questions early in a questionnaire might cause participants to form opinions or attitudes that would affect their answers later in the questionnaire), instability of measures (the degree to which inconsistent or unreliable measurements affect the study), and *instability of study results* (the degree to which the results of a study are likely to occur again if the study were replicated).

For the most part, extraneous variables are a threat to the internal reliability and validity of a research project. Essentially, such extraneous variables, if not controlled, or otherwise accounted for in a study, are all potential *intervening variables* (i.e., unanticipated variables that could explain the outcomes of a study as well as the conclusions drawn by the authors). As I put it in my 1988 book, "In statistical studies, there are a number of problems that can arise—both within a study and from outside of it—that may create major flaws in its *validity*, i.e., the degree to which a study and its results correctly lead to, or support, exactly what is claimed. The problems themselves result from extraneous variables that are relevant to a study but are not noticed or controlled."

What is "washback" and why do some language researchers avoid the term?

For readers who may not be familiar with the term "washback", let's look briefly at some definitions. Shohamy, Donitsa-Schmidt and Ferman (1996) define washback as "the connections between testing and learning" (p. 298). Gates (1995) defines washback as "the influence of testing on teaching and learning" (p. 101). Messick (1996) refers to washback as ". . . the extent to which the introduction and use of a test influences language teachers and learners to do things they would not otherwise do that promote or inhibit language learning" (p. 241). Washback clearly has to do with the effect of external testing on the teaching and learning processes in language classrooms. An example that often comes up in Japan is the effect of the university entrance examinations in Japan on high school language teaching and learning.

I wasn't aware that some researchers in our field are avoiding the term "washback". However, I can see how that might be the case, for two reasons. First, the very existence of the concept of washback has been questioned (see for instance, Alderson & Wall, 1993). However, since 1993, a considerable literature has emerged on the topic of washback, which seems to indicate that washback does exist (see, for example, Cheng & Watanabe, 2004). As shown in Table 8.1, washback can be analyzed into aspects of a curriculum that negative washback can affect and ways that positive washback can be fostered (see Brown, 1999c, for discussion of both positive and negative washback, or Brown, 2000a [Chapter 9] for more details on fostering positive washback).

Table 8.1. *Negative and Positive Effects of Washback*

−	+
Negative washback can affect:	Ways positive washback can be fostered:
• Teaching	• Alter test design factors
• Course content	• Change test content factors
• Course characteristics	• Adjust test logistic factors
• Class time	• Modify test interpretation factors

Second, many authors simply use other terms for the same basic concept as washback and thereby avoid the term. For example, in the general education literature, this concept is sometimes referred to as *backwash*, while elsewhere it is referred to variously as *test impact, test feedback, curriculum alignment,* and *measurement-driven instruction.* So, in direct answer to your question, I'm not sure language researchers are avoiding the concept of washback, but, as with so many concepts in the language teaching literature, various authors may be using different terminology to discuss it.

Washback, whether it is positive or negative, can be a potential boon or threat to language teaching curriculum (broadly defined) because, through washback, a test can steer a curriculum in one direction or another (in terms of teaching, course content, course characteristics, and/or class time) either with or against the better judgment of the administrators, teachers, students, parents, etc. From the point of view of testing, thinking about washback can help us to think about test validity. Washback becomes negative washback when there is a mismatch between the construct definition and the test, or between the content (e.g., the material/abilities being taught) and the test. Given that the definition of validity is the degree to which a test is measuring what it claims to measure, any such mismatch between a test and the construct or content that the test is designed to measure, would be a threat to the test's validity.

For example, as long as the official English language teaching curriculum in Japan was *yakudoku* (roughly translated as the grammar-translation reading method), those university entrance examinations that tested in ways consistent with *yakudoku* could be viewed as valid to the degree that they matched the curriculum. However, once the government ministry issued the 1993 guidelines for communicative language teaching, a mismatch was created between the *yakudoku* entrance examinations and any curricula that had actually responded to the ministry's guidelines. Thus, the *yakudoku* entrance examinations are seen by some to be creating negative washback on the communicative curriculum.

Thinking about washback can also lead us to considering the consequential basis for test validity in terms of the social consequences of test score use and the values implications of test interpretations, but that is a story for another day (for more on these topics, see Messick, 1988, 1989; Brown, 1999c).

What is the relationship between extraneous variables and washback?

Before I received your questions, I had never previously considered the relationship between the extraneous variables listed in the first section of this article and the concept of washback discussed in the second section. To be perfectly honest, when I first considered the question, I didn't see any connection whatsoever. After all, the effect of extraneous variables is a *research* issue, and the washback effect of test results is a *curriculum* issue.

However, as often happens, in writing about the relationship between extraneous variables and washback, I began to see that there was a connection: extraneous variables can have unintended, but nonetheless important, consequences on research very much in the way that test washback can have unintended, but nonetheless important, consequences on curriculum. Looking at the connection from another angle, extraneous variables can be seen as having a sort of washback effect on research, either in positive or negative ways, depending on whether such variables were accounted for in the research. Similarly, washback can be viewed as an extraneous variable affecting curriculum, either in positive or negative ways, depending on whether washback was accounted for in the curriculum and anticipated in the test design and use.

While I may be stretching things a bit here, there is no question that extraneous variables are an important aspect of the research endeavor and that washback is an important aspect of the testing/curriculum endeavor. So thank you for raising these questions.

(updated and reprinted from Brown, 2002b)

CHAPTER 9

UNIVERSITY ENTRANCE EXAMINATIONS: STRATEGIES FOR CREATING POSITIVE WASHBACK ON ENGLISH LANGUAGE TEACHING IN JAPAN

QUESTION:[1] For many years, you have been criticizing the English entrance examinations used by Japanese universities. Has any of that taught you what kinds of positive responses might be useful for solving the problems these tests create?

ANSWER: I think the best strategy that can be used at the moment to solve the university entrance examination problem would be to work to turn them into positive forces for change. Thus, this chapter explores some of the ways the university entrance examinations in Japan could be used to foster positive washback effects on English language instruction. During the last twelve years, a great deal has been written about the quality and appropriateness of examinations in Japan.

As far back as 1987, the possibility of including listening tests in Japanese university English language entrance examinations became an issue (Brown & Christensen, 1987). Other issues that have arisen over the years include ways to improve the testing of false beginners (Brown, 1987), ways to improve the fit of tests to language programs (Brown, 1990a), and ways that standardized test results are sometimes misinterpreted in Japan (Brown, 1993a).

---

[1] Note that this question as well as the question/answer format were added to what was a *Shiken* article (rather than one of my columns) to make it conform to the other 40 chapters in this book.

Beginning in 1995, the problems of examination hell and the appropriateness of the university entrance examinations for testing English language skills in Japan became issues of discussion (Brown, 1995a, 1995b; Brown & Kay, 1995; Brown & Gorsuch, 1995). Also in 1995, Brown and Yamashita (1995a, 1995c) began publishing the results of their analyses of the English language parts of twenty-one university entrance examinations, including ten private universities, ten public, plus the center exam. These studies did not go entirely without criticism (see for instance, O'Sullivan, 1995, answered in Brown & Yamashita, 1995b).

In 1996, discussion of the issue of the English language parts of the Japanese university entrance examinations came to a head when Brown (1996b) delivered his plenary speech at the annual JALT Conference in 1995. Stapleton (1996) offered a reaction to some of Brown's points, arguing basically that Brown was ignorant of the Japanese perspective. Yoshida (1996a) started a series of articles when he offered the view that Brown was practicing "cultural imperialism" by ignoring important cultural differences between Japan and the United States. Brown (1996c) answered Yoshida's arguments point-by-point and Yoshida (1996b) gave a final response (because, perhaps mercifully, the Daily Yomiuri would not accept an additional response article by Brown). A recent addition to the literature on this topic also came from the ever-persistent Brown (1998b), in which he discussed the general effects of university entrance examinations on English language teaching in Japan.

In the articles above, a number of criticisms were leveled and problems identified, but a few solutions were also offered. In this short paper, I hope to expand the solutions by summarizing some of the positive aspects of two other papers wherein I dealt with the washback effect in general (Brown, 1997c) and the washback effect and its relationship to Japanese university English language entrance exams (Brown, 1998b). Before doing that, however, it would be useful to define the notion of washback.

Promoting positive washback

In the previous chapter, washback was defined as the effect of external testing on the teaching and learning processes in language classrooms. A classic example is the ways in which university entrance examinations in Japan affect high school language teaching and learning. In searching the literature on washback, I found that Hughes (1989), Heyneman and Ransom (1990), Shohamy (1992), Kehaghan and Greaney (1992), Bailey (1996), and Wall (1996) all provided lists of strategies for using the washback effect to positively influence language teaching. For more extensive discussion of these lists, see Brown, 1997c, 1998b. However, no two lists agreed on what those strategies should be or how they are related to each other.

In the following outline, I attempt to summarize and organize the strategies proposed in the literature into four different categories that language educators in Japan can use to promote positive washback: test design strategies, test content strategies, logistical strategies, and interpretation strategies:

A. *Test design strategies*
   1. Sample widely and unpredictably (Hughes, 1989)
   2. Design tests to be criterion-referenced (Hughes, 1989; Wall, 1996)
   3. Design the test to measure what the programs intend to teach (Bailey, 1996)
   4. Base the test on sound theoretical principles (Bailey, 1996)
   5. Base achievement tests on objectives (Hughes, 1989)
   6. Use direct testing (Hughes, 1989; Wall, 1996)
   7. Foster learner autonomy and self-assessment (Bailey, 1996)

B. *Test content strategies*
   1. Test the abilities whose development you want to encourage (Hughes, 1989)
   2. Use more open-ended items (as opposed to selected-response items like multiple choice) (Heyneman & Ransom, 1990)
   3. Make examinations reflect the full curriculum, not merely a limited aspect of it (Kehaghan & Greaney, 1992)
   4. Assess higher-order cognitive skills to ensure they are taught (Heyneman & Ransom, 1990; Kehaghan & Greaney, 1992)
   5. Use a variety of examination formats, including written, oral, aural, and practical (Kehaghan & Greaney, 1992)
   6. Do not limit skills to be tested to academic areas (they should also relate to out-of-school tasks) (Kehaghan & Greaney, 1992)
   7. Use authentic tasks and texts (Bailey, 1996; Wall, 1996)

C. Logistical strategies

1. Ensure that test-takers, teachers, administrators, and curriculum designers understand the purpose of the test (Bailey, 1996; Hughes, 1989)

2. Make sure language learning goals are clear (Bailey, 1996)

3. Where necessary, provide assistance to teachers to help them understand the tests (Hughes, 1989)

4. Provide feedback to teachers and others so that meaningful change can be effected (Heyneman & Ransom, 1990; Shohamy, 1992)

5. Provide detailed and timely feedback to schools on levels of pupils' performance and areas of difficulty in public examinations (Kehaghan & Greaney, 1992)

6. Make sure teachers and administrators are involved in different phases of the testing process because they are the people who will have to make changes (Shohamy, 1992)

7. Provide detailed score reporting (Bailey, 1996)

D. Interpretation strategies

1. Make sure exam results are believable, credible, and fair to test takers and score users (Bailey, 1996)

2. Consider factors other than teaching effort in evaluating published examination results and national rankings (Kehaghan & Greaney, 1992)

3. Conduct predictive validity studies of public examinations (Kehaghan & Greaney, 1992)

4. Improve the professional competence of examination authorities, especially in test design (Kehaghan & Greaney, 1992)

5. Ensure that each examination board has a research capacity (Kehaghan & Greaney, 1992)

6. Have testing authorities work closely with curriculum organizations and with educational administrators (Kehaghan & Greaney, 1992)

7. Develop regional professional networks to initiate exchange programs and to share common interests and concerns (Kehaghan & Greaney, 1992)

Discussion

In view of the points made in the literature on positive washback, we have to ask ourselves how such test design, test content, logistical, and interpretation strategies could be applied to the university entrance examinations in Japan as well as who would implement them. Clearly, some of the strategies listed above would have to be the responsibility of the people who design and write the university English language entrance exams, but the majority of these strategies would probably only work if there was comprehensive teamwork and collaboration between the university examination writers and the instructors who teach high school English. Such large-scale cooperation to achieve positive washback from the entrance examinations in Japan could probably only be organized by the Ministry of Education [Sports, Science and Technology] or the National Center for University Entrance Examinations. Even then, such reforms would probably only be effective if they were applied to a single, centralized university entrance examination. As Watanabe (1996, p. 332) points out:

> A large amount of time, money and energy is spent on entrance examinations every year at individual, school and national levels. In order to make the best use of such an investment, we need to be empirical, rational and well-informed.

In this chapter, I have listed some of the strategies available for promoting positive washback effects from the university entrance examinations. Such strategies could help improve the teaching and learning that is going on in Japan's junior and senior high school English language classrooms and at the same time help make the entrance examination process fairer and more relevant. I leave one question with the reader: Is Japan ready and willing to reform the current entrance examination system in order to foster positive washback effects that will help improve language education?

(updated and reprinted from Brown, 2000a)

PART I: SECOND LANGUAGE TESTING

SECTION B: ITEM ANALYSES

CHAPTER 10

NORM-REFERENCED ITEM ANALYSIS: ITEM FACILITY AND ITEM DISCRIMINATION

QUESTION: A few years ago in your *Shiken* column, you showed how to do item analysis for weighted items using a calculator (Brown, 2000b, pp. 19-21 [Chapter 14]). In a later column (Brown, 2002c, pp. 20-23 [Chapter 13]), you showed how to do distracter efficiency analysis in a spreadsheet program. But, I don't think you have ever shown how to do regular item analysis statistics in a spreadsheet. Could you please do that? I think some of your readers would find it very useful.

ANSWER: Yes, I see what you mean. In answering questions from readers, I explained more advanced concepts of item analysis without laying the groundwork that other readers might need. To remedy that, in this chapter, I will directly address your question, but only with regard to norm-referenced item analysis. In the next chapter, I will address another reader's question, and in the process show how criterion-referenced item analysis can be done in a spreadsheet.

The overall purpose of item analysis

Let's begin by answering the most basic question in item analysis: Why do we do item analysis? We do it as the penultimate step in the test development process. Such projects are usually accomplished in the following steps:

1. Assemble or write a relatively large number of items of the type you want on the test.

2. Analyze the items carefully using item format analysis to make sure the items are well written and clear (for guidelines, see Brown, 1996a; Brown & Hudson, 2002).

3. Pilot the items using a group of students similar to the group that will ultimately be taking the test. Under less than ideal conditions, this pilot testing may be the first operational administration of the test.

4. Analyze the results of the pilot testing using item analysis techniques. These are described below for norm-referenced tests (NRTs) and in the next chapter for criterion-referenced tests (CRTs).

5. Select the most effective items (and get rid of the ineffective items) to make a shorter, more effective revised version of the test.

Basically, those five steps are followed in any test development or revision project.

Item analysis statistics for norm-referenced tests

As indicated above, the fourth step, item analysis, is different for NRTs and CRTs, and in this chapter, I will only explain item analysis statistics as they apply to NRTs. The basic purpose of any NRT is to spread students out along a general continuum of language abilities, usually for purposes of making aptitude, proficiency, or placement decisions (for much more on this topic, see Brown, 1996a; Brown & Hudson, 2002). Two item statistics are typically used in the item analysis of such norm-referenced tests: item facility and item discrimination.

Item facility (IF) is defined here as the proportion of students who answered a particular item correctly. Thus, if 45 out of 50 students answered a particular item correctly, the proportion would be 45/50 = .90. An IF of .90 means that 90% of the students answered the item correctly, and by extension, that the item is very easy for them. In Figure 10.1, you will see one way to calculate *IF* using the *Excel*® spreadsheet for Item 1 in a small example data set coded 1 for correct and 0 for incorrect answers. Notice the cursor has outlined cell C21 and that the function/formula typed in that cell (shown both in the row above the column labels and in cell B21) is =AVERAGE(C2:C19), which tells the computer to average the ones and zeros in the range between cells C2 and C19. The result in this case is .94, a very easy item because 94% of the students are answering correctly.

All the other NRT and CRT item analysis techniques that I will discuss here and in the next chapter are based on this notion of item facility. For instance, item discrimination can be calculated by first figuring out who the upper and lower students are on the test (using their total scores to sort them from the highest score to the lowest). The upper and lower groups should probably be made up of equal numbers of students who represent approximately one third of the total group each. In Figure 10.1, I have

Norm-Referenced Item Analysis: Item Facility and Item Discrimination 65

	A	B	C	D	E	F	G	H	I	J	K	L	M	N
1	STUDENT		Item1	Item2	Item3	Item4	Item5	Item6	Item7	Item8	Item9	Item10	etc…	Total
2	Hide		1	1	0	1	1	1	0	1	1	1	etc…	77
3	Tomoko		1	1	0	1	1	1	0	1	1	1	etc…	75
4	Kunio		1	1	0	1	1	1	0	1	0	1	etc…	72
5	Naoko		1	1	0	1	1	1	0	0	0	1	etc…	72
6	Eriko		1	1	0	1	0	0	0	1	0	1	etc…	70
7														
8	Kimi		1	1	0	1	0	1	1	1	1	0	etc…	70
9	Kazumoto		1	1	0	0	1	1	0	1	0	1	etc…	69
10	Kako		1	1	0	0	1	0	0	1	1	0	etc…	69
11	Joji		1	1	0	1	0	1	1	1	1	1	etc…	69
12	Mitsuko		1	1	0	0	0	1	0	0	1	0	etc…	69
13	Issaku		1	1	0	1	0	1	1	0	0	1	etc…	68
14														
15	Naoyo		1	1	0	0	0	1	1	1	1	0	etc…	68
16	Yuki		1	1	0	0	0	0	1	0	1	1	etc…	67
17	Mariko		1	1	0	0	0	1	0	0	0	0	etc…	64
18	Toshi		1	1	0	0	0	0	1	0	1	1	etc…	61
19	Hachiko		0	1	0	0	0	0	1	1	0	0	etc…	61
20		Formulas for Item1												
21	IF	=Average(C2:C19)	0.94	1.00	0.00	0.50	0.38	0.63	0.50	0.63	0.56	0.63		
22	IFupper	=Average(C2:C6)	1.00	1.00	0.00	1.00	0.80	0.80	0.00	0.80	0.40	1.00		
23	IFlower	=Average(C15:C19)	0.80	1.00	0.00	0.00	0.00	0.20	1.00	0.40	0.60	0.40		
24	ID	= C22-C23	0.20	0.00	0.00	1.00	0.80	0.60	-1.00	0.40	-0.20	0.60		
25	Keepers		*			*	*	*		*		*		
26														

Figure 10.1. The NRT Item Analysis

sorted the students from high to low based on their total test scores from 77 for Hide down to 61 for Hachiko. Then I separated the three groups such that there are five in the top group, five in the bottom group, and six in the middle group. Notice that Issaku and Naoyo both had scores of 68 but ended up in different groups (as did Eriko and Kimi with their scores of 70). The decision as to which group they were assigned to was made with a coin flip.

To calculate *item discrimination* (ID), I started by calculating IF for the upper group using the following: =AVERAGE(C2:C6), as shown in row 22. Then, I calculated IF for the lower group using the following: = AVERAGE(C15:C19), as shown in row 23. With IFupper and IFlower in hand, calculating ID simply required subtracting IFupper - IFlower. I did this by subtracting C22 minus C23, or =C22-C23, as shown in row 24, which resulted in an ID of .20 for Item 1.

Once I had calculated the four item analysis statistics shown in Figure 10.1 for Item 1, I then simply copied them and pasted them into the spaces below the other items, which resulted in all the other item statistics you see in Figure 10.1. [Note that the statistics didn't always fit in the available spaces, so I got results that looked like ### in some cells; to fix that, I blocked out all the statistics and typed **alt oca** and thus adjusted the column widths to fit the statistics. You may also want to adjust the number of decimal places, which is beyond the scope of this article. You can learn about this by looking in the **Help** menu or in the *Excel*® manual.

Ideal items in an NRT should have an average *IF* of .50. Such items would thus be well centered, i.e., 50 percent of the students would have answered correctly, and by extension, 50 percent would have answered incorrectly. In reality however, items rarely have an *IF* of exactly .50, so those that fall in a range between .30 and .70 are usually considered acceptable for NRT purposes.

Once those items that fall within the .30 to .70 range of *IF*s are identified, the items among them that have the highest *ID*s should be further selected for inclusion in the revised test. This process would help the test designer to keep only those items that are well centered and discriminate well between the high and the low scoring students. Such items are indicated in Figure 10.1 by an asterisk in row 25 (cleverly labeled "Keepers").

For more information on using item analysis to develop NRTs, see Brown (1995c, 1996a). For information on calculating NRT statistics for weighted items (i.e., items that cannot be coded 1 or 0 for correct and incorrect), see Brown (2000b). For information on calculating item discrimination using the point-biserial correlation coefficient instead of *ID*, see Brown (2001d [Chapter 12]). For an example NRT development and revision project, see Brown (1989).

Conclusion

I hope you have found my explanation of how to do norm-referenced item analysis statistics (item facility and item discrimination) in a spreadsheet clear and helpful. I must emphasize that these statistics are only appropriate for developing and analyzing norm-referenced tests, which are usually used at the institutional level, like, for example, overall English language proficiency tests (to help with, say, admissions decisions) or placement tests (to help place students into different levels of English study within a program). However, these statistics are not appropriate for developing and analyzing classroom oriented criterion-referenced tests like the diagnostic, progress, and achievement tests of interest to teachers. For an explanation of item analysis as it is applied to CRTs, read the next chapter in this book, where I will explain the distinction between the difference index and the *B*-index.

(updated and reprinted from Brown, 2003b)

CHAPTER 11

CRITERION-REFERENCED ITEM ANALYSIS: THE DIFFERENCE INDEX AND B-INDEX

QUESTION: Can you explain the distinction between a difference index and a *B*-index? When should these indices be used? When should they not be used? (You mentioned the use of *B*-index on page 212 of your article (Brown, 2001f) in the book *A Focus on Language Test Development* that you edited with Thom Hudson.)

ANSWER: Your question fits neatly with the question I addressed in the last chapter. I really can't answer your question without first repeating the brief introduction (from the previous chapter) about the purpose of item analysis in revising and improving language tests.

The purpose of item analysis

The development of any language test is a major task just like other aspects of language curriculum development. Such projects are usually accomplished in the following steps:

1. Assemble or write a relatively large number of items of the type you want on the test.

2. Analyze the items carefully using item format analysis to make sure they are well-written and clear (for guidelines, see Brown, 1996a; Brown & Hudson, 2002).

3. Pilot the items using a group of students similar to the group that will ultimately be taking the test (under less than ideal conditions, this may actually be the first operational administration of the test).

4. Analyze the results statistically using item analysis techniques. These were described in the previous chapter for norm-referenced tests (NRTs) and are described below for criterion-referenced tests (CRTs).

5. Select the most effective items (and get rid of the ineffective items) and make a shorter, more effective revised version of the test.

Item analysis statistics for criterion-referenced tests

The fourth step in the above list—item analysis—is different for NRTs and CRTs. In the previous chapter, I explained how that step works for NRTs. In this chapter, I will explain item analysis for CRTs. Recall that the basic purpose of CRTs is to measure the amount (or percent) of material in a course or program of study that students know (or can do), usually for purposes of making diagnostic, progress, or achievement decisions (for much more on this topic, see Brown, 1995d, 1996a; Brown & Hudson, 2002). Two item statistics are often used in the item analysis of such criterion-referenced tests: the difference index and the *B*-index.

The *difference index* is defined as the item facility on the particular item for the posttest minus the item facility for that same item on the pretest. [Recall that the definition of item facility is the proportion of students who answered a particular item correctly.] In other words, the difference index shows the gain, or difference in performance, on each item between the pretest and posttest. Calculating the difference index (DI) goes like this: if 10 out of 50 students answered Item 1 correctly on the pretest for a course, the pretest item facility ($IF_{pretest}$) would be 10/50 = .20; if 45 out of the same 50 students answered that same item correctly on the posttest, the posttest item facility ($IF_{posttest}$) would be 45/50 = .90. Given that $IF_{posttest}$ = .90 and $IF_{pretest}$ = .20, the DI would be .70 ($DI = IF_{posttest} - IF_{pretest}$ = .90 - .20 = .70).

Notice in Figure 11.1 that I have calculated the DI for Item 1 using my spreadsheet program. I did so by typing in the item numbers, then lining up my posttest and pretest item facilities as shown. Then, in cell F2, I typed =B2-D2 and hit the ENTER key. In other words, I subtracted the $IF_{posttest}$ minus the $IF_{pretest}$ and got .70 as my result. Once the calculation in cell F2 was completed, I blocked and copied that cell (using CONTROL C to do so) and pasted that into cells F3 to F11 (by blocking them out and hitting CONTROL V). That copying yielded the other DI values. The DI tells me how much the students are improving between the pretest and posttest on each item (and by extension, on the related curriculum objective). Like the item discrimination statistic discussed in the previous chapter, the higher the value of the DI, the better. Indeed a value of 1.00 is a perfect difference index.

Thus, in Figure 11.1, Items 1, 3, and 7-10 are much better related to the curriculum than are Items 2, and 4-6 because they have higher values. Items 4-6 are not fitting because they reflect only small gains (i.e., their values are very low); Item 2, which has a negative value, indicates that, somehow, during the course, 80% of the students who started out knowing this item unlearned it by the end of the course.

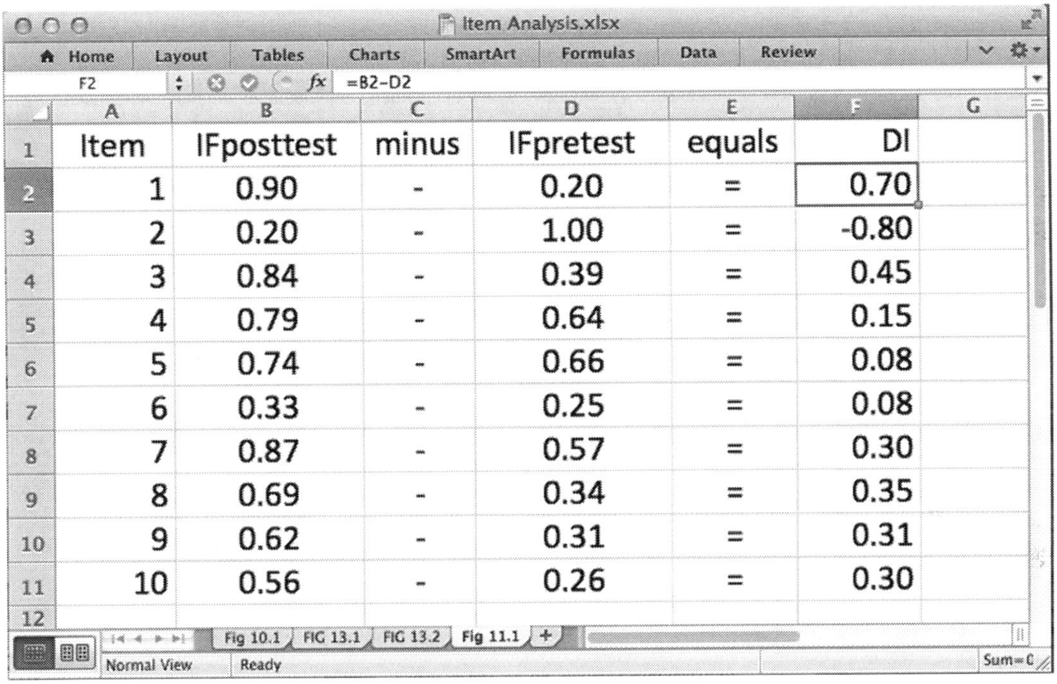

Item	IFposttest	minus	IFpretest	equals	DI
1	0.90	-	0.20	=	0.70
2	0.20	-	1.00	=	-0.80
3	0.84	-	0.39	=	0.45
4	0.79	-	0.64	=	0.15
5	0.74	-	0.66	=	0.08
6	0.33	-	0.25	=	0.08
7	0.87	-	0.57	=	0.30
8	0.69	-	0.34	=	0.35
9	0.62	-	0.31	=	0.31
10	0.56	-	0.26	=	0.30

Figure 11.1. The CRT Item Analysis

In contrast, the *B*-index is defined as the item facility on the particular item for the students who passed the test minus the item facility for the students who failed. In other words, the *B*-index shows how well each item is contributing to the pass/fail decisions that are often made with CRTs. For example, if 14 out of the 14 students who passed the test answered Item 1 correctly, the item facility for students who passed (IF_{pass}) would be 14/14 = 1.00; if none of the six students who failed the test answered that same item correctly, the item facility for students who failed (IF_{fail}) would be 0/6 = .00. Given that IF_{pass} = 1.00 and IF_{fail} = .00, the *B*-index for this particular item would be 1.00 (*B*-index = $IF_{pass} - IF_{fail}$ = 1.00 - .00 = 1.00).

Notice in Figure 11.2 that I have calculated the *B*-index for Item 1 using my spreadsheet program. I arranged my data by typing labels for Student ID and the item numbers across the first row. Then, I typed in all the students' names, as well as 1s for items they answered correctly and 0s for items they answered incorrectly. I next calculated the total score for each student and sorted the students from highest to lowest scores. Finally, to make it easy to visualize the passing and failing groups, I put a blank row between those who passed (i.e., scored above the 60% cut-point in this case) and those who failed.

	A	B	C	D	E	F	G	H	I	J	K	L	M	N
1	Student ID		Item1	Item2	Item3	Item4	Item5	Item6	Item7	Item8	Item9	Item10	Score	Percent
2	Kimi		1	0	1	1	1	1	1	1	1	1	9	90
3	Kazumoto		1	0	1	1	1	1	1	1	1	1	9	90
4	Kako		1	0	1	1	1	1	1	1	1	1	9	90
5	Joji		1	0	1	1	0	1	1	1	1	1	8	80
6	Mitsuko		1	0	1	1	1	1	1	1	0	1	8	80
7	Issaku		1	0	1	1	1	0	1	1	1	1	8	80
8	Kensaku		1	0	0	1	1	1	1	1	1	1	8	80
9	Yurikio		1	0	0	1	1	1	1	1	1	1	8	80
10	Minoru		1	0	0	1	0	1	1	1	1	1	7	70
11	Hide		1	0	1	1	1	1	1	0	1	0	7	70
12	Tomoko		1	0	1	1	1	1	1	0	0	1	7	70
13	Kunio		1	0	0	1	0	1	1	1	1	0	6	60
14	Naoko		1	0	0	1	1	1	0	1	0	1	6	60
15	Eriko		1	0	0	1	1	1	1	1	0	0	6	60
16												60% Cut-Point (for Passing)		
17	Yoshi		0	1	1	1	0	0	1	1	0	0	5	50
18	Naoyo		0	1	0	1	0	1	1	0	0	1	5	50
19	Yuki		0	1	0	1	0	1	0	0	1	1	5	50
20	Mariko		0	1	1	1	1	1	0	0	0	0	5	50
21	Toshi		0	1	1	1	0	0	1	0	0	0	4	40
22	Hachiko		0	1	0	1	0	0	0	0	0	0	2	20
23		Functions/Formulas for Item 1												
24	IFpass	= Average (C2:C15)	1.00	0.00	0.57	1.00	0.79	0.93	0.93	0.86	0.71	0.79	7.57	76	MeanPass
25	IFfail	= Average (C17:C22)	0.00	1.00	0.50	1.00	0.17	0.50	0.50	0.17	0.17	0.33	4.33	43	MeanFail
26	B-index	= C24-C25	1.00	-1.00	0.07	0.00	0.62	0.43	0.43	0.69	0.55	0.45	3.24	32	Pass-Fail

Figure 11.2. Calculating the B-index in a Spreadsheet

To calculate the *B*-index, I began by labeling the three rows from A24 to A26 as follows: IFpass, IFfail, and B-index. Then I typed functions/formulas into cells C24, C25, and C26 as shown next to each cell in Figure 11.2. After typing each formula, I hit the ENTER key and moved on to the next one. Once the three formulas were typed into cells C24 to C26, I blocked them, copied them (I used CONTROL C to do so), and pasted them into cells D24 to L26 (by hitting CONTROL V). For each item, I now had the item facility for those students who passed the test, the item facility for those who failed, and the B-index for each item. The B-index tells me how well each item is contributing to the pass/fail decision on this test at this cut-point. Like the item discrimination and difference index statistics, the higher the *B*-index, the better. A perfect *B*-index would be 1.00.

Conclusion

In direct answer to your question: yes, I can explain the distinction between a difference index and a *B*-index, as you can see above.

When should these indices be used? They should be used to analyze the items on a criterion-referenced test for purposes of revising the test. In both cases, the items with the highest values should generally be kept. However, making these decisions is not nearly as simple as it is for NRT development because a CRT item may not be performing well in terms of these statistics for many reasons: (a) perhaps the item is written/working poorly, (b) maybe the objective the item is testing is vague, (c) perhaps the students are not yet ready to learn this particular objective, (d) maybe one - or all - of the teachers are not teaching this particular objective, or are teaching it poorly, (e) perhaps the materials are confusing with regard to this particular objective, or (f) maybe some combination of the above factors is at work. So, these item statistics can point you to places in your curriculum where something is not working well, but they cannot tell you exactly what is wrong. You will have to do some common-sense analysis of the entire situation in deciding how to revise your criterion-referenced test and/or other aspects of your curriculum (aspects like the objectives themselves, the materials, or the teaching; for more on these curriculum elements, see Brown, 1995e).

However, the statistics explained in this chapter should help you figure out where to focus your energies. Generally, the difference index will tell you how well each item fits the objectives of your curriculum, and the *B*-index will tell you how well each item is contributing to the pass/fail decision that you must make at whatever cut-point you are using.

The word *criterion* in criterion-referenced test has been defined in two ways in the literature. One definition is that criterion refers to the material being taught in the course. Thus criterion-referenced testing would assess the particular learning points of a particular course or program. This definition fits very well with the difference index, which indicates how well each item fits the objectives of the curriculum.

The other definition is that the criterion is the standard of performance (or cut-point for decision making) that is expected for passing the test/course. Thus criterion-referenced testing would be used to assess whether students pass or fail at a certain criterion level (or cut-point). This definition fits very well with the *B*-index, which indicates how well each item is contributing to the pass/fail decision that you must make at whatever cut-point you are using.

Clearly, if you are primarily interested in the degree to which your items are reflecting the material in your courses (the first definition), you should focus on the difference index. If you are primarily interested in the degree to which your items are helping you make decisions at a certain cut-point (the second definition), you should focus on the *B*-index. If you are interested in both aspects of criterion-referenced testing at the same time, you will need to use both statistics.

When should they not be used? These particular statistics should probably not be used to analyze the effectiveness of norm-referenced items. However, see Brown (1989) for one exception where the *DI* statistic was used in combination with item facility and discrimination to develop an NRT that "fit the curriculum." The ultimate goal is to produce a curriculum and CRTs that match each other such that you get high difference indexes and high *B*-indexes.

For more information on using item analysis to develop CRTs, see Brown (1996a) or Brown and Hudson (2002). For information that will help you calculate CRT item statistics for weighted items (i.e., items that cannot be coded 1 or 0 for correct and incorrect), see Brown (2000b [Chapter 14]). For examples of CRT development and revision projects, see Brown (1993c, 2001f).

(updated and reprinted from Brown, 2003c)

CHAPTER 12

POINT-BISERIAL CORRELATION COEFFICIENTS

QUESTION: Recently on the email forum LTEST-L, there was a discussion about point-biserial correlation coefficients, and I was not familiar with this term. Could you explain what point-biserial correlation coefficients are and how they are important for language testers?

ANSWER: To adequately explain the point-biserial correlation coefficient, I will need to address four questions: (a) What is the point-biserial correlation coefficient? (b) How is the point-biserial correlation coefficient related to other correlation coefficients? (c) How is the point-biserial correlation coefficient calculated? And, (d) how is the point-biserial correlation coefficient used in language testing?

What is the point-biserial correlation coefficient?

As I defined it in Brown (1988, p. 150), the point-biserial correlation coefficient (symbolized as r_{pbi}) is a statistic used to estimate the degree of relationship between a naturally occurring dichotomous nominal scale and an interval (or ratio) scale. For example, a researcher might want to investigate the degree of relationship between gender (that is, being male or female—a naturally occurring dichotomous nominal scale) and achievement in English as a second language as measured by scores on the end-of-the-year departmental examination (an interval scale).

Aside from the types of scales involved, the interpretation of the resulting coefficient is very similar to that for the more commonly reported Pearson product-moment correlation coefficient (sometimes referred to as Pearson r, or simply r). In brief, like the Pearson r, the r_{pbi} can range from 0 to +1.00 if the two scales are related positively (that is, in the same direction) and from 0 to -1.00 if the two scales are related negatively (that is, in opposite directions). The higher the value of r_{pbi} (positive or negative), the stronger the relationship between the two variables. [For more detailed explanations of the interpretation and assumptions of Pearson r and r_{pbi}, see Brown, 1996a.]

How is the point-biserial correlation coefficient related to other correlation coefficients?

In distinguishing the point-biserial from other correlation coefficients, I must first point out that the point-biserial and biserial correlation coefficients are different. The biserial correlation coefficient (or r_{bi}) is appropriate when you are interested in the degree of relationship between two interval (or ratio) scales but for some logical reason one of the two is more sensibly interpreted as an artificially created dichotomous nominal scale. For instance, you might be interested in determining the degree of relationship between passing or failing a first year university ESL course and language aptitude test scores. To do this, grades at the end of the course (A, B, C, D and F, often converted to a 4.00, 3.00, 2.00, 1.00, & 0.00 interval scale) might be artificially separated into a nominal scale made up of two groups: pass (A to D, or 1.00 to 4.00) and fail (F or 0.00). The degree of relationship between this new, artificially created dichotomy and the interval scores on the language aptitude test could then be determined by using the r_{bi} coefficient. Thus the biserial correlation coefficient is appropriately applied when the nominal variable is artificially created (as in the pass-fail variable created from grade points), while the point-biserial correlation coefficient is appropriately applied when the nominal variable occurs naturally (as in the naturally occurring male-female gender distinction).

A variety of different correlation coefficients have been developed over the years for various combinations of scale types, as summarized in Table 12.1. The point-biserial is just one of these statistical tools (see the fifth row of correlation coefficients).

Table 12.1. *Types of Correlation Coefficients*

Correlation Coefficient	Types of Scales
Pearson product-moment	Both scales interval (or ratio)
Spearman rank-order	Both scales ordinal
Phi	Both scales are naturally dichotomous (nominal)
Tetrachoric	Both scales are artificially dichotomous (nominal)
Point-biserial	One scale naturally dichotomous (nominal), one scale interval (or ratio)
Biserial	One scale artificially dichotomous (nominal), one scale interval (or ratio)
Gamma	One scale nominal, one scale ordinal

How is the point-biserial correlation coefficient calculated?

The data in Table 12.2 are set up with some obvious examples to illustrate the calculation of r_{pbi} between items on a test and total test scores. Notice that the items have been coded 1 for correct and 0 for incorrect (a natural dichotomy) and that the total scores in the last column are based on a total of 50 items (most of which are not shown).

Table 12.2. *Example Student Data*

Student	Item 1	Item 2	Item 3	Items 4,5,6, ...	Total Score
Hachiko	1	0	1	...	50
Kazuko	1	0	1	...	45
Toshi	1	0	1	...	45
Yoshi	1	0	1	...	40
Tomoko	0	1	1	...	35
Yasuhiro	0	1	1	...	30
Yuichi	0	1	1	...	30
Masa	0	1	1	...	25
M_p	45	30	37.5	Total mean	37.50
M_q	30	45	.00	Total SD	8.29
p	.50	.50	1.00		
q	.50	.50	.50		
r_{pbi}	.91	-.91	.00		

To calculate the r_{pbi} for each item use the following formula:

$$r_{pbi} = \frac{M_p - M_q}{S_t}\sqrt{pq}$$

Where:
    r_{pbi} = point-biserial correlation coefficient
    M_p = whole-test mean for students answering item correctly (i.e., those coded as 1s)
    M_q = whole-test mean for students answering item incorrectly (i.e., those coded as 0s)
    S_t = standard deviation for whole test
    p = proportion of students answering correctly (i.e., those coded as 1s)
    q = proportion of students answering incorrectly (i.e., those coded as 0s)

For example, let's apply the formula for r_{pbi} to the data for Item 1 in Table 12.2 (which we would expect to correlate highly with the total scores), where the whole-test mean for students answering correctly is 45; the whole-test mean for students answering incorrectly is 30; the standard deviation for the whole test is 8.29; the proportion of students answering correctly is .50; and the proportion answering incorrectly is .50.

$$r_{pbi} = \frac{M_p - M_q}{S_t}\sqrt{pq} = \frac{45-30}{8.29}\sqrt{(.50)(.50)} = \frac{15}{8.29}\sqrt{.2500} = 1.81(.50) = .91$$

Thus the correlation between item 1 and the total scores is a very high .91, and this item appears to be spreading the students out in very much the same way as the total scores are. In this sense, the point-biserial correlation coefficient indicates that item 1 discriminates well among the students in this group (at least in terms of the way the total test scores discriminate).

As another example, let's apply the formula for r_{pbi} to the data for Item 2 in Table 12.2 (which we would expect to be highly but negatively correlated with the total scores), where the whole-test mean for students answering correctly is 30; the whole-test mean for students answering incorrectly is 45; the standard deviation for the whole test is still 8.29; the proportion of students answering correctly is still .50; and the proportion answering incorrectly is still .50.

$$r_{pbi} = \frac{M_p - M_q}{S_t}\sqrt{pq} = \frac{30-45}{8.29}\sqrt{(.50).50} = \frac{-15}{8.29}\sqrt{.2500} = -1.81(.50) = -.91$$

Thus the correlation between item 2 and the total scores is a very high negative value of -.91, and this item appears to be spreading the students out opposite to the way the total scores are. In other words, the point-biserial correlation coefficient shows that item 2 discriminates in a very different way from the total scores at least for the students in this group.

As one last example, let's apply the formula for r_{pbi} to the data for Item 3 in Table 12.2 (which we would expect to have no correlation with the total scores), where the whole-test mean for students answering correctly is 37.5; the whole-test mean for students answering incorrectly is 0.00 because it is non-existent; the standard deviation for the whole test is still 8.29; the proportion of students answering correctly is 1.00; and the proportion answering incorrectly is .00.

$$r_{pbi} = \frac{M_p - M_q}{S_t}\sqrt{pq} = \frac{37.5 - .00}{8.29}\sqrt{(1.00)(.00)} = \frac{37.5}{8.29}\sqrt{.00} = 4.52(.00) = .00$$

Thus the correlation between item 3 and the total scores is zero, and this item does not appear to be spreading the students out in the same way as the total scores. In other words, item 3 is not discriminating at all among the students in this particular group—in this case because there is no variation in their answers.

How is the point-biserial correlation coefficient used in language testing?

As mentioned above, the point-biserial correlation coefficient can be used in any research where you are interested in understanding the degree of relationship between a naturally occurring nominal scale and an interval (or ratio) scale. For instance, I might be interested in the degree of relationship between being male or female and language aptitude as measured by scores on the Modern Language Aptitude Test (or MLAT; Carroll & Sapon, 1958). The point-biserial correlation coefficient could help you explore this or any other similar question. For examples of other uses for this statistic, see Guilford and Fruchter (1973).

However, language testers most commonly use r_{pbi} to calculate the item-total score correlation as another, more accurate, way of estimating item discrimination. The correlation coefficient being calculated here is between a naturally occurring dichotomous nominal scale (the correct or incorrect answer on the items, usually coded as 1 or 0) with the interval scale test scores. Such item-total correlations are often used to estimate item discrimination. Consider the item analysis results shown in Table 12.3.

The goal of the analysis shown in Table 12.3 is to estimate how difficult each item is (the IF, or item facility, shown in the second column) and how highly each item is correlated with the total scores (the r_{pbi} shown in the third column). The item facility, as estimated by the IF, ranges from 0.00 (everybody answered incorrectly) to 1.00 (everyone answered correctly) and shows how easy (or difficult) each item is. The r_{pbi} shows the degree to which each item is separating the better students on the whole test from the weaker students. Thus the higher the r_{pbi}, the better the item is discriminating. Notice in Table 12.3 that asterisks refer to the $p < .05$ at the bottom of the table and thereby indicate the items with point-biserial correlation coefficients that are significant at the .05 level (in other words, those items with correlations that have only a five percent chance of having occurred for chance reasons alone). (For more information on how to determine these p values for r_{pbi}, see Brown, 1996a, p. 178; for more information on item analysis for norm-referenced testing purposes, see Brown, 1996a (pp. 64-74), or 2003b [Chapter 10].)

Table 12.3. *Example Item Analysis (for 32 students)*

Item #	IF	r_{pbi}	
1	0.930	0.153	
2	0.656	0.295	*
3	0.882	0.122	
4	0.738	0.189	
5	0.455	0.310	*
6	0.838	0.394	*
7	0.684	0.469	*
8	0.552	0.231	
9	0.581	0.375	*
10	0.398	0.399	*
11	0.926	0.468	*
12	0.774	0.468	*
13	0.663	0.414	*
14	0.862	0.276	
15	0.624	0.205	

*$p < .05$

Certainly, if you are interested in creating a shorter, more efficient, norm-referenced version of the test, you might be wise to select those items with the highest point-biserial correlation coefficients from among those that are significant (numbers 2, 5-7, & 9-13) for the new revised version of the test. At the same time, you should keep an eye on the item facility index shown in the first column so that you select a balance of items that average out to make a test that is neither too difficult nor too easy. This strategy is very similar to the way the discrimination index is used (for more on this statistic, see Brown, 1996a, pp. 66-70). Such statistics can even be useful if what you need is a longer test: simply examine those items that appear to be discriminating well and write more items like them.

One important caveat: remember that item analysis statistics, like the r_{pbi}, are only tools that can help you in selecting the best items for a norm-referenced test, but they should never be used to replace the common sense notions involved in developing sound language test items. In other words, use these statistics to help you understand how students perform on your test items and then use that information to help you design a better test next time, while always keeping in mind your theoretical and practical reasons for writing the items you did and designing the test the way you did.

(updated and reprinted from Brown, 2001d)

CHAPTER 13

DISTRACTOR EFFICIENCY ANALYSIS IN A SPREADSHEET

QUESTION: In your testing book (Brown, 1996a), you show an example of distractor efficiency analysis, and you explain that you do it by calculating the proportion of people who chose each option on each item. How can I do such an analysis in my spreadsheet program, and how should it be interpreted?

ANSWER: Let me rephrase your questions a bit and address them in the following order: For multiple option items like multiple-choice items, the traditional item analysis for norm-referenced tests, including item facility and item discrimination analyses, can usefully be supplemented by a distractor efficiency analysis. Basically, you just need to (a) calculate the item analysis statistics (including item facility and item discrimination), (b) compute the proportion of people in the High, Middle, and Low groups who selected each option (say, A, B, C, & D), and then (c) use that information to help you decide which items and options are working and which are not. Let's look at those three steps one at a time from the perspective of the spreadsheet approach you asked about.

Setting up the spreadsheet

To begin with, look at the very small data set shown in Figure 13.1. This data set was created using the *Excel*® spreadsheet. Notice that the students are arranged from the best student, Hide, at the top with his score of 94, to the worst student, poor hapless Hachiko, who (though dogged and loyal) scored a miserable 25 points. Notice also that I formed three groups along the range of abilities: the High, Middle, and Low groups with 5, 6, and 5 students, respectively, and that I left empty rows between groups so I can see them easily. Much of traditional norm-referenced item analysis involves comparing the performances of the High and Low ability groups. Note also that each student's A, B, C, or D choice is entered as the data instead of the 1s and 0s that are often used to code correct and incorrect answers in such spreadsheet analyses.

Finally, notice that I have spread the items out with four blank columns between items to make room to work on my distractor efficiency analysis, which you see at the bottom of the spreadsheet.

Item analysis in a spreadsheet

Let's begin with the item analysis statistics. The first step is to put labels in the first column for *IF*, *IF*upper, *IF*lower, and *ID*. If you need a review of these norm-referenced item analysis statistics see Brown 1996a, or the first page of Chapter 14. In Figure 13.1, the cursor is in cell B21 (as indicated by the darkened edges of that cell). You can see in the formula box in the third row at the top of the spreadsheet that the formula being used in cell B21 is =COUNTIF(B2:B19,"A")/16. This means: count up all the cells containing "A" in the range between B2 and B19, then divide the result by 16. Since "A" is the correct answer, the result of this formula will be the item facility value (i.e., count up the number of correct answers in the range between B2 and B19, then divide the result by the total number of students taking the test).

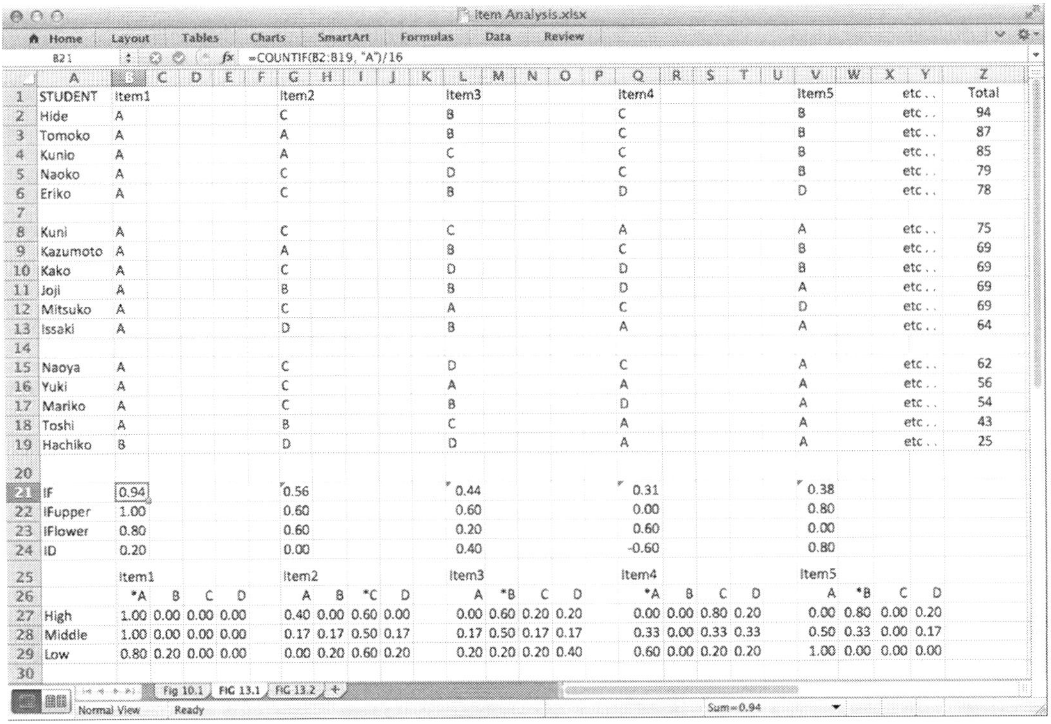

	A	B	C	D	E	F	G	H	I	J	K	L	M	N	O	P	Q	R	S	T	U	V	W	X	Y	Z
1	STUDENT	Item1					Item2					Item3					Item4					Item5			etc . .	Total
2	Hide	A					C					B					C					B			etc . .	94
3	Tomoko	A					A					B					C					B			etc . .	87
4	Kunio	A					A					C					C					B			etc . .	85
5	Naoko	A					C					D					C					B			etc . .	79
6	Eriko	A					C					B					D					D			etc . .	78
7																										
8	Kuni	A					C					C					A					A			etc . .	75
9	Kazumoto	A					A					B					C					B			etc . .	69
10	Kako	A					C					D					D					B			etc . .	69
11	Joji	A					B					B					D					A			etc . .	69
12	Mitsuko	A					C					A					C					D			etc . .	69
13	Issaki	A					D					B					A					A			etc . .	64
14																										
15	Naoya	A					C					D					C					A			etc . .	62
16	Yuki	A					C					A					A					A			etc . .	56
17	Mariko	A					C					B					D					A			etc . .	54
18	Toshi	A					B					C					A					A			etc . .	43
19	Hachiko	B					D					D					A					A			etc . .	25
20																										
21	IF	0.94					0.56					0.44					0.31					0.38				
22	IFupper	1.00					0.60					0.60					0.00					0.80				
23	IFlower	0.80					0.60					0.20					0.60					0.00				
24	ID	0.20					0.00					0.40					-0.60					0.80				
25		Item1					Item2					Item3					Item4					Item5				
26		*A	B	C	D		A	B	*C	D		A	*B	C	D		*A	B	C	D		A	*B	C	D	
27	High	1.00	0.00	0.00	0.00		0.40	0.00	0.60	0.00		0.00	0.60	0.20	0.20		0.00	0.00	0.80	0.20		0.00	0.80	0.00	0.20	
28	Middle	1.00	0.00	0.00	0.00		0.17	0.17	0.50	0.17		0.17	0.50	0.17	0.17		0.33	0.00	0.33	0.33		0.50	0.33	0.00	0.17	
29	Low	0.80	0.20	0.00	0.00		0.00	0.20	0.60	0.20		0.20	0.20	0.20	0.40		0.60	0.00	0.20	0.20		1.00	0.00	0.00	0.00	
30																										

Figure 13.1. The Setup for Distractor Efficiency Analysis

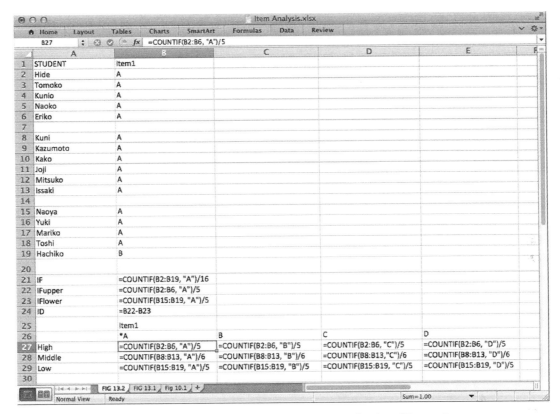

Figure 13.2. Formulas for Distractor Efficiency Analysis of Item 1

Cell B21 of Figure 13.2 shows how the *IF* for Item 1 is calculated using = COUNTIF (B2:B19, "A")/16, or the average of correct answers for all students taking the item. Simply enter the formula shown in cell B21 and hit the <enter> key. The number .94 should appear (as shown in the same cell in Figure 13.1). Figure 13.2 also shows the calculation of *IF_upper* using a similar formula in cell B22, but for the range that includes only the top five students (B2:B6); calculation of *IF_lower* in cell B23 is similar, but for the bottom five students (B15:B19). Cell B24 shows the calculation of ID, which is *IF_upper - IF_lower*, or in this case, =B22-B23. In the process of doing the above, you may have one of the following two problems:

1. Your numbers may have the wrong number of digits to the right of the decimal place. To get two digits to the right of the decimal use the following menus: **Format, Cells**, select Number, **Category**, again select Number, **Decimal**, and change the number in the box to 2; then click the **okay** button.

2. Your columns may be too wide or two narrow (especially if a series of number signs, ###, appear in some cells) in which case you should try **Format, Column, Width**, and changing the number in the box to a larger number; then click the **okay** button].

Once you have done the item analysis statistics for Item 1 and you are completely satisfied with it, the next step is to copy the block of statistics from B21 to B24 to the same position below Item 2, then copying that block to the same position below Item 3, and so forth. Unfortunately, since the option that is correct is different for each item, to finish this process, you will have to manually change the portion in quotes in the IF_{upper}, IF_{lower}, and ID formulas to reflect the correct answer for each item. In Windows, use F2 key to show the formula and edit it within the cell. In the Mac version, use control + U. In either version, you can also edit formulas by clicking in the formula bar (go to the view menu and click on formula bar if it is not showing).

Distractor efficiency analysis in a spreadsheet

To do the distractor efficiency analysis, you will need to type in the formulas you see for Item 1 in the bottom three rows of Figure 13.2. Notice that the formulas are the same from column to column for the A, B, C, and D options except that the letter in quotes varies, and that the formulas are the same from row to row for the High, Middle, and Low groups, except for differences in the ranges and number used to divide.

Once you have typed in the labels and formulas for all four options and three groups for Item 1 (those shown in the rectangular set of cells with B25 and E29 at the corners), your next step is to block out the same cells and copy them to exactly same position below Item 2, then copy that block to the same position below Item 3, and so forth. With a few changes to the item numbers and the placement of the asterisk indicating the correct answer, you should now have a complete distractor efficiency analysis for this extremely short example test.

Interpreting item and distractor efficiency analyses

The next step is to interpret the results of your distractor efficiency analysis. If you have been following this example in your spreadsheet, your results should look like those in Figure 13.1. Notice that the analysis of the proportion of students selecting each option in each group for Item 1 indicates that 100 percent of the students in the high and middle groups chose A, while 80 percent of the students in the low group chose A. The other 20 percent of the low students apparently chose option B. Since the asterisk indicates the option that was correct, this item appears to have been very easy with even the vast majority of the low students answering it correctly. This is confirmed by the high *IF* value of .94, which in turn indicates that the item was easy overall because 94 percent of the students answered it correctly. Note also that subtracting the percent of students in the upper group who correctly answered minus the same figure for the lower group corroborates the *ID* reported for this first item ($ID = IF_{upper} - IF_{lower} = 1.00 - .80 = .20$).

At first glance, this item might seem too easy for norm-referenced purposes with the group of students involved, and since it is not discriminating well and options C and D appear to be drawing no students, you might want to eliminate it from future versions of the test. However, from a commonsense point of view, you might instead decide that you want to have an easy first item so that students can get off to a good start. As with all item analyses, the decision is yours, but the *IF*, *ID*, and distractor analyses can certainly help in making such decisions.

For instance, in Item 2, option C is the correct answer with the majority (60 percent) of the high group choosing that answer. However, the other 40 percent of the high group selected a wrong answer, option A. In a situation like this, you might want to go back to the original item and examine it carefully from both format and content points of view. The high group may be attracted to both A and C because both are correct answers (or very nearly correct). If this is the case, the best strategy is to change option A so that it is more clearly wrong or revise C so that it is more clearly correct. Doing either should help strengthen the item and increase its *ID* in future administrations of the test.

Item 3 looks like a good item with a reasonably well centered *IF* (.44) and relatively high *ID* (.40). This item seems to be a bit difficult, but the distractor efficiency analysis indicates that a majority of the high group is answering this item correctly with the middle group doing less well and the low group doing poorly. This is the sort of pattern of answers I like to see for a norm-referenced test. Note also that all three distractors seem to be about equally attractive to those students who did not answer correctly. If item three continues to look good in terms of content and format, then I would probably keep it in the revised version of the test even though it is a bit difficult.

Item 4 provides an example of an item with one distractor that is not attracting any of the students. Clearly, distractor B is not carrying its weight in the process of testing the students. But, since the item is very difficult (*IF* = .31) and appears to be discriminating in the opposite direction from the rest of the test (*ID* = -.60), the weakness of option B is the least of my problems. However, a quick look at option C makes me wonder why it looks like the pattern I might expect for a correct answer (High group doing best, then Middle group, then Low group). Is it possible that this item is miskeyed? Option C is behaving more like the correct answer than A is, even though A has the asterisk. If examination of the item itself confirms that Item 4 is miskeyed, then changing the answer key and reanalyzing the item would be in order (in this case resulting in an *IF* of .44 and an *ID* of .60 for the newly keyed item).

Item 5 looks like a reasonably sound item, though option C is not attracting any students, so I would want to have a look at that option to see if I can make it more attractive to those students who do not know the correct answer.

Note that the approach employed here (i.e., using the =COUNTIF function) is just one way to do these analyses. By experimenting with the various functions in your spreadsheet program, you may find a strategy that you like much better.

Conclusion

Generally speaking, the item analysis statistics of *IF* and *ID* help me to decide which items to keep and which to discard in creating a new revised version of the test. However, the distractor efficiency analysis is also useful for spotting items that are miskeyed and for tuning up those items that have options that are not working as would be expected. Naturally, whether or not I decide to keep an item depends on how high the *ID*s are for all the other items and how many items I need in the revised version of the test. If many other items have *ID*s that are higher than the item I am examining, I may decide to throw it out, even though it is not such a bad item, because it is adding very little to the test (other than length). Again, the content and format analyses by direct observation of the items themselves should figure into all of these decisions.

Please keep in mind that my example items in this article were designed to exemplify certain types of problems that distractor efficiency analysis can help you solve. As a result, most of the items were not functioning very well. Typically, in the real world, when a set of items is carefully developed by experienced teachers to suit a particular group of students in a particular situation, a much higher percentage of the items will be found to be working and can therefore be retained in the revised version of the test. However, the types of problems exemplified here do arise and distractor efficiency analysis in your spreadsheet can help you spot them.

(updated and reprinted from Brown, 2002c)

CHAPTER 14

HOW CAN WE CALCULATE ITEM STATISTICS FOR WEIGHTED ITEMS?

QUESTION: I have read your testing book (Brown, 1996a), and I understand how to do item analysis for norm-referenced tests using item facility and item discrimination statistics and for criterion-referenced tests using the difference index and B-index. But all of the examples in your book are for tests that are scored right/wrong with the students' answers coded "1" for right and "0" for wrong. My question is: What can you do when you want to do item analysis for items that have weighted scores instead of right/wrong scorings? (This question was raised by Dr. Kimi Kondo of the University of Hawai'i at Mānoa.)

ANSWER: To review briefly, *item facility* is typically defined as the proportion of students who answered a particular item correctly. Thus, if 45 out of 50 students answered a particular item correctly, the item facility for that item would be 45/50 = .90, meaning that 90% of the students answered the item correctly and it is very easy. All the other classical test theory statistics for norm-referenced and criterion-referenced item analysis techniques that I give in my book are based on that notion of item facility. For example, *item discrimination* is defined as the item facility on the particular item for the upper group (usually the top 33% or so, based on their total test scores) minus the item facility for the lower group (usually the lower 33% or so); the *difference index* is defined as the item facility on the particular item for the posttest minus the item facility for that item on the pretest; the *B-index* is defined as the item facility on the particular item for the students who passed the test minus the item facility for the students who failed. Calculating these statistics is easy as long as the definition of item facility remains the proportion of students who answered a particular item correctly.

However, in some cases, especially in classroom criterion-referenced tests, teachers want to give partial credit for items (i.e., give 1, 2, or 3 points for a particular item depending on how well students answer it or give half a point for a partially correct answer and a full point for a fully correct answer). In that case, because the item is not clearly right or wrong for each student, the definition of item facility given at the end of the previous paragraph does not work, and as a result, none of the other item statistics can be calculated either. In such cases of partial credit, a somewhat different definition of item facility could be used: item facility is the average proportion of correctness for a particular item.

The trick to calculating this version of item facility is to put each student's answer to each question on a proportion score scale from 0 to 1. The scoring of each item on the actual test can be on a 0 - 3 integer scale, a 1 - 5 scale, a 0 - ½ - 1 scale, or a 0 - 3 decimal scale, but for purposes of item analysis, they all need to be converted to a 0 to 1 scale by dividing each student's item score by the total possible for that item. Thus a 0 - 3 integer scale (i.e., a 0, 1, 2, 3 scale) could be converted to .00 for a student who answered completely wrong (0/3 = .00), .33 for a student who got 1 point and answered one-third correctly (⅓ = .33), .67 for a student who got 2 points and answered two-thirds correctly (⅔=.67), and 1.00 for a student who got all 3 points and answered completely correctly (3/3 = 1.00). The same principle could be applied to a 1- 5 scale, with scores of .00, .20, .40, .60, .80, and 1.00 being possible. For a 0 - ½ - 1 scale, the points on the scale could be converted to .00, .50, and 1.00. And so forth.

Once each student's proportion score for each item is coded in this way, item facility is simply the average of all these values across students for each item. For instance, let's say that ten students took a four-item test scored with different weightings for each item (regular right/wrong for the first item, a 1 - 3 integer scale for the second question, a 1 - 5 scale for the third question, and a 0 - ½ -1 scale for the fourth question. The item results might look like the raw scores in Table 14.1.

The results in Table 14.1 would be converted into proportion scores as described above for each person on each item as shown in Table 14.2. Then, with item facility redefined in this way, the item analysis could proceed with only slight variations from the usual classical test theory calculations. Item facility (IF) becomes the average of the proportion scores. For instance, for Item 2 in Table 14.2, the calculations would be as follows:

$$IF = (1.00+1.00+.67+.67+1.00+.67+.33+.33+.00+.00)/10=.57$$

Table 14.1. *Actual Scoring of the Example Test*

Student	Item 1	Item 2	Item 3	Item 4	...	Total Scores
Kimi	1	3	5	1	...	100
Sachiko	1	3	5	1	...	89
Keiko	1	2	4	½	...	85
Rieko	1	2	4	½	...	80
Mitsue	1	3	3	½	...	79
Hitoshi	1	2	3	½	...	70
Hide	0	1	2	½	...	64
Yoshi	0	1	2	0	...	50
Toshi	0	0	1	0	...	37
Hachiko	0	0	0	0	...	13

Table 14.2. *Proportion Score Equivalents for Each Item (and Item Statistics)*

Student	Item 1	Item 2	Item 3	Item 4	...	Total Scores
Kimi	1.00	1.00	1.00	1.00	...	100
Sachiko	1.00	1.00	1.00	1.00	...	89
Keiko	1.00	0.67	0.80	0.50	...	85
Rieko	1.00	0.67	0.80	0.50	...	80
Mitsue	1.00	1.00	0.60	0.50	...	79
Hitoshi	1.00	0.67	0.60	0.50	...	70
Hide	0.00	0.33	0.40	0.50	...	64
Yoshi	0.00	0.33	0.40	0.00	...	50
Toshi	0.00	0.00	0.20	0.00	...	37
Hachiko	0.00	0.00	0.00	0.00	...	13
IF	0.60	0.57	0.58	0.45	...	
ID	1.00	0.78	0.73	0.83	...	

Then, the item discrimination statistic (ID) could be based on the average proportion score for the upper group minus the average for the lower group. Where the upper group is defined as the top three students in Table 14.2 and the lower group is defined as the lower three students. ID for Item 2 would be calculated as follows:

$$IF_{upper} - IF_{lower} = (1.00+1.00+.67)/3 - (.33+.00+.00)/3 = 2.67/3 - .33/3 = 89 - .11 = .78$$

Exactly the same principles could be applied to calculating the difference index (DI) and the B-index. Note that the results for IF, ID, DI, and B would be interpreted very much in the same way they are normally interpreted.

Other strategies exist for dealing with weighted items in item analysis. For instance, item facility could be calculated as a simple average of the weighted scores shown in Table 14.1. In such a case, the values would simply be reported and interpreted relative to the possible values in the scale. For instance, the average for Item 2 in Table 14.1 would be 17/10 = 1.7, which could then be compared to the total possible for that item of 3 to determine whether or not it was difficult. However, using this method, the interpretation would be different for each type of item weighting, which could prove confusing. An alternative strategy for calculating *item discrimination* for weighted items would be to use computer power to calculate the item-total correlations.

However, the proportion score strategies that I explained in the body of this article seem to me to be the easiest to understand and carry out. I hope that you will find them practical and useful ways of dealing with item analysis for tests with weighted scores.

(updated and reprinted from Brown, 2000b)

CHAPTER 15

WHAT ISSUES AFFECT LIKERT ITEM QUESTIONNAIRE FORMATS?

QUESTION: Recently I came across a survey which attempted to evaluate student interest about a range classroom topics. Students were asked to rank their interest in various potential topics according to this scale:

    10   if they felt a topic was very interesting

    6   if they felt a topic was above average interest

    4   if they felt a topic was below average interest

    1   if they felt a topic was not worth studying in class

Please note that only four responses were permitted: 10, 6, 4, and 1. Is this an acceptable survey design? Should the scale reflect the number of permissible responses, rather than an arbitrary figure of 10?

ANSWER: To begin with, I find it difficult to answer your question because I do not know the context in which the scale was used. Nonetheless, I will try to respond, based on what I do know, because it affords me an opportunity to write a little bit about the problems of designing such scales. I hope you will find this information useful.

The general type of questionnaire item you refer to in your question is called a Likert item (named after Rensis Likert with the *i* in Likert pronounced with a short *i* as in *it*). Likert items are most often used to investigate how respondents rate a series of statements by having them circle or otherwise mark numbered categories (for instance, 1 2 3 4 5). Likert items are useful for gathering respondents' feelings, opinions, attitudes, etc. on any language-related topics. Typically, the numbered categories are on continua like the following four: very serious to not at all serious; very important to very unimportant; strongly like to strongly dislike; or strongly agree to strongly disagree. Two problems commonly arise when trying to use Likert items: (a) you may encounter some students who prefer to "sit the fence" by always marking the most neutral possible answer, and (b) you may find it difficult to decide what kind of scale the data coming from such an item represents. I will address both of those issues by of providing background for a direct answer to your question.

Students who "sit the fence"

The first problem is dealing with those students who tend to "sit the fence" on Likert items. Given the possibility of a neutral option (like the 3 for don't know in a five-point strongly agree to strongly disagree), such students will tend to take that neutral option. If you need to force respondents to express a definite opinion one way or the other, you may want to use an even number of options (say four options like, 1 2 3 4) from which they must choose either in the positive or negative direction. When using such four-option Likert items at the University of Hawai'i, I have found that most students will pick 2 or 3, but they are at least expressing some opinion, one way or the other. However, even so, I have found a few students so prone to selecting the neutral answer that they circle the space between the 2 and the 3. I have therefore had to code some of the answers as 2.5. Nonetheless, using an even number of options forced the majority of students to go one way or the other.

Unfortunately, by doing that I may have been forcing students who did not really have an opinion to express one nevertheless. That, of course, is another facet of this problem that you must consider when you are deciding whether to use an even or odd number of options; that is, some students really do feel neutral, or have no opinion about a particular issue, and you may want to know that. In such a case, you will want to give the respondents an odd number of options with a neutral position in the middle, or offer 1 2 3 4 as choices along with another option that is no opinion. The call is yours, and what you decide will depend on the kinds of information you want to get from your questionnaire.

Deciding the type of scale

The second problem is that you may find it difficult to decide what kind of scale the data coming from such a Likert item represents. Three scales of measurement are often described in books on statistical analyses of surveys: categorical, rank-ordered, and continuous.

Categorical scales, also called nominal scales, quantify by tallying up the number in each of two or more categories. For example, a group might be made up of 21 females and only 10 males. That information taken together is a nominal scale with two categories (female and male). Other variables with more than two categories, like nationality, first language background, educational background, etc., are all potential categorical scales if the number of people in each category is being tallied.

Rank-ordered scales, also called ordinal scales, quantify by giving each data point a rank. For example, the students in a class might be ranked from 1st to 30th in terms of their test scores. That, or any other such ranking, would be a rank-ordered scale. Thus, any variable for which ordinal numbers are being used (1st, 2nd, 3rd, 4th, etc.) is a rank-ordered scale.

Continuous scales, also sometimes separated into interval and ratio scales, quantify at equal intervals along some yardstick. Thus inches, feet, and yards are equal intervals along a real yardstick and represent a continuous scale. Similarly, we treat IQ scores, TOEFL scores, and even classroom test scores as points along a continuum of possible scores. Hence, they are continuous, too. One other characteristic of continuous scores is that calculating means and standard deviations makes sense (which is not true of categorical or rank-ordered scales). (For much more on scales, see Brown, 1988, pp. 20-28; 1996a, pp. 93-98; or Hatch & Lazaraton, 1991).

Unfortunately, many a novice teacher-researcher has trouble deciding whether Likert items are categorical, rank-ordered, or continuous. Sometimes, Likert items are treated as categorical scales. For example, a researcher might report that five people chose 1, sixteen selected 2, twenty-six preferred 3, fourteen decided on 4, and three picked 5. Other times, Likert scales are referred to as a rank-order. For instance, again using the example in the previous sentence, five people would be reported as ranking the statement 1st, sixteen ranking it 2nd, twenty-six ranking it 3rd, fourteen ranking it 4th, and three ranking it 5th. Still other times, Likert scales are analyzed as continuous, with each set of 1 2 3 4 5 treated as equal points along a continuum. In such cases, a mean and standard deviation is often reported for each of the Likert items. Using the same example that runs throughout this paragraph, the mean would be 2.91 and the standard deviation would be .98.

A direct answer to your question

The 1, 4, 6, 10 scale you referred to in your question at the top of this article is a strange scale indeed. The scale cannot be considered continuous because the points on the scale are not equally spaced, as you can see if you examine where they sit along the continuum from one to ten: *1* 2 3 *4* 5 *6* 7 8 9 *10*. Clearly, there are two numbers between the 1 and 4, one number between the 4 and 6, and three numbers between the 6 and 10. Thus the numbers are not equally spaced along a continuum and therefore do not form a continuous scale. Similarly, these four numbers are not rank-ordered because they are not ordinal in nature; that is, saying 1st, 4th, 6th, and 10th would make absolutely no sense. At best this scale might be analyzed as categorical, but convincing readers that the categories make sense might be difficult, because they are not evenly spaced along a continuum. Thus, whoever the researcher was who used the 1 4 6 10 Likert-like item took a scale which is already difficult to analyze and made it even more difficult to deal with.

In short, the scale probably would have been better as a more traditional 1 2 3 4 5, or 1 2 3 4, or either of those options with an additional no opinion option. Any of those alternative scales could have been analyzed as a categorical, rank-ordered, and/or continuous scale. But, the scale the 1 4 6 10 researcher chose to use is neither fish nor fowl, and must have been very difficult indeed to analyze and interpret.

For more on Likert scales see Brown (2001e, 2011a [Chapter 16]), and for an example of Likert item questionnaires used in a Japanese-language needs analysis at the University of Hawai'i at Mānoa and how results can be reported from them, see Iwai, et al. (1999) at www.lll.hawaii.edu/nflrc/NetWorks/NW13/.

(updated and reprinted from Brown, 2000c)

CHAPTER 16

LIKERT ITEMS AND SCALES OF MEASUREMENT

QUESTION: Many people have asked me this seemingly simple question: Are "Likert-scale" questions on questionnaires nominal, ordinal, interval, or ratio scales?

ANSWER: In preparing to answer this seemingly easy question, I discovered that the answer is far from simple. To explain what I found, I will have to address the following sub-questions: (a) what are scales of measurement? (b) what does the literature say about Likert items and scales of measurement? and (c) what does common sense tell us about Likert items and scales of measurement?

What are scales of measurement?

Language researchers commonly describe the different ways they measure things numerically in terms of *scales of measurement*, which come in four flavors: nominal, ordinal, interval, and ratio scales. Each is useful in its own way for quantifying different aspects of language teaching and learning.

Nominal scales categorize. A nominal scale can used for natural categories like gender (male or female) or artificial categories like proficiency (elementary, intermediate, or advanced proficiency groups). Nominal scales are also sometimes called *categorical scales*, or *dichotomous scales* (when there are only two categories).

Ordinal scales order or rank things. For instance, an item might ask students to rank ten types of classroom activities from most to least interesting (from 1 through 10). The most interesting activity would be first, followed by second, third, etc. (sensibly, ordinal scales are most often expressed as ordinal numbers). While the order is clear on such a scale, it is not clear what the distances are along the ordering. Thus the 1st activity might be much more interesting than the 2nd, but the 2nd activity might be only a little more interesting than the 3rd, and so forth. In short, ordinal scales show us the order, but not the distances between the rankings. Such ordinal scales are also sometimes called *ranked scales*.

Interval scales show the order of things, but with equal intervals between the points on the scale. Thus, the distance between scores of 50, 51, 52, 53 and so forth are all assumed to be the same all along the scale. Test scores are usually treated as interval scales in language research. Scales based on Likert items are also treated as interval scales in our field.

Ratio scales differ from interval scales in that they have a zero value and points along the scale make sense as ratios. For example, a scale like age can be zero, and it makes sense to think of four years as twice as old as two years.

Researchers are often concerned with the differences among these scales of measurement because of their implications for making decisions about which statistical analyses to use appropriately for each. At times, they are discussed in only three categories: nominal, ordinal, and *continuous* (i.e., interval and ratio are collapsed into one category as in the previous chapter). [For more on scales of measurement, see Brown, 1988, pp. 20-24; 2001e, pp. 17-18.]

What does the literature say about Likert items and scales of measurement?

Likert items were first introduced by Rensis Likert (1932). The following is an example of three Likert (pronounced /lɪkərt/) items:

	Strongly disagree	Disagree	Neutral	Agree	Strongly agree
1. I understand the difference between Likert items and Likert scales.	1	2	3	4	5
2. I understand how to analyze Likert items.	1	2	3	4	5
3. I like using Likert items.	1	2	3	4	5

The example items have five options. These items could equally well have had 3, 4, 6, 7, or more options. [For more information on choosing the number of options and on how to write sound Likert items, see Brown, 2001e, pp. 40-42, 44-54.]

When I first delved into the general literature on Likert items and scales of measurement, I found most articles were counter-intuitive and confusing. A number of articles argued or assumed that Likert items do not form an interval scale, but instead should be considered ordinal scales and should be analyzed accordingly (e.g., Coombs, 1960; Vigderhous, 1977; Jakobsson, 2004; Jamieson, 2004; Knapp, 1990; Kuzon, Urbanchek, & McCabe, 1996). Other articles proposed ways to get around this perceived ordinal/interval scale "problem" by proposing alternative Likert-like item formats such as the two-stage alternative offered by Albaum (1997) or the phrase completion alternative offered by Hodge and Gillespie (2003).

Despite all this discussion of the ordinal nature of Likert items and scales, most of the research based on Likert items and scales that I have seen in our field treats them as interval scales and analyzes them as such with descriptive statistics like means, standard deviations, etc. and inferential statistics like correlation coefficients, factor analysis, analysis of variance, etc. So you can see why I found the general literature counter-intuitive and confusing. For the most part, it says that we should treat Likert scales as ordinal scales, yet the research in my field consistently treats them as interval scales. How can these two positions be reconciled?

I believe that much of this ordinal/interval confusion arises from the fact that many authors use *Likert scale* to refer to both the Likert item type (items of the form shown above) and Likert scales (sums or averages of the results on sets of Likert items). For example, a questionnaire might have a total of 120 Likert items, divided into 12 Likert scales of 10 items each. If we carefully differentiate between Likert *items* and Likert *scales*, as I have done throughout this article (and this book), I think that much of the confusion will dissipate.

In addition, several papers have shown that *Likert scales* can indeed be analyzed effectively as interval scales (see for instance, Baggaley & Hull, 1983; Maurer & Pierce, 1998; and Vickers, 1999). Also, Allen and Seaman (1997, p. 2) support treating Likert scales as interval data with certain rather sensible provisos:

> The "intervalness" here is an attribute of the data, not of the labels. Also, the scale item should be at least five and preferably seven categories. Another example of analyzing Likert scales as interval values is when the sets of Likert items can be combined to form indexes. However, there is a strong caveat to this approach: Most researchers insist such combinations of scales pass the Cronbach alpha or the Kappa test of intercorrelation and validity. Also, the combination of scales to

form an interval level index assumes this combination forms an underlying characteristic or variable."

In another vein, a number of authors have shown how Rasch analysis can be used to analyze and improve Likert scales as well as transform them into *true* interval scales. For more on this topic in the general literature, see Andrich (1978), Hagquist and Andrich (2004), Linacre (2002), Van Alphen, Halfens, Hasman, and Imbos (1994), and Waugh (2002); in the area of language research, see Sick (2006, 2009) or Weaver (2005, 2010).

What does common sense tell us about Likert items and scales of measurement?

Because they confuse Likert items with Likert scales, many authors look at a single Likert item and conclude that the 1 2 3 4 and 5 options form an ordinal scale at best, and therefore data based on these items must be analyzed as though they are ordinal. I have two responses to that form of "logic."

When you read that MacArthur graduated first in the West Point class of 1903, that means he was at the top of his class ahead of whoever was second, third, fourth, fifth, etc. What is it about any Likert item 1 2 3 4 5 (much less a Likert scale) that can be expressed in ordinal numbers? Is *strongly agree* fifth, ahead of *agree* at fourth, and *neutral* at third, *disagree* at 2nd, and *strongly disagree* at 1st? This doesn't make sense, even at the Likert item level, much less at the Likert scale level.

From a Likert scale perspective, even if we were to accept the erroneous idea that Likert items are ordinal, saying that the resulting data must be analyzed as though they too are ordinal is like saying that test items that are scored right or wrong are nominal so data based on them must be analyzed as though they are nominal. Test scores are usually based on nominal right/wrong items, yet the total scores are always treated as interval data in our field. If the single argument (that Likert item options are ordinal) is wrong, then the compound argument (that Likert scales are ordinal [sic] because Likert items are ordinal [sic]) is doubly wrong.

The one 100% sensible treatment I have found for this set of issues is found in Carifio and Perla (2007). On page 114, they list "the top ten myths and urban legends about 'Likert scales' and the counter argument and 'antidote' for each myth and urban legend." According to the authors, the following myths are **WRONG**:

Myth 1—There is no need to distinguish between a scale and response format; they are basically the same "thing" and what is true about one is true about the other.

Myth 2—Scale items are independent and autonomous with no underlying conceptual, logical or empirical structure that brings them together and synthesizes them.

Myth 3—Likert scales imply Likert response formats and vice versa as they are isomorphic.

Myth 4—Likert scales cannot be differentiated into macro and micro conceptual structures.

Myth 5—Likert scale items should be analyzed separately.

Myth 6—Because Likert scales are ordinal-level scales, only non-parametric statistical tests should be used with them.

Myth 7—Likert scales are empirical and mathematical tools with no underlying and deep meaning and structure.

Myth 8—Likert response formats can without impunity be detached from the Likert scale and its underlying conceptual and logical structure.

Myth 9—The Likert response format is not a system or process for capturing and coding information the stimulus questions elicit about the underlying construct being measured.

Myth 10—Little care, knowledge, insight or understanding is needed to construct or use a Likert scale.

Notice in particular Myths 1, 5, and 6, which are directly related to the topic of this chapter. For more details about these 10 myths, you should of course refer to the original article.

Conclusion

The original question was: Are "Likert-scale" questions on questionnaires nominal, ordinal, interval, or ratio scales? My experience and my take on the literature lead me to believe that the following are true:

With regard to Likert items:

1. We must think about individual Likert items and Likert scales (made up of multiple Likert items) in different ways.

2. Likert items represent an item format, not a scale.

3. Whether Likert *items* are interval or ordinal is irrelevant in using Likert *scale* data, which can be taken to be interval.

4. If a researcher presents the means and standard deviations (interval scale statistics) for individual Likert items, he/she should also present the percent or frequency of people who selected each option (a nominal scale statistic) and let the reader decide how to interpret the results at the Likert-item level.

5. In any case, we should not rely too heavily on interpreting single items because single items are relatively unreliable.

With regard to Likert scales:

1. Likert scales are totals or averages of answers to multiple Likert items.

2. Likert scales contain multiple items and are therefore likely to be more reliable than single items.

3. Naturally, the reliability of Likert scales should be checked using Cronbach alpha or another appropriate reliability estimate.

4. Likert scales contain multiple items and can be taken to be interval scales, so descriptive statistics can be applied, as well as correlational analyses, factor analyses, analysis of variance procedures, etc. (if all other design conditions and assumptions are met).

(updated and reprinted from Brown, 2011a)

Part I: Second Language Testing

Section C: Reliability Issues

CHAPTER 17

THE CRONBACH ALPHA RELIABILITY ESTIMATE

QUESTION: For what kind of test would a coefficient alpha reliability be appropriate? How does one interpret reliability coefficients?

ANSWER: Coefficient alpha is one name for the Cronbach alpha reliability estimate. Cronbach alpha is one of the most commonly reported reliability estimates in the language testing literature. To adequately explain Cronbach alpha, I will need to address several sub-questions: (a) What are the different strategies for estimating reliability? (b) Where does Cronbach alpha fit into these strategies for estimating reliability? And, (c) how should we interpret Cronbach alpha?

What are the different strategies for estimating reliability?

Testing books (e.g., Brown 1996a) usually explain three strategies for estimating reliability: (a) test-retest reliability (i.e., calculating a reliability estimate by administering a test on two occasions and calculating the correlation between the two sets of scores), (b) equivalent (or parallel) forms reliability (i.e., calculating a reliability estimate by administering two forms of a test and calculating the correlation between the two sets of scores), and (c) internal consistency reliability (i.e., calculating a reliability estimate based on a single form of a test administered on a single occasion using one of the many available internal consistency equations). Clearly, the internal consistency strategy is the easiest logistically because it does not require administering the test twice or having two forms of the test.

Where does Cronbach alpha fit into these strategies for estimating reliability?

Internal consistency reliability estimates come in several flavors. The most familiar are the (a) split-half adjusted (i.e., adjusted using the Spearman-Brown prophecy formula, which is the focus of Brown, 2001a [Chapter 20]), (b) Kuder-Richardson formulas 20 and 21 (also known as K-R20 and K-R21, see Kuder & Richardson, 1937), and (c) Cronbach alpha (see Cronbach, 1970).

The most frequently-reported internal consistency estimates are the K-R20 and Cronbach alpha. Either one provides a sound under-estimate (that is conservative or safe estimate) of the reliability of a set of test results. However, the K-R20 can only be applied if the test items are scored dichotomously (i.e., right or wrong). Cronbach alpha can also be applied when test items are scored dichotomously, but alpha has the advantage over K-R20 of being applicable when items are weighted (as in an item scored 0 points for a functionally and grammatically incorrect answer, 1 point for a functionally incorrect, but grammatically correct answer, 2 points for a functionally correct but grammatically incorrect answer, and 3 points for a functionally and grammatically correct answer). Hence, Cronbach alpha is more flexible than K-R20 and is often the appropriate reliability estimate for language test development projects and language testing research.

How should we interpret Cronbach alpha?

A Cronbach alpha estimate (often symbolized by the lower-case Greek letter α) should be interpreted just like other internal consistency estimates, that is, it estimates the proportion of variance in the test scores that can be attributed to true score variance. Put more simply, Cronbach alpha is used to estimate the proportion of variance that is systematic or consistent in a set of test scores. It can range from 0.00 (if no variance is consistent) to 1.00 (if all variance is consistent) with all values between 0.00 and 1.00 also being possible. For example, if the Cronbach alpha for a set of scores turns out to be .90, you can interpret that as meaning that the test is 90% reliable, and by extension that it is 10% unreliable (100% - 90% = 10%).

However, when interpreting Cronbach alpha, you should keep in mind at least the following four concepts:

1. Cronbach alpha provides an estimate of the internal consistency of the test scores, thus (a) alpha does not indicate the stability or consistency of the scores over time, which would be better estimated using the test-retest reliability strategy, and (b) alpha does not indicate the stability or consistency of the test scores across test forms, which would be better estimated using the equivalent forms reliability strategy.

2. Cronbach alpha is appropriately applied to norm-referenced tests and norm-referenced decisions (e.g., admissions and placement decisions), but not

to criterion-referenced tests and criterion-referenced decisions (e.g., diagnostic and achievement decisions).

3. All other factors held constant, tests that have normally-distributed scores are more likely to have high Cronbach alpha reliability estimates than tests with positively or negatively skewed distributions, and so alpha must be interpreted in light of the particular distribution involved.

4. All other factors held constant, Cronbach alpha will be higher for longer tests than for shorter tests as shown and explained in Brown 1998a [Chapter 18]) & 2001a [Chapter 20], and so alpha must be interpreted in light of the particular test length involved.

The standard error of measurement (or SEM) is an additional reliability statistic calculated from the reliability estimate (as explained in Brown, 1999a [Chapter 19]) that may prove more useful than the reliability estimate itself when you are making actual decisions with test scores. The SEM's usefulness arises from the fact that it provides an estimate of how much variability in actual test score points you can expect around a particular cut-point due to unreliable variance (with 68% probability if one SEM plus or minus is used, or with 95% if two SEMs plus or minus are used, or 98% if three are used). (For more on this topic, see Brown 1996a).

Conclusion

Clearly, Cronbach alpha is a useful and flexible tool that you can use to investigate the reliability of your language test scores. In the process, it is important to remember that reliability, regardless of the strategy used to obtain it, is not a characteristic inherent in the test itself, but rather is an estimate of the consistency of the scores that result from a set of items when they are administered to a particular group of students at a specific time under particular conditions for a specific purpose. Extrapolating from reliability results obtained under a particular set of circumstances to other situations must be done with great care.

(updated and reprinted from Brown, 2002a)

CHAPTER 18

CLOZE TESTS AND OPTIMUM TEST LENGTH

QUESTION: I am interested in including a cloze section in the entrance exam for our university. I know that the longer the test (that is, the more items) the more reliable, but I also need to keep the test as short as possible. Is there a point at which the increasing length of the test has diminishing returns? If so, how can I figure that out?

ANSWER: You are absolutely right that, in general, all other factors held constant, longer tests tend to be more reliable than shorter ones (as explained in Brown, 1996a, pp. 194-195). Naturally, there is a point at which adding more items can have the opposite effect, as fatigue sets in and the students begin to get discouraged or stop taking the test seriously. However, unfortunately, reliability is not just a function of test length with cloze tests. At least three factors substantially affect the reliability of cloze tests: (a) variations in student ability levels and score ranges, (b) differences in passage difficulties, and (c) changes in numbers of items.

Variations in student ability levels and score ranges

Reliability results for the scores on any test can vary markedly across groups of students who have different proficiency levels or ranges of language abilities. In Brown (1984a), I showed how cloze test results could vary considerably for different groups. The results of that study are summarized in Table 18.1. Notice in Table 18.1 that the reliabilities (in this case, Cronbach alpha estimates) range from .31 to .95 in the fourth row of numbers. Thus, this table reports one of the highest reliability estimates ever published for a cloze test (at .95) and one of the lowest (.31). The startling thing is that all of these results are based on exactly the same cloze passage, but it was administered to different groups of students (at UCLA and Zhongshan University in Guangzhou, China). So you can see that reliability results can vary considerably for different groups of students. More interesting, these results do not vary solely because they are produced by different groups of students. Notice how the standard deviations and ranges in the second and third rows of numbers of Table 18.1 systematically decrease as you look across the table in much the same way as the reliability estimates in the fourth row of numbers.

Clearly, the magnitude of the reliability estimates is directly related to the amount of variation in abilities in the various groups as that variation is reflected in the standard deviation and range of scores.

Table 18.1. *Ranges of Talent in Relationship to Reliability and Validity of Cloze (adapted from Brown, 1984a)*

Scoring Method	AC	EX	AC	EX	EX	AC	AC	EX
Sample	1978	1978	1981	1981	1982a	1982b	1982c	1982d
SD	12.45	8.56	6.71	5.59	4.84	4.48	4.07	3.38
Range	46	33	29	22	22	20	21	14
r_{xx}	.95	.90	.83	.73	.68	.66	.53	.31
r_{xy}	.90	.88	.79	.74	.59	.51	.40	.43

Differences in passage difficulties

Reliability estimates can also vary markedly for cloze tests developed from passages of varying difficulty. In Brown (1993b), I showed how passage difficulty is related to reliability by administering 50 cloze tests to equivalent groups (2298 Japanese university students were randomly assigned to the 50 passages). The results from that study are summarized in Table 18.2.

Notice that the reliability estimates in the bottom row of Table 18.2 (labeled alpha) range from .816 to .283. Notice also that the standard deviations and ranges in the third and fourth rows systematically decrease as you read across those rows, in much the same way that the reliability coefficients decrease.

Similarly, but to a somewhat lesser degree, the means shown in the second row of Table 18.2 also decrease similarly to the reliability estimates. A relatively high mean on a cloze test would indicate that it is based on a relatively easy passage because the students are scoring higher on average, and a low mean would indicate a relatively difficult passage because the students are scoring lower on average. Thus there appears to be some relationship between the difficulty of the cloze passages and the reliabilities that result when students of similar ability take them as cloze tests. In Table 18.2, the most difficult passages appear to be producing skewed distributions, a sort of "floor" effect, and are also producing commensurately low reliability estimates (as low as .283 in this case), while the easiest passages appear to be better centered and are also producing higher reliability estimates (as high as .816 in this case). Thus, in addition to varying across groups of different ability levels and ranges, cloze test reliability estimates can vary according to how well the difficulty of the particular passage is related to the ability levels of the group of students being tested.

Table 18.2. *Passage Difficulty in Relationship to Reliability of Cloze, arranged from high to low reliability (adapted from Brown, 1993b)*

test	21	12	37	50	27	45	20	2	31	4	22
	11	35	15	9	6	7	1	41	42	49	19
	10	5	32	14	44	30	8	3	47	34	23
	24	48	25	28	33	39	29	38	16	46	43
	36	40	13	18	17	26					
mean	9.92	8.98	5.46	2.49	2.34	6.55	4.38	4.21	3.78	7.54	3.70
	5.94	6.63	9.18	2.85	5.11	6.14	5.23	2.87	4.41	4.56	4.76
	2.54	3.98	3.83	3.23	3.24	9.56	3.16	2.02	3.79	5.87	3.64
	2.96	2.69	5.36	2.58	2.14	2.51	2.32	1.71	1.36	2.16	1.43
	5.00	3.49	2.87	1.02	1.38	2.68					
SD	4.44	3.97	3.66	2.70	2.72	3.87	3.24	3.42	3.08	3.87	2.86
	3.36	3.66	3.42	2.46	3.23	3.41	3.16	2.51	3.10	2.81	2.88
	2.31	2.79	2.53	2.50	2.52	3.28	2.27	2.13	2.33	2.91	2.40
	2.26	2.12	2.74	2.17	1.87	1.98	1.77	1.57	1.41	1.82	1.45
	2.05	1.90	1.71	1.09	1.25	1.56					
range	19	21	13	12	13	16	15	13	15	14	11
	16	17	14	11	14	16	15	10	18	11	10
	8	13	9	9	10	13	8	10	11	13	11
	9	11	12	8	6	9	7	8	6	7	7
	9	9	8	3	5	5					
alpha	.816	.798	.788	.775	.774	.766	.763	.762	.750	.748	.742
	.734	.733	.727	.724	.723	.716	.711	.711	.710	.696	.682
	.675	.663	.663	.656	.653	.645	.644	.643	.638	.637	.622
	.622	.612	.607	.607	.604	.547	.533	.532	.500	.482	.465
	.452	.434	.347	.317	.313	.283					

Note. The 50 cloze passages have been compressed into 11 columns and 4 rows, read from right to left then back to the beginning of the next row. Test 11 thus corresponds to a mean of 5.94, a SD of 3.36, a range of 16, and an alpha of .734.

Changes in numbers of items

One study by Rand (1978) at UCLA directly addressed the issue of the effect of test length on the reliability of cloze tests. Based on a cloze passage that I developed for my MA thesis (Brown, 1978, also reported in Brown, 1980), Rand calculated the reliabilities for various lengths of that cloze test for three scoring methods: exact-answer (wherein only the original word found in the blank is counted as correct), acceptable-answer (wherein any answer judged as correct by native speakers for a give blank is counted as correct), and multiple-choice (wherein students are given three or four choices to select from for each blank). He found that the reliability for all three scoring methods began to "level off" at 20 items and the maximum reliability was nearly achieved at 25 items. He rather rashly concluded that: "This study has shown that the examiner using cloze tests can most efficiently use his own resources and his examinees' time by giving a cloze test of only twenty-five deletions and employing the acceptable-word method of scoring" (pp. 65-66). Unfortunately, Rand based his results on a single cloze test and single population; he therefore overlooked the importance of variations in student ability levels and score ranges as well as differences in passage difficulties.

Determining the best length of cloze test for your students

Clearly then, cloze tests can vary dramatically depending on which group of students is taking the test and which passages are being used. To answer your question directly, in order to determine the best length of cloze test for your students, given a particular passage, you might want to take the following steps:

- Develop a cloze passage of say 50 items that is at roughly at the correct level of difficulty.

- Administer the test to students of the same abilities and range as those for whom the test will eventually be used to make decisions.

- Score the test using whichever scoring method makes more sense in your situation (for instance, the exact-answer scoring may make more sense if you are doing large scale placement testing and the students will never see the tests again, or the acceptable-answer scoring method may make more sense if you are going to give the tests back to the students and go over the answers).

- Enter the results as 1s and 0s (1 for correct answers, 0 for incorrect or blank answers) in your spreadsheet program.

- Use a K-R20 formula to calculate the reliability of the test scores with all items included (after Brown, 1996a, pp. 199-202). Then copy and modify that formula so that you figure the reliabilities for decreasing lengths of the cloze test (by excluding the last item from the previous analysis each time you do so). In other words, figure out the reliability for the entire 50 item cloze, then for a 49 item cloze (by excluding the last item), then for a 48 item cloze, a 47 item cloze, etc.

- Examine the reliability estimates that you get for the various lengths of cloze test (either by simply inspecting the values or by using the spreadsheet to plot reliability vs. length in a scatterplot). Determine the reliability at which it is no longer worthwhile to add more items. In other words, find the reliability above which little more reliability is gained by adding more items.

- Retype the cloze test so that it has only the number of blanks you have determined to be best.

Following the above steps will allow you to create a cloze test that is maximally efficient for your particular group of students. Good luck with it!

(updated and reprinted from Brown, 1998a)

CHAPTER 19

STANDARD ERROR VERSUS STANDARD ERROR OF MEASUREMENT

QUESTION: One of the statistics my spreadsheet gives me is Standard Error. Is that the same as the Standard Error of Measurement?

ANSWER: The most direct answer to your question is "no." Most likely, you are referring to the STEYX function in the ubiquitous *Excel*® spreadsheet. The statistic calculated by the STEYX function is commonly referred to as the standard error of estimate and that is not the standard error of measurement. As your question suggests, the standard error of estimate is often confused with the standard error of measurement that is reported by some test analysis software, or even with the standard error of the mean that is reported by more sophisticated statistical packages like SPSS, SAS, or SYSTAT. Let me try to unscramble all of this step by step by first reviewing what the standard deviation is. Then I will be able to explain the definitions and differences among the standard error of the mean, the standard error of estimate, and the standard error of measurement.

Standard Deviation

As I defined it in Brown (1988, p. 69), the *standard deviation* "provides a sort of average of the differences of all scores from the mean." This means that it is a measure of the dispersion of scores around the mean. The standard deviation is related to the *range* (another indicator of dispersion based on the distance between the highest and lowest score), but has the advantage over the range of not being affected as much as the range by aberrant scores that are exceptionally high or low. Generally, a low standard deviation means that a set of scores is not very widely dispersed around the mean, while a high standard deviation indicates that the scores are more widely dispersed. [For more information on calculating and interpreting standard deviations see Brown, 1988]

It turns out that, in a normal distribution, about 68% of the students can be expected to fall in the range of scores between minus one standard deviation below the mean and plus one standard deviation above the mean, and that about 95% of the students can be expected to fall in the range of scores between minus two standard deviations below the mean and plus two standard deviations above the mean. So on a test with a mean of 51 and standard deviation of 10, you can expect about 68% of the students to score between 41 and 61, and about 95% of the students to score between 31 and 71. This use of percentages with the standard deviation will become important in interpreting all three of the standard error statistics described below. Now, having reviewed the basic concept of standard deviation, it is possible to consider the concept of standard error of the mean.

To begin with, if you were to select random samples of 50 students one after the other until you had 100 such random samples and administered the same test to all the students, you would find that the 100 samples would have many different means. Moreover, if you were to plot the means for the 100 random samples, you would find that a histogram of those means would probably be normal in distribution, and that the means themselves would have a mean (this mean of means, by the way, would probably be the best estimate of the population mean). The standard deviation of such a distribution of means is referred to as the standard error of the mean because it represents the distribution of errors (or random fluctuations) in estimating the population mean. Thus the standard error of the mean is the standard deviation for the distribution of errors or random fluctuations that are likely to occur in estimating the population mean from sample means in a particular situation. Based on the percentages discussed in the previous section for the standard deviation, we can expect about 68% of the errors to be distributed within one standard error plus or minus of the population mean, and about 95% to be distributed within two standard errors plus or minus of the population mean. Normally, you will not have the time or resources to actually take 100 samples. Instead, you may want to use the following formula to estimate the standard error of the mean from a single sample:

$$S_M = \frac{S}{\sqrt{N}}$$

Where:
    S_M = standard error of the mean
    S = standard deviation
    N = number of scores on the test

So, if you had 50 students (N) on a test with a standard deviation (S) of 4.89, the standard error of the mean (S_M) would turn out to be as follows:

$$S_M = \frac{S}{\sqrt{N}} = \frac{4.89}{\sqrt{50}} = \frac{4.89}{7.07} = .6917 \approx .69$$

For further explanation of standard error of the mean, see Hatch & Lazaraton (1991).

Standard Error of Measurement

Conceptually, the *standard error of measurement* is related to test reliability in that it provides an indication of the dispersion of the measurement errors when you are trying to estimate students' true scores from their observed test scores. In order to understand the previous sentence you will first need to understand three bits of jargon: sampling errors, true scores, and test scores. I will deal with them in reverse order.

Students' test scores are not a mystery: they are simply the observed scores that the students got on whatever test is being considered. However, those same students' true scores are a bit more difficult to understand. Let's say that you can give a test an infinite number of times to a group of students (I know fatigue would probably become a problem sometime before infinity, but this is just for the sake of argument). If you could average a student's scores over the infinite number of administrations, the average of that person's scores would probably be the best estimate of that person's true ability/knowledge in whatever is being tested, or that person's true score. The standard deviation of all those scores after they have been averaged across test administrations and persons is the standard error of measurement.

Of course, it is humanly impossible to administer a test an infinite number of times while holding testing effect, fatigue, and other variables constant. So we settle for second best. We assume that each student's test score is our best estimate of the true score, but we recognize that there are sampling errors in that estimate, just as there were for estimating the population mean. Those sampling errors are normally distributed and have a standard deviation called the standard error of measurement.

Fortunately, an estimate of the standard error of measurement can be calculated from the test score standard deviation and reliability estimate using the following formula:

$$SEM = S\sqrt{1 - r_{xx}}$$

Where:
    SEM = standard error of measurement
    S = standard deviation of the test
    r_{xx} = reliability of the test

So, if you have a test with a standard deviation (S) of 4.89, and a Cronbach alpha reliability estimate (r_{xx}) of .91, the standard error of measurement would be calculated as follows:

$$SEM = S\sqrt{1 - r_{xx}} = 4.89\sqrt{1 - .91} = 4.89\sqrt{.09}$$

$$4.89(.3) = 1.467 \approx 1.47$$

One useful application of the standard error of measurement is that it can be used to estimate a band of scores around any cut-point wherein students are treated with special care. For instance, if the test in question had a cut-point for failing of 30, you should recognize that, if you want to be 68% sure of your decision, the standard error of measurement indicates that the students within one *SEM* of the cut point (i.e., 30 +- 1.47, or 28.53 to 31.47) might fluctuate randomly to the other side of the cut point if they were to take the test again, so it might behoove you to gather additional information (e.g., other test scores, homework grades, interviews with the students, or whatever is appropriate) in deciding whether or not they should pass the test.

By extension, if you want to be 95% sure of your decision, the standard error of measurement indicates that the students within two *SEMs* of the cut point (i.e., 30 +- 2.94, or 27.06 to 32.94) might randomly fluctuate to the other side of the cut point, and you may want to act accordingly. [For further explanation of the standard error of measurement, see Brown, 1996a].

Standard Error of Estimate

Conceptually, the *standard error of estimate* is related to regression analysis in that it typically provides an estimate of the dispersion of the prediction errors when you are trying to predict *Y* values from *X* values in a regression analysis. In order to understand the previous sentence, you will first need to understand three bits of jargon: prediction errors, *Y* values, and *X* values. Again, I would like to deal with those terms in reverse order. In a regression analysis, X values are any values from which you want to predict, and Y values are any values to which you want to predict. Unfortunately, those predictions are never perfect because prediction errors occur. Such errors may be due to unreliable measurement in either the Y or X variable, or due to unsystematic differences between the two sets of numbers. When you are trying to predict Y values from X values, it would be useful to know what the distribution of those prediction errors is so you can interpret your predictions wisely.

An example of such a situation might be a case where you use regression analysis to predict TOEFL scores from the PERFECT test at your institution. You must first conduct a study based on a large number of students who took both tests. Then using regression analysis, you build a regression equation of the form Y = a + bX. Based on your analysis, you will know the values of a (the intercept) and b (the slope), and can then plug in the X value (or PERFECT test score) for a student who has never taken the TOEFL. Solving for Y will then give you that student's predicted Y (or predicted TOEFL score). All of this is beyond the scope of this explanation, but is necessary in order to get even a basic understanding of what the standard error of estimate is. [For more on regression analysis, see Brown, 1988, or Hatch and Lazaraton, 1991].

We assume that any student's predicted Y score is our best estimate of that score, but we recognize that there are sampling errors around that estimate, just as there were for estimating the population mean and true scores. Those sampling errors are normally distributed and, in this case, have a standard deviation called the standard error of estimate.

Fortunately, you can use the following simple formula to calculate the standard error of estimate from the standard deviation of the Y values in the original regression analysis and the correlation coefficient between the X and Y values in that analysis:

$$see = S_y \sqrt{1 - r_{yx}^2}$$

Where:
    see = standard error of estimate
    S_y = standard deviation of the *y* values in the original regression analysis
    r_{yx}^2 = correlation squared of *y* and *x* values in the original regression analysis

So, if you have a set of Y values (say test scores) with a standard deviation (S_y) of 10.21 and a correlation squared with the X values of .84, the standard error of estimate would be calculated as follows:

$$see = S_y\sqrt{1 - r_{yx}^2} = 10.21\sqrt{1 - .84} = 10.21\sqrt{.16}$$

$$10.21(.4) = 4.084 \approx 4.08$$

One useful application of the standard error of estimate is that it can be used to create a band of scores around any predicted score. For instance, if a student's predicted Y score is 35, the *see* (just calculated) of 4.08 would tell you that the student's predicted score is likely to vary within plus or minus 4.08 points on Y 68% of the time. So you know that the prediction would fall between 30.92 and 39.08 with 68% confidence. At this point, you can probably guess how you would go about establishing bands of scores for 95% confidence. Such bands of confidence intervals around predictions are very useful in making decisions based on predictions. [For further explanation of the standard error of estimate, see Brown, 1988 or Hatch and Lazaraton, 1991].

Conclusion

Quite obviously, the standard deviation, standard error of the mean, standard error of measurement, and standard error of estimate are quite different things. They are all based on the simple notions of the normal distribution, but they have quite different applications. In a nutshell:

1. The standard deviation helps you estimate the dispersion in a given distribution;

2. The standard error of the mean helps you to estimate the dispersion of sampling errors when you are trying to estimate the population mean from a sample mean;

3. The standard error of measurement helps you estimate the dispersion of the measurement errors when you are making decisions about students' scores at a certain cut-point; and

4. The standard error of estimate helps you estimate the dispersion of prediction errors when you are trying to predict Y values from X values in a regression analysis.

They are all useful statistical tools, and now you are in a position not only to understand the differences and similarities among these four concepts, but also to know when and where to apply them.

(updated and reprinted from Brown, 1999a)

CHAPTER 20

CAN WE USE THE SPEARMAN-BROWN PROPHECY FORMULA TO DEFEND LOW RELIABILITY?

QUESTION: Can we defend a low (or undesirable) reliability coefficient by estimating the ideal number of test items with the Spearman-Brown prophecy formula? Hirai (1999) used the Spearman-Brown prophecy formula to defend her test's moderate reliability this way: with two sets of 8 MC [multiple-choice] questions, her Cronbach alpha was .70, which is moderate. This is hardly surprising considering the small number of items. If the standard Spearman-Brown prophecy formula for 30 items is applied to this test, however, the Cronbach's alpha estimated jumps to .81 (p. 375). So, her point may be that the reliability of .70 is good for a small number of test items. In other words, for a 30-item test, .81 is enough: therefore, for 16 items, .70 is adequate.

I have never seen the formula used like this. Hirai indicated that she got a hint from your book [Brown, 1996a] regarding this. To my knowledge, no one else has adapted the Spearman-Brown formula as she did. How common is this practice?

I know that Spearman-Brown formula is used as a split-half method to double a reliability coefficient after splitting the test into two; however, I didn't know that this formula might also be applicable to more than double the reliability coefficient for estimation.

ANSWER: I find three separate questions in what you wrote above, two that you yourself posed in your first and second paragraphs and a third that is implied in your third paragraph: (a) Can we defend a low (or undesired level of) reliability coefficient by estimating the ideal number of test items on the Spearman-Brown prophecy formula? (b) Is this technique commonly used? (c) Can this formula be applied to more than double the reliability coefficient for estimation?

Can we defend a low (or undesired level of) reliability coefficient by estimating the ideal number of test items on the Spearman-Brown prophecy formula?

Hirai (1999) does indeed use the Spearman-Brown prophecy formula in discussing the reliability of her multiple-choice questions. The fact that you and other readers may interpret this use of the Spearman-Brown formula as a defense of her "moderate" reliability points to one danger in making this kind of argument. No, we cannot defend a low reliability in that way. However, since Hirai presents the original Cronbach reliability estimate of .70, I cannot fault her for making that argument. She was open and honest in her approach and can be said to be simply demonstrating that the reason for her "moderate" reliability was probably the relatively small number of items. The reader is still free to interpret the .70 she reported as indicating 70% reliability and 30% error.

Is this technique commonly used?

I wouldn't say that this strategy is commonly used, but it is sometimes used to make demonstrations of the sort Hirai did. I myself have used it several times. Most recently, I used it in Brown, Cunha, and Frota (2001), where we were examining the reliability of the subscales (of various lengths) on the QEMA (a Portuguese version of the Motivated Strategies for Learning Questionnaire, or MSLQ) as shown in Table 20.1.

To illustrate the relationship between the number of items and reliability, columns five and six of Table 20.1 give estimates of what the reliability would be if the subscales were all 12 items in length and 50 items in length, respectively. These adjustments were calculated using the Spearman-Brown prophecy formula (S-B). Notice that the reliabilities for each of the subscales are predictably higher for all of the subscales when adjusted to 12 items and are even very high when adjusted to 50 items. However, since such long subscales are clearly impractical, the demonstration here is simply meant to be illustrative and is not meant to suggest that the subscales actually be lengthened to 12 or 50 items.

Table 20.1. *Subscale and Cloze Reliabilities for a Portuguese Learning Questionnaire. (Adapted from Brown, Cunha, & Frota, 2001)*

Subscale	k	MSLQ Alpha	QUEMA Alpha	S-B (k=12)	S-B (k=50)	SEM
INTR	4	.71	.55	.79	.94	.70
EXTR	4	NG	.59	.81	.95	.76
TASK	6	.91	.79	.88	.97	.44
CONT	8	NG	.38	.48	.79	.53
SELF	5	.89	.82	.92	.98	.45
EXPT	3	NG	.66	.89	.95	.53
TEST	5	.82	.45	.67	.89	.86
REHR	4	.65	.61	.82	.95	.86
ELAB	6	.75	.68	.81	.95	.63
ORGS	4	.73	.66	.85	.96	.74
CRIT	5	.83	.78	.90	.97	.63
META	12	.83	.79	.79	.94	.47
TIME	8	.82	.58	.67	.90	.60
EFFT	4	.70	.43	.70	.91	.93
PEER	3	NG	.60	.86	.96	.91
HELP	4	.70	.42	.68	.90	.97

Since Brown, Cunha, and Frota (2001) did include the original reliability estimates and since they, like Hirai, were simply demonstrating what the reliability would have been under various conditions, I personally think they were within logical and ethical bounds. However, I may not be an impartial judge in this case.

Can this formula be applied to more than double the reliability coefficient for estimation?

As you mentioned the Spearman-Brown prophecy formula is commonly used for adjusting split-half reliability estimates for full test reliability. To review briefly, split-half reliability is an internal consistency estimate. Split-half reliability is typically calculated in the following steps:

1. Divide whatever test you are analyzing into two halves and score them separately (usually the odd-numbered items are scored separately from the even-numbered).

2. Calculate a Pearson correlation coefficient between the students' scores on the even-numbered items and their scores on the odd-numbered items. The resulting coefficient is an estimate of the half-test reliability of your test (i.e., the reliability of the odd-numbered items, or the even-numbered items, but not both combined).

3. Apply the Spearman-Brown prophecy formula to adjust the half-test reliability to full-test reliability. We know that, all other factors being held constant, a longer test will probably be more reliable than a shorter test. The Spearman-Brown prophecy formula was developed to estimate the change in reliability for different numbers of items. The Spearman-Brown formula that is often applied in the split-half adjustment is as follows:

$$reliability = \frac{2 \times r_{half-test}}{1 + r_{half-test}}$$

For example, if the half-test correlation (for a 30-item test) between the 15 odd-numbered and 15 even-numbered items on a test turned out to be .50, the full-test (30-item) reliability would be .67 as follows:

$$reliability = \frac{2 \times r_{half-test}}{1 + r_{half-test}} = \frac{2 \times .50}{1 + .50} = \frac{1.00}{1.50} = .666 \approx .67$$

However, there is another version of the formula (where n is the number of times the length of the test is to be increased or decreased), which can be applied to situations other than a simple doubling of the number of items:

$$reliability = \frac{n \times r}{1 + (n-1)r}$$

Using the more complex formula, we get the same answer as we did with the simpler formula for the split-half reliability adjustment example as follows:

$$reliability = \frac{n \times r}{1 + (n-1)r} = \frac{2 \times .50}{1 + (2-1).50} = \frac{2 \times .50}{1 + .50} = \frac{1.00}{1.50} = .666 \approx .67$$

We can also use the more complex formula to estimate what the reliability for that same test would be if it had 60 items by using $n = 4$ (for the number of times we must multiply 15 to get 60; 4 x 15 = 60) as follows:

$$reliability = \frac{n \times r}{1 + (n-1)r} = \frac{4 \times .50}{1 + (4-1).50} = \frac{4 \times .50}{1 + (3).50} = \frac{4 \times .50}{1 + 1.50} = \frac{2.00}{2.50} = .80$$

Or we can estimate what the reliability would be for various fractions of the test length. For instance, we could estimate the reliability for a 63 item test by using $n = 4.2$ (for the number of times we must multiply 15 to get 63; 4.2 x 15 = 63) as follows:

$$reliability = \frac{n \times r}{1 + (n-1)r} = \frac{4.2 \times .50}{1 + (4.2-1).50} = \frac{4.2 \times .50}{1 + (3.2).50} = \frac{4.2 \times .50}{1 + 1.60} = \frac{2.10}{2.60} = .807 \approx .81$$

We can even estimate the reliability for a shorter version of the test, say a 5-item version by using a decimal fraction, that is, $n = .33$ (for the number of times we must multiply 15 to get 5; .33 x 15 = 4.95 or about 5), as follows:

$$reliability = \frac{n \times r}{1 + (n-1)r} = \frac{.33 \times .50}{1 + (.33-1).50} = \frac{.33 \times .50}{1 + (-.67).50} = \frac{.33 \times .50}{1 + (-.335)} = \frac{.165}{.665} = .248 \approx .25$$

We might want to use this last strategy if we were trying to figure out how short we could make our test and still maintain decent reliability. [For more on the Spearman-Brown formula, see Brown, 1996a, pp. 194-196, 204-205]

Conclusion

The Spearman-Brown prophecy formula can be used for adjusting split-half reliability, but more importantly, it can be used for answering what-if questions about test length when you are designing or revising a language test. Unfortunately, the Spearman-Brown formula is limited to estimating differences on one dimension (usually the number of items, or raters). For those interested in doing so on more than one dimension, generalizability theory (G Theory) provides the same sort of answers, but for more dimensions (called facets in G Theory). For instance, in Brown (1999b), I used G Theory to examine (separately and together) the effects on reliability of various numbers of items and subtests on the TOEFL, and numbers of languages among the persons taking the test.

In any case, the sentence taken from Hirai (1999) about her use of the Spearman-Brown formula is just one sentence, indeed just one small detail, taken from a larger study that has much to offer readers interested in statistical research design, and/or the relationship between listening and reading rates for EFL learners in Japan. Sometimes, it is important to look past a single tree in order to see the entire forest clearly.

(updated and reprinted from Brown, 2001a)

CHAPTER 21

GENERALIZABILITY AND DECISION STUDIES

QUESTION: Recently, I read a paper in the *2004 JALT Pan-SIG Proceedings* by Lars Molloy and Shimura about situational sensitivity in medium-scale interlanguage pragmatics research. They analyzed how three situationally-sensitive measures (word count, speech act features, and a coded set of actions) vary among Japanese university-age students when initiating twelve scripted complaints in English. They used G- and D-studies to analyze the data. My question is threefold: Basically what are "G-studies" and "D-studies"? How do they differ? When should they be used?

ANSWER: My guess is that most readers of *Shiken* probably have no idea what generalizability theory is, so I will first provide some background material on that topic. I will then proceed to answer your three questions more directly, and finally I will have some concluding thoughts.

Generalizability theory

The reliability of measures in social sciences research has typically been estimated using a classical test theory (CTT) approach (replete with statistical estimates of reliability based on test-retest, parallel forms, split-half, K-R20, K-R21, Cronbach alpha, etc.). One useful extension of CTT reliability is called generalizability theory (G theory).[1]

G theory was pioneered by Cronbach, Rajaratnam, and Gleser (1963). In G theory, reliability becomes an issue of the degree to which we can generalize from one

---

[1] G theory should not be confused with the *G factor*, which is the *general intelligence factor* that some researchers believe in.

observation to a universe of observations (Cronbach, Gleser, Nanda, & Rajaratnam, 1972, p. 15). Hence, G theory takes the view that the observed score is a universe score and permits generalizing from a specific sample to the universe of interest through the use of clearly defined procedures (Shavelson & Webb, 1981, pp. 133-137). These procedures involve the use of a conceptual framework to estimate sources of measurement error in the measurement context. Analysis of variance (ANOVA) procedures are used to segregate and estimate the variance components associated with whatever facets of measurement the tester wants to examine. The mean squares values found in the ANOVA procedure are used to estimate the components of variance in a potentially multifaceted way, which provides a more comprehensive and detailed explanation of test variance than was ever possible in CTT reliability (Shavelson & Webb, 1981, p. 133). The variance components are then used to study how various test designs affect the *generalizability coefficient* (also known as the G *coefficient*, which is analogous to a *reliability coefficient*). Test design decisions can then be based on more accurate estimations of the effects of various sources of testing error. Shavelson and Webb (1991) describe G Theory techniques in theoretical terms, and Brennan (1983) describes ways to do G-studies in somewhat more practical terms. The single most comprehensive book on G theory currently in print is Brennan (2001). G theory has been applied in many fields other than language measurement research. Naturally, I cannot include all of those references here.

What are G-studies and D-studies?

The various procedures described in the previous section can be broken up into two distinct stages: the generalizability study (G study) and the decision study (D study). In the *G-study stage*, the ANOVA techniques are used to estimate components of variance for whatever testing facets are of interest in the study. This involves running the ANOVA, using the resulting mean squares to calculate the estimated variance components (one for each facet and one for each of the possible interactions among facets), and interpreting those variance components. Note that the testing facets of interest to a particular researcher may involve one, two, or more of the following sorts of variables: numbers of items, subtests, task types, passages, testing occasions, raters, etc. All of this is explained in great detail in the books cited above.

The Molloy and Shimura (2005) study (mentioned in your question at the top of this article) provides an appropriate and innovative use of G theory to explore the relative effects of situations (i.e., prompts in interlanguage pragmatics research) on the results for individuals (the participants being studied) in three one-facet (situations) G studies, one for each of three sets of measures (number of words, number of speech acts, and number of actions). Their interpretations of the three sets of G-study variance components are correct and useful as far as they go:

> Roughly, in this study, the variance components estimates for individuals can be interpreted as an estimate of how much the individuals in the study varied in terms of the three measures; that is, roughly this shows simple differences between individuals. The situation variance component estimates how much prompts affect the scores. Roughly, this shows how much situations affect scores. The interaction variance components estimates [sic] the extent to which the relative ranking of individuals changes according to prompts. Basically, this shows the extent to which the scores depended on differing reactions to the 12 complaint-initiation prompts (p. 19).

This explanation could have been a bit more explicit and clear in terms of prose explanations of the relative magnitude of the variance components, the percentages of variance accounted for in each study, the meaning of the signal-to-noise ratio, and so forth. But on the whole, as I pointed out above, the authors do provide correct and useful interpretations of the three sets of G-study results, as far as they go.

In the *D-study stage* that follows the G-study, the values determined for the estimated variance components are used to further calculate estimates of the effects of various measurement designs on the *dependability* (analogous to *reliability*) of the scores. Decisions about alternative test designs and score uses can be rationally made based on estimates of the error involved in whatever choices are involved. Then, the *dependability coefficients* (analogous to *reliability coefficients*) for these various possible alternatives can be calculated, examined, and compared.

Once again turning to the Molloy and Shimura (2005) example, the researchers present their D study results in the last two columns of their Tables 2, 4, and 6. Unfortunately, they do nothing with those results, not even explaining what they indicate, thereby missing important opportunities to explore and illustrate the effects of numbers of situations on the dependability of their measures. Consider the results (for number of words) reported in their Tables 1 and 2. The authors show D-study variance component estimates for individuals, situations, and the individuals-by-situations interaction of 25.7197, .85747, and 3.19213, respectively (apparently for the current design with 12 situations). Based on these results, I was able to calculate the values shown in my Table 21.1 in about 45 minutes using my spreadsheet program.

Table 21.1. *Estimated Generalizability Coefficients for Relative and Absolute Decisions for All Three Measures*

	Number of Words		Number of Speech Acts		Number of Actions	
Situations	Relative Decisions	Absolute Decisions	Relative Decisions	Absolute Decisions	Relative Decisions	Absolute Decisions
1	0.4017	0.3461	0.3671	0.3491	0.3188	0.2961
2	0.5732	0.5142	0.5371	0.5175	0.4834	0.4570
3	0.6682	0.6136	0.6351	0.6167	0.5840	0.5580
4	0.7287	0.6792	0.6988	0.6820	0.6518	0.6273
5	0.7705	0.7258	0.7436	0.7283	0.7006	0.6778
6	0.8011	0.7605	0.7768	0.7629	0.7374	0.7163
7	0.8246	0.7875	0.8024	0.7896	0.7661	0.7465
8	0.8431	0.8089	0.8227	0.8110	0.7892	0.7710
9	0.8580	0.8265	0.8393	0.8284	0.8081	0.7911
10	0.8704	0.8411	0.8530	0.8428	0.8239	0.8080
11	0.8808	0.8534	0.8645	0.8550	0.8373	0.8223
12	*0.8896*	*0.8640*	*0.8744*	*0.8655*	*0.8488*	*0.8347*
13	0.8972	0.8731	0.8829	0.8745	0.8588	0.8454
14	0.9038	0.8811	0.8904	0.8825	0.8676	0.8549
15	0.9097	0.8881	0.8969	0.8894	0.8753	0.8632
20	0.9307	0.9137	0.9207	0.9147	0.9035	0.8938
30	0.9527	0.9408	0.9457	0.9415	0.9335	0.9266
40	0.9641	0.9549	0.9587	0.9555	0.9493	0.9439
50	0.9711	0.9636	0.9667	0.9640	0.9590	0.9546
60	0.9758	0.9695	0.9721	0.9699	0.9656	0.9619
70	0.9792	0.9737	0.9760	0.9741	0.9704	0.9672
80	0.9817	0.9769	0.9789	0.9772	0.9740	0.9711
90	0.9837	0.9794	0.9812	0.9797	0.9768	0.9743
100	0.9853	0.9815	0.9831	0.9817	0.9791	0.9768
150	0.9902	0.9876	0.9886	0.9877	0.9860	0.9844
200	0.9926	0.9906	0.9915	0.9908	0.9894	0.9883

Table 21.1 shows the dependability coefficients for various numbers of situations for relative decisions (i.e., norm-referenced decisions) and absolute decisions (i.e., criterion-referenced decisions) for each of the three measures. The table clearly

illustrates the effect of increasing the number of situations on the dependability for each measure. Notice that, for 12 situations (in boldfaced italics), the results in Table 21.1 match those reported by Molloy and Shimura, which were .88959, .86379, 87493, .86550, .84883, and .83469 for relative and absolute decisions for number of words, number of speech acts, and number of actions, respectively. Notice also, however, that this table shows estimates for other possible numbers of situations, thereby allowing me to explore and illustrate the effect of numbers of situations on the dependability of each of the measures. For instance, the table shows that designing a measure for number of words (columns 2 & 3) with only one situation results in low dependability (.4017 and .3461 for relative and absolute decisions, respectively). However, adding only one more situation increases the dependability considerably to .5732 and .5142, respectively. Notice also, for number of words, that considerable gains in dependability are garnered by adding additional situations all the way up to about 5 or 6 situations, but that thereafter the bang-for-the-buck gained by adding situations decreases considerably. If a particular group of researchers is (a) going to be using this measure for relative decisions, (b) has limited time for gathering data, and (c) feels that dependability of .80 is sufficient, they may decide, on the basis of these D-study results, to design their measure with six situations, with which they can reasonably expect to produce dependability of about .80 if their participants are similar to those studied in Molloy and Shimura.

Columns 4 through 7 provide equivalently useful D-study information for the other two measures. Notice that each of these sets of results is interesting in its own right, but also that comparing the three measures can provide useful insights into the relative number of situations needed to produce such-and-such dependability with each of the three measures. For example, for relative decisions, only six situations are needed for the number of words measure to produce dependability of .80 (see column 2), while seven situations are required for the number of speech acts measure to reach the same level (see column 4), and nine situations are needed for the number of actions measure to reach .80 (see column 6).

In short, using the sort of D-study information shown in Table 21.1, the designer of a measure can decide, in terms of the type of decision (relative or absolute) and any practical considerations, how many situations will be needed to produce the necessary level of dependability for a given measure in a given research project; the researcher can also compare the relative efficiency of several measures. Clearly, such information can be very helpful in making design decisions about research instruments (even if, or especially if, there are two, three, or even more facets in the G study).

How do G-studies and D-studies differ?

It should be clear from the previous section that the *G study stage* involves using ANOVA procedures to determine and interpret the variance components. Then, the *D study stage* takes over to use those variance components to estimate the effects of various design conditions (numbers of situations, items, subtests, testing occasions, etc.) on dependability (for relative decisions, absolute decisions, or both).

When should G-studies and D-studies be used?

Clearly, the G study should be used first; then and only then, a follow-up D study should be applied. To do either without the other makes little sense. Hence, there are no "merits or demerits" involved in using either method of analysis. They should both be used together, and they should be applied sequentially.

Conclusion

Molloy and Shimura (2005) made an excellent contribution to pragmatics research in their article. They provided an appropriate and innovative use of G theory analysis to explore the relative effects of situations for individuals in a one-facet G study for each of three different measures. With the additional D-study results in Table 21.1, researchers (with research participants similar to those used by Molloy and Shimura) will now be able to plan how many situations they will need to include in their studies to achieve whatever dependability they feel is adequate and necessary given their practical constraints. G theory can be applied to many sorts of measurement problems in language testing, measurement, and research. Anyone interested in pursuing similar sorts of research may want to visit:

> www.education.uiowa.edu/centers/casma/computer-programs

At the time of this writing, GENOVA software (in both PC and Mac versions) and manuals are free and downloadable at that website.

Those researchers intrigued by the possibilities inherent in G theory should definitely try to get copies of Shavelson and Webb (1991) and Brennan (1983, 2001), but they may also find a number of language testing studies interesting. Bolus, Hinofotis, and Bailey

(1982) were the first to suggest the usefulness of G theory to language testing. Brown (1984b) was the first to actually use G theory in language testing (to study the effects of numbers of items and passages on the dependability of an engineering English reading comprehension test). Brown and Bailey (1984) examined the effects of numbers of raters and scoring categories on the dependability of essay ratings. Brown (1991, and elsewhere) applied G theory to studying the effects of numbers of raters and topic types on L1 writing placement test scores. Stansfield and Kenyon (1992) used G theory to investigate the effects of numbers of tests and raters on the dependability of oral interview scores. Brown (1990b, 1993c) used G theory to examine score dependability in criterion-referenced tests. Kunnan (1992) also used G Theory to investigate the dependability of a criterion-referenced test. Bachman, Lynch, and Mason (1995) used G Theory to study the effects of test tasks and rater judgments on speaking test dependability. Brown and Ross (1996) investigated the relative contributions of numbers of item types, sections, and tests to the dependability of TOEFL scores. Brown (1999b) examined the relative contributions of numbers of items, subtests, languages, and their various interactions to TOEFL score dependability. And finally, Brown and Hudson (2002) explained how to apply G theory to criterion-referenced tests in both domain score approaches and squared-error loss approaches.

(updated and reprinted from Brown, 2005a)

CHAPTER 22

HOW DO WE CALCULATE RATER/CODER AGREEMENT AND COHEN'S KAPPA?

QUESTION: I am working on a study in which two raters coded answers to 6 questions about study abroad attitudes/experience for 170 Japanese university students. The coding was done according to a rubric in which there were 4-8 possible responses per question. Since most—if not all—of the data is categorical, I have heard that Cohen's Kappa is the most common way of ascertaining inter-rater agreement. What is the best way to actually calculate that? Since more and more people are moving away from single-rater assessments to multi-rater assessments, this question should be relevant to *Shiken* readers.

ANSWER: In order to address your question, I will have to describe the *agreement coefficient* as well as the *kappa coefficient*. I will do so with a simple example, then with the more complex data that you have in your study.

Simple agreement coefficient example

In the realm of ratings or codings (hereafter simply called codings) of various categories, an *agreement coefficient* can be used to estimate the proportion of codings assigned by two raters or coders (hereafter simply called coders) that coincide. In the simplest scenario, let's say that two coders listen to the interview data of 120 students who were interviewed just after returning from a study abroad experience. After listening to each interview, each of the two coders is required to decide if the student was generally positive about the living abroad experience or generally negative. In other words, the coders are required to code each student's experience as positive or negative. Figure 22.1 illustrates how we need to lay out the results for the two coders in order to calculate an agreement coefficient.

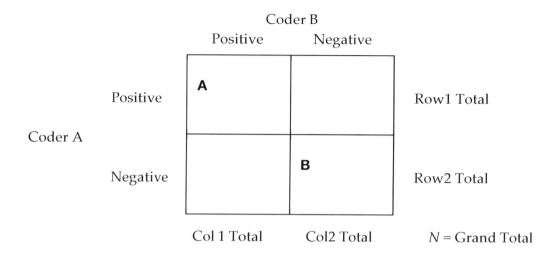

Figure 22.1. Layout for Positive and Negative Coding Data for Two Coders

In some cases, the codings agree between the two coders. When the two assigned codings for a student are both positive, that student is counted in cell A; when the two assigned codings for a student are both negative, that student is counted in cell B. The other cells indicate that the two coders disagreed in their codings (i.e., Coder A assigned a positive coding, but Coder B assigned a negative one, or vice versa). Notice that the row totals Row1 and Row2 are given to the right of Figure 22.1, and column totals Col1 and Col2 are given at the bottom. Notice also that the grand total (also affectionately known as N) is shown at the bottom right.

Coming back to our imaginary scenario, notice in Figure 22.2 that 65 out of the 120 students were classified as positive by both coders, while 30 others were classified as negative by both coders. In addition, 25 students (10 + 15 = 25 students) are classified differently by the two coders.

How Do We Calculate Rater/Coder Agreement and Cohen's Kappa? 141

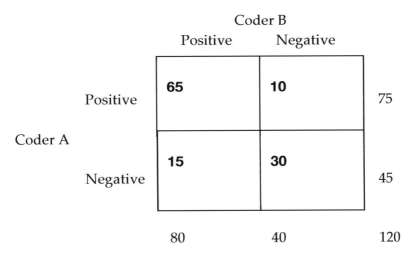

Figure 22.2. Sample Data for Positive and Negative Coding Data for Two Coders

With this information in hand, the following formula can be used to calculate the agreement coefficient:

$$p_o = \frac{A + B}{N}$$

Where:
p_o = agreement coefficient (or proportion observed)
A = number of agreed codings in cell A
B = number of agreed codings in cell B
N = total number of codings

Substituting the values found in Figure 22.2 into the equation, we get:

$$p_o = \frac{65 + 30}{120} = \frac{95}{120} = .7916666 \approx .79$$

Thus, the agreement coefficient in this case is about .79, which means that the coders classified the students in the same way about 79% of the time. Note that by extension, the coders disagreed 21% of the time (100% - 79% = 21%).

If all students were coded exactly the same way by both coders, the coefficient would be 1.00 [e.g., $(A + B) / N = (70 + 50) / 120 = 1.00$], so 1.00 is the maximum value the agreement coefficient can have. However, unlike the reliability coefficients (for more on this concept, see Brown, 1997b [Chapter 23], 2002a [Chapter 17]) that researchers often use, the agreement coefficient can't be lower than what would result by chance. Put another way, with 120 students, we might reasonably expect 30 students per cell by chance alone. This would result in a coefficient of .50 [(A + B) / N = (30 + 30)/120 = 60/120 = .50]. Thus, no agreement coefficient can logically be any lower than what would occur by chance alone—in this case, no lower than .50. This is very different from reliability estimates, which can go as low as .00.

Simple kappa coefficient example

The *kappa coefficient* (κ) arose (due to Cohen, 1960) to adjust for this chance-lower-limit problem by providing an estimate of the proportion of agreement in classifications beyond what would be expected to occur by chance alone. The adjustment is given in the following formula:

$$\kappa = \frac{(p_o - p_e)}{(1 - p_e)}$$

Where:
- κ = the kappa coefficient
- p_o = agreement coefficient (or proportion observed)
- p_e = proportion classification agreement that could occur by chance alone,

In this case: p_e = (Row1 × Col1) + (Row2 × Col2) / N^2

Before calculating κ, a researcher must calculate p_o and p_e for the particular data involved. We have already calculated p_o = .7916666 for the data in Figure 22.2; the calculations for p_e for the same data are as follows:

$$p_e = \frac{(Row1 \times Col1) + (Row2 \times Col2)}{N^2} = \frac{(75 \times 80) + (45 \times 40)}{120^2} = \frac{6000 + 1800}{14400}$$

$$= \frac{7800}{14400} = .5416666$$

Notice that we are calculating p_e by (a) multiplying the total for the row in which cell A is found by the column for cell A (Row1 x Col1), (b) multiplying the row total for cell B times the column total for cell B (Row2 x Col2), then (c) adding the two results together

[(Row1 x Col1) + (Row2 x Col2)], and (d) dividing the whole thing by N^2. In doing so, we are calculating the proportion of the expected frequencies for cells A and B.

Since the p_o for the data in Figure 22.2 was .7916666 and now we know that p_e is .5416666, kappa turns out to be: [1]

$$\kappa = \frac{(p_o - p_e)}{(1 - p_e)} = \frac{(.7916666 - .5416666)}{(1 - .5416666)} = \frac{(.25)}{(.4583334)} = .5454544 \approx .55$$

This kappa coefficient is an estimate of the coding agreement that occurred beyond what would be expected to occur by chance alone. It can also be interpreted as a proportion of agreement, .55 in this case, or as a percentage of agreement, 55% in this case. Unlike the agreement coefficient, kappa represents the percentage of classification agreement beyond chance, so it is not surprising that kappa is lower than the agreement coefficient. Like the agreement coefficient, kappa has an upper limit of 1.00, but unlike the agreement coefficient, kappa has the more familiar .00 lower limit.

Your more complex agreement coefficient example

In the case of your more complex coding criteria, your data should be laid out as shown in Figure 22.3 for your Question 1. Figure 22.4 shows the labels and examples you sent me for your Question 1 rubric. Notice that instead of cells A and B (as in the simpler example), we are focused here on agreements in cells A, B, C, D, E, and F.

---

[1] Note that, for the sake of accuracy, I keep all the decimal places that my 100-Yen-shop calculator gives me until the very last step where I round the result off to two-places in order to be consistent with APA formatting.

		Coder B					
		5	4	3	2	1	0	
Coder A	5	A						Row1
	4		B					Row2
	3			C				Row3
	2				D			Row4
	1					E		Row5
	0						F	Row6
		Col1	Col2	Col3	Col4	Col5	Col6	N

Figure 22.3. Layout for Categories 5, 4, 3, 2, 1, and 0 Data for Two Coders for Question 1 in Your Study.

5 = A strong interest in SA	Ex: *I'm very interested in abroad study because I want to speak English fluently* [T1]
4 = A mild interest in SA	Ex: *A little. But, I like to go abroad.* [K4]
3 = Neutral and/or ambivalent	Ex: *It's so so. I want to study abroad, but I don't have money. And you?* [T80]
2 = Little interest in SA	Ex: *I have just little interested about study abroad.* [K28]
1 = A strong disinterest in SA	Ex: *I'm nothing. I like Japan school. And you?* [T90]
0 = No response	

Figure 22.4. Coder Options for Question 1 in Your Study[2]

---

[2] You asked me in an aside if this could be a Likert item (see Brown, 2000c [Chapter 15], 2011a [Chapter 16]). I'm inclined to say *no* because you really are interested in how consistently the coders judged data to be in these different categories (including *no response*). If you had been asking the students themselves to rate their experience using this scale, then I would say that it should be analyzed as a Likert item. Even if all the above were not true, your other questions

Your actual data are displayed in Figure 22.5. Notice that the agreements in cells A, B, C, D, E, and F (at 74, 21, 1, 9, 20, and 25, respectively) are fairly high relative to the other cells. That is an indication that the two raters tend to agree with each other in their ratings.

		Coder B						
		5	4	3	2	1	0	
Coder A	5	74	0	0	0	0	0	74
	4	0	21	0	1	1	0	23
	3	1	5	1	3	0	0	8
	2	0	2	0	9	0	0	11
	1	0	0	0	2	20	0	22
	0	3	1	0	1	0	25	30
		78	29	10	16	21	25	170

Figure 22.5. Data for Categories 5, 4, 3, 2, 1, and 0 for Two Coders for Question 1 in Your Study.

With Figures 22.3 and 22.5 in hand, the calculation of the agreement coefficient is simple with the following equation:

---

are all clearly nominal in nature, so it is probably best if you use agreement and Kappa to consistently analyze all of your questions the same way.

$$p_o = \frac{A + B + C + D + E + F}{N}$$

Where:
p_o = agreement coefficient (or proportion observed)
A to F = number of agreed codings in cells A to F
N = total number of codings

Substituting the values found in Figure 22.5 into the equation, we get:

$$p_o = \frac{74 + 21 + 1 + 9 + 20 + 25}{170} = \frac{150}{170} = .88235294 \approx .88$$

Thus, the agreement coefficient is about .88, which indicates that the coders agreed in their classifications of students about 88% of the time (and that they disagreed 12% of the time).

Your more complex kappa coefficient example

Recall that the kappa coefficient arose to adjust for this chance-lower-limit problem by providing the proportion of consistency in classifications beyond what would be expected to occur by chance alone and that the adjustment is given in the following formula:

$$\kappa = \frac{(p_o - p_e)}{(1 - p_e)}$$

Where:
κ = the kappa coefficient
p_o = agreement coefficient (or proportion observed)
p_e = proportion classification agreement that could occur by chance alone

In this case: p_e = [(Row1 x Col1) + (Row2 x Col2) + (Row3 x Col3) + (Row4 x Col4) + (Row5 x Col5) + (Row6 x Col6)] / N^2

Before calculating κ, we must calculate p_o for the particular data table involved. For the data in Figure 22.5, the calculations would be as follows:

$$p_e = \frac{(Row1 \times Col1) + (Row2 \times Col2) + (Row3 \times Col3) + (Row4 \times Col4) + (Row5 \times Col5) + (Row6 \times Col6)}{N^2}$$

Notice that this time we are calculating p_e by multiplying the row and column totals for cells A, B, C, D, E, and F and adding them up before dividing by N^2. In doing so, we are calculating the proportion of the expected frequencies for cells A through F. Substituting in the values from Figure 22.5, we get:

$$p_e = \frac{(74 \times 78) + (23 \times 29) + (8 \times 10) + (11 \times 16) + (22 \times 21) + (30 \times 25)}{170^2}$$

$$= \frac{5772 + 667 + 80 + 176 + 462 + 750}{28900} = \frac{7907}{28900} = .2735986$$

Given that p_o for the data in Figure 22.5 is .88235294 and p_e is .2735986, kappa turns out to be:

$$\kappa = \frac{(p_o - p_e)}{(1 - p_e)} = \frac{(.88235294 - .2735986)}{(1 - .2735986)} = \frac{(.6087543)}{(.7264014)} = .8380411 \approx .84$$

This kappa coefficient shows that the proportion of coding agreement that occurred beyond what we would expect by chance alone is .84, so the percentage of agreement is a respectable 84%, and we know that it could have fallen anywhere between .00 to 1.00.

Conclusion

This chapter described how to calculate rater/coder agreement and Cohen's kappa. I have shown here how to lay out the data and calculate agreement and Kappa coefficients for a simple set of data based on binary decisions by two coders, as well as for the data generated in your study for six-category decisions by two coders. I hope you see how you need to arrange your data for Questions 2 to 6 in order to calculate p_o, and more importantly, how to calculate p_e from the row and column totals associated with each agreement cell (regardless of the number of decisions involved) in the process of then calculating agreement and kappa coefficients for each question in your study. Please note that I would generally report both the agreement and kappa coefficients because they provide different types of information, both of which may be interesting to some readers.

(updated and reprinted from Brown, 2012b)

CHAPTER 23

RELIABILITY OF SURVEYS

QUESTION: In a JALT Journal article I recently read (Sasaki, 1996), the author wrote about a teacher survey. In it, she reported that she used the Cronbach alpha statistic to measure internal consistency, with a resulting alpha value of 0.70 (p. 232). When should this internal consistency measure be used and how good is a reliability figure of 0.70?

ANSWER: To fully answer your question, I need to first address several sub-questions:

- Why is consistency important?
- Does the notion of consistency vary in different situations?
- What do norm-referenced reliability statistics mean?
- What factors affect the reliability of an instrument?
- And what kinds of norm-referenced reliability statistics are appropriate for questionnaires?

Before I am finished here, I do promise to come back to your original question.

Why is consistency important?

For language surveys, like any other measurement instrument, we need to be concerned about the consistency of measurement. This concern should apply to all observations or measurements that we make, whether they be qualitative or quantitative, and whether they be for pedagogical/curriculum purposes or for research purposes.

In a sense, we are no different from a post office that weighs letters and packages. The customers at a post office quite reasonably expect the scales to be consistent. If they take a package to the post office and weigh it on two different occasions, they expect the two weights to be the same, or at least very similar. Thus measurement consistency is an important issue in everyday life. In fact, measurement consistency is such an important issue that national governments have established departments of weights and measures to ensure measurement consistency. Similarly, we would like our measurements in language teaching to be consistent.

Does the notion of consistency vary in different situations?

Measurement consistency may be defined differently depending on the situation involved. Qualitative researchers refer to the consistency concept as dependability and will stress the importance of using multiple sources of information, especially triangulation (wherein different types of information are gathered to cross-validate each other; for instance, three different kinds of information, say interviews, observations, and questionnaires, might be gathered from three different sources, say students, teachers, and administrators).

Quantitative researchers also refer to the consistency concept as dependability for criterion-referenced assessments, but they call it reliability for norm-referenced assessments. Criterion-referenced dependability typically involves one or more of the following three strategies (these three will not be defined here because they are not directly germane to the discussion at hand): threshold-loss agreement, squared-error loss, or domain-score dependability. Norm-referenced reliability usually involves one or more of the following three strategies: test-retest reliability, equivalent forms reliability, or internal consistency reliability (these three strategies will be defined below). Like qualitative researchers, quantitative researchers should stress the importance of multiple sources of information, especially in making important decisions about students' lives. (For much more information, including how to calculate the various reliability and dependability estimates, see Brown, 1996a).

Clearly, for any observations or measurements (whether qualitative or quantitative), consistency is a crucial concept for language teachers, administrators, and researchers of all kinds. Equally clear is the fact that the concept of consistency is approached differently depending on the type of measurement involved and the purposes of that measurement.

What do norm-referenced reliability statistics mean?

Zeroing in on the meaning of reliability statistics for norm-referenced purposes, they are most commonly reported as the proportion of consistent variance on whatever instrument is being examined. These reliability statistics range from zero (for a totally unreliable measure) to 1.00 (for a measure that is 100% reliable). Thus, an estimate of .70, like the one you asked about, indicates that the questionnaire is 70% reliable. Note that a .70 estimate also means that the measure is 30% unreliable (1 - .70 = .30, or 30%). The question of whether such a value is good or bad can only be answered in relative terms depending on a number of factors.

What factors affect the reliability of an instrument?

Reliability is affected by many factors, but from the researcher's point of view, the three most important factors are the length (or total number of questions), the quality of the questions, and the fit to the group being measured. If a test or questionnaire is reasonably long (say at least 30 questions) and is well-written, it should be fairly reliable, but if the instrument is short and/or the questions are not effective, it will not be reliable at all.

Furthermore, even if sufficient well-written questions are used, an instrument may prove to be unreliable if it does not fit the group of people involved in the measurement process. So a test like the TOEFL that has repeatedly been shown to be highly reliable (in excess of .90 when administered to students ranging from near zero English to native-like proficiency) may be much less reliable if used in a local English language program where it doesn't fit very well, that is, where the range of abilities is very restricted or where the scores are skewed. [Restricted range means the scores don't vary much. Skewed, in non-technical terms, means that the scores are scrunched up toward the top or bottom of the score range. [For more complete definitions, see Brown, 1996a.] We will return to these issues, as they apply to the .70 reported in Sasaki's (1996) study, at the end of this article.

What kinds of norm-referenced reliability statistics are appropriate for questionnaires?

Testing books (e.g., Brown, 1996a) typically discuss test-retest reliability (where the researcher administers a measure on two occasions and calculates the correlation between the two sets of scores as a reliability estimate), equivalent forms reliability (where the researcher administers two forms of a measure and calculates the correlation between the two sets of scores as reliability a estimate), and internal consistency reliability (where the researcher estimates the reliability of a single form administered on a single occasion). Obviously the internal consistency estimates are the easiest to get because it is not necessary to administer the measure twice or to have two forms.

Internal consistency reliability estimates come in many forms, e.g., the split-half adjusted (using the Spearman-Brown prophecy formula), the Kuder-Richardson formulas 20 and 21 (aka, K-R20 and K-R21), and Cronbach alpha. The most commonly reported of these are the K-R20 and the Cronbach alpha. Either one provides a sound estimate of reliability. However, the K-R20 is applicable only when questions are scored in a binary manner (i.e., right or wrong). Cronbach alpha has the advantage of being applicable when question responses form a graded scale (i.e., 1 2 3 4 5), such as the Likert scale items found on many questionnaires. Hence, Cronbach alpha is most often the reliability estimate of choice for survey research.

A direct answer to your question

Coming back to your question, the central parts were "Why would someone want to use a measure of internal consistency for survey data, and is 0.70 good or bad?"

Why measure internal consistency for survey data? A direct answer to this question is that the researcher probably wanted to know about the consistency of her survey instrument because the results of her study rested entirely on that measurement. If the consistency of her instrument was questionable, then all of her results would be equally questionable. Put another way, her results could be no more reliable than the instrument upon which they were based.

Is .70 good or bad? The answer to this part of your question is *it depends*. Ultimately, you, the reader of such an article, must decide whether you think .70 is good or bad. Is 70% reliability good? That will depend on the length of the questionnaire, the quality of the questions, and their fit to the group being measured. For what they are worth, my reactions as a reader of Sasaki's article are as follows:

- In terms of length, there are 25 questions, which would lead me to think that the reliability might be higher if she had just a few more questions.

- Looking at question quality, I note that the questionnaire was developed solely out of the researcher's experience and was a first attempt, so I would not expect it to be extremely reliable.

- In her favor, she does present the actual questions (in her Tables 1 and 2), so readers can directly inspect them. And, the questions strike me as being reasonably well-crafted.

- In addition, considering the fit to the group, the questionnaire appears to fit the group in the sense that it produced considerable systematic variance as indicated by the fact that the mean answers on the various five-point Likert items ranged from 1.48 to 4.83 with many different values in between.
- Finally, the results of the questionnaire are systematic enough to have produced significant differences between preferred and perceived student behaviors on 24 out of the 25 questions. So the fit of the questionnaire appears to be fairly good.

But, that is just one man's opinion. What do you think? Whatever you decide will (and should) affect the way you read and interpret the rest of the study. So this is a rather critical decision.

Maybe the question shouldn't be so much whether .70 is good or bad (in absolute terms), but rather whether 70% reliability is sufficient for the purposes of the study involved. From that perspective, I would have to say that 70% reliability is not spectacular, but it does seem sufficiently high for the purposes of Sasaki's survey study.

In any case, my hat is off to her for reporting the reliability of her instrument. Such statistics are seldom reported in language teaching journals. Thus we often have no idea how good the instruments (upon which entire studies are based) really are in terms of reliability. I also congratulate the author for showing her questions directly to the readers. There is no better way to decide for yourself whether a questionnaire makes sense to you and to your teaching situation, than to inspect the questions directly. By reporting her reliability and including her questions, Sasaki was being open and honest about her study and giving her readers sufficient information to judge its quality. Bravo!

(updated and reprinted from Brown, 1997b)

PART II: SECOND LANGUAGE RESEARCH

SECTION D: PLANNING RESEARCH

CHAPTER 24

CHARACTERISTICS OF SOUND QUALITATIVE RESEARCH

QUESTION: Many *Shiken* readers have never undertaken a qualitative research project, and they probably need to know something about triangulation. Could you briefly outline why triangulation is important, what the main types of triangulation are, and some of the most common triangulation procedures?

ANSWER: Certainly, let me begin with a definition of what I think *research* is. Then I will turn to the issues that qualitative researchers need to address in order to produce sound qualitative research. As I proceed through these explanations, you will see how triangulation fits into the whole picture.

What is research?

In a survey that I conducted years ago for the TESOL organization (reported in Brown, 1992a), I asked the respondents for their definitions of research. The results? A surprising variety of answers ranging from short, idealistic definitions (e.g., "Careful, thorough study" and "The search for the truth") to cynical ones (e.g., "Ignoring the obvious"). More recently in an article about applied linguistics research (Brown, 2004d), I was able to settle on a single definition for research that was broad enough to include all the definitions listed in Brown (1992a): research is "any systematic and principled inquiry."

How can we know if qualitative research is systematic and principled?

Research can be systematic and principled in many different ways. Brown (2004d) discusses those different ways in terms of what Newman and Benz (1998) called the qual-quant continuum. In general terms, *good quantitative research* (at one end of the qual-quant continuum) will be judged in terms of its reliability, validity, replicability, and generalizability, while *sound qualitative research* (at the other end of the continuum) will be judged in term of its dependability, credibility, confirmability, and transferability. Naturally, much of our research falls somewhere in between those two end points of the qual-quant continuum, or combines aspects of both. In this chapter, I will focus on the qualitative end of the continuum, and therefore on dependability, credibility, confirmability, and transferability.

Dependability

Dependability involves accounting for all the changing conditions in whatever is being studied as well as any changes in the design of the study that were needed to get a better understanding of the context. Dependability can be enhanced by using overlapping methods, stepwise replications, and/or inquiry audits (e.g., see Denzin, 1994, p. 513).

- *Overlapping methods* use carefully planned *methodological triangulation*, or multiple data gathering procedures (e.g., observations, interviews, and questionnaires), used in order to create overlapping (and therefore cross-validating) data.

- *Stepwise replications* involve *time triangulation*, that is, gathering data on multiple occasions (e.g., at the beginning, middle, and end of a school year), which helps in examining the consistency of the data and interpretations over time.

- *Inquiry audits* involve enlisting an outside expert *auditor* to verify the consistency of agreement among data, research methods, interpretations, conclusions, etc.

Where appropriate, confidence in the dependability of a study can also be improved by doing quantitative analyses like *intercoder/interrater agreement coefficients* or other *reliability estimates*.

Credibility

Credibility requires demonstrating, in one or more ways, that the research was designed to maximize the accuracy of identifying and describing whatever is being studied, especially as judged by the groups of people being studied. Credibility can be enhanced by using one or more of the following strategies: prolonged engagement, persistent observation, triangulation, peer debriefing, negative case analysis, and/or member checking (see Denzin, 1994, p. 513).

Prolonged engagement involves investing sufficient time and *persistent observation* involves using adequate numbers of observations, meetings, interviews, etc. so that participants feel enough confidence and trust in the researcher to allow for adequate study of the cultural context and adequate checks for misinformation (Davis, 1992, p. 606; 1995, p. 445).

Various forms of *triangulation* may also enhance credibility: *source triangulation* involves gathering data from multiple sources (e.g., people in different roles, like students, teachers, and administrators) in order to minimize and understand any differences/biases held by people in various roles. *Investigator triangulation* involves using multiple researchers to interpret the data in order to minimize and understand any differences/biases the researchers may have. *Location triangulation* involves gathering data at multiple sites (e.g., three different schools) in order to minimize and understand any differences/biases that might be introduced by the participants in each of the institutions.

Credibility can also be enhanced by using *peer debriefing* (i.e., critical examination and evaluation by a qualified outside researcher of the study design, data collection, analyses, etc.); *negative case analysis* (i.e., intentionally searching for and analyzing examples of data or participants that contradict the overall interpretations in a study); and *member checking* (i.e., verifying the researcher's interpretations and conclusions with the various groups of participants themselves).

Confirmability

Confirmability entails full revelation of the data upon which all interpretations are based, or at least the availability of the data for inspection. In other words, the reader of the research report should be able to examine the data to confirm the results/interpretations. Confirmability is sometimes enhanced by using *audit trails* (i.e., a "residue of records stemming from inquiry", Lincoln & Guba, 1985, p. 319). According to Denzin (1994, p. 513), "confirmability builds on audit trails...and involves the use of written field notes, memos, a field diary, process and personal notes, and a reflexive journal." Clearly, thorough record keeping and preservation of data for potential inspection are crucial to this strategy. Some researchers will append their data (including transcripts, instructions, etc.) to their report, or at least include crucial examples for inspection by the reader. Naturally, if the reader can inspect the data, the interpretations and results will be maximally confirmable.

Transferability

Transferability involves demonstrating the applicability of the results of the study in one context to other contexts. Transferability can be enhanced by providing what is often referred to as *thick description* (i.e., giving enough details so the readers can decide for themselves if the results are transferable to their own contexts). Thick description also "involves an emic perspective, which demands description that includes the actors' interpretations and other social and/or cultural information" (Davis, 1995, p. 434). Marshall and Rossman (1989, p. 145) note that transferability is the responsibility of the person seeking to apply the results of the study to a new context, that is, it is the responsibility of the reader. "In this way, the responsibility of the original investigator ends in providing sufficient descriptive data to make such similarity judgments possible" (Davis 1992, p. 606).

Conclusion

In direct answer to your original question, triangulation is a key concept in qualitative research. Variants of triangulation are used to enhance both the dependability (i.e., methodological and time triangulation) and credibility (i.e., source, investigator, and location triangulation) of such research. Other types of triangulation exist (e.g., theory triangulation and interdisciplinary triangulation) that serve additional purposes (see Brown 2001e, pp. 227-231). However, the issue of triangulation is not that simple: as Fielding and Fielding (1986) point out, "the important feature of triangulation is not the simple combination of different kinds of data, but the attempt to relate them so as to counteract the threats to validity identified in each" (p. 31). Hence, to be used effectively, triangulation must be carefully thought through and planned.

Those who find qualitative research methods intriguing may benefit from reading some or all of the following general qualitative research books: Denzin and Lincoln (1994), Fetterman (1989), Glesne (1998), Huberman and Miles (2002), Marshall and Rossman (1989), Maxwell (2004), and Miles and Huberman (1984). Five other books provide at least a chapter length treatment of qualitative language research methods: Brown (2001e), Brown and Rodgers (2002), Freeman (1998), Johnson (1992), and Nunan (1992).

(updated and reprinted from Brown, 2005b)

CHAPTER 25

CHARACTERISTICS OF SOUND QUANTITATIVE RESEARCH

QUESTION: In Brown, 2005b [Chapter 24], you explained the characteristics of well-done qualitative research by explaining the importance of dependability, credibility, confirmability, and transferability. You mentioned in passing that the parallel characteristics for quantitative research were reliability, validity, replicability, and generalizability. But you never really explained those quantitative research characteristics. I think it would be useful to know more about those characteristics of sound quantitative research and maybe even something about the characteristics of good quality mixed-methods research. Could you talk about these other research paradigms?

ANSWER: Certainly, let me begin by reviewing my definition of what I think *research* is. Then I will turn to the issues that quantitative researchers need to address in order to produce sound quantitative research by explaining four concepts: reliability, validity, replicability, and generalizability. As I proceed through these explanations, you will see how similar and yet different the qualitative and quantitative sets of characteristics are. I will focus on the characteristics of quantitative research here and save the characteristics of mixed-methods research for a subsequent chapter (Brown, 2016 [Chapter 26]).

What is research?

In the chapter you refer to (Brown, 2005b [Chapter 24]), I defined *research* very broadly as "any systematic and principled inquiry" (based on Brown, 1992a, 2004d). Research can be systematic and principled in many different ways. As I discussed in Brown (2005b), *sound qualitative research* (at one end of the continuum) can be systematic in terms of its dependability, credibility, confirmability, and transferability, while *sound quantitative research* can be systematic in terms of its reliability, validity, replicability, and generalizability—four characteristics that will serve as the focus of the rest of this chapter.

Reliability

In quantitative research, at a micro level, *reliability* can be defined as something like the degree to which the results of research measurements and observations are consistent. The reliability of a study's measurements and observations can be enhanced by carefully designing and creating them, piloting them beforehand, and revising them with an eye toward increasing their reliability before they are ever used in the main study. In cases where humans will be rating or coding data, reliability may be enhanced by giving the raters/coders clear guidelines, carefully training them, and periodically retraining them (especially if the ratings will be done over a long period of time).

The reliability of a study's measurements and observations can be checked in cases where test items or Likert-item questionnaires are involved, either by calculating test-retest reliability (i.e., examining the degree of correlation between the scores produced by two administrations of the same test or questionnaire), parallel forms reliability (i.e., examining the degree of correlation between the scores produced by two forms of the same test or questionnaire), or more easily, by calculating internal consistency reliability estimates (e.g., Cronbach alpha, K-R20, etc.), as appropriate. Alternatively, in cases where the measurements or observations are being assigned by raters, interrater reliability can be used (typically by examining the degree of correlation between ratings assigned by pairs of raters), and when the measures or observations are being coded by human coders, intercoder agreement will be used (typically, by calculating the percent of codings that agree between two coders).

However, at a macro level, the *reliability of a study* can be defined as the degree to which the results of a study are consistent. This type of macro reliability can be enhanced by: (a) carefully sampling, (b) thoughtfully planning and controlling the conditions under which the study is conducted, and (c) meticulously designing, piloting, and revising all measurement and observation tools. In general, then, the reliability of a study should be examined in terms of how well the results of the study are internally consistent and make sense in terms of sampling, study conditions, and instrumentation.

Validity

In quantitative research, at a micro level, *validity* can be defined as the degree to which a study's measurements and observations represent what they are supposed to characterize. The validity of a study's measurements and observations can be enhanced by carefully designing and creating them based on the best available language learning theories, piloting them beforehand, and revising them with an eye toward increasing their validity in terms of how accurately they are measuring what they were intended to measure.

The validity of the scores or other values obtained from any instrumentation in a study can be checked and/or defended by studying evidence and developing arguments for the content, criterion-related, and construct validity of the resulting scores or other values, as well as their social consequences and values implications within the study and more broadly.

At a macro level, the *validity of a study* can be defined as the degree to which the results of a study represent what the researcher thinks they represent. This type of macro validity can be enhanced by initially designing a study to maximally approximate *natural* conditions; by carefully prearranging and controlling study conditions; and by guarding against effects like the Hawthorne effect, halo effect, subject expectancy effect, researcher expectancy effect, practice effect, and reactivity effect (see Brown, 1988, or many other sources).

Replicability

Replicability can be defined as the degree to which a study supplies sufficient information for the reader to verify the results by replicating or repeating the study. The replicability of a study can be enhanced by writing a clear and complete research report in the style of a recipe that tells readers about: the *participants* (including who they were and how they were selected), the *materials* (including what measurements and observations were used in the study and why they were reliable and valid for that purpose), the *procedures* (including all of the steps in how the study was conducted), and the *analyses* (including how the variables were defined and arranged, as well as how all of the analyses were performed to address the research questions). Indeed, the study should be so clearly described that a reader could in fact repeat the study if they were so inclined. One way to check this is to ask a colleague to read the report and give you feedback with the notion of replicability (as described here) in mind.

Generalizability

Generalizability can be defined as the degree to which the results of a study can be generalized, or are meaningful, beyond the sample in a study to the population that the sample represents. Unfortunately, it is often very difficult to define a general population in second language studies. For example, in an ESL study, can we ever say that a sample of students selected from the English Language Institute at the University of Hawai'i at Mānoa (UHM) is representative of all ESL students studying in the US? Or even all ESL university students studying in Hawai'i? Can we say that this predominantly Asian sample of international students is the same or even similar to ESL students studying at a US East Coast university, where students might tend to be predominantly European and Middle Eastern? I think you can see the problem.

However, there is no reason to lose hope because the generalizability of a study can be enhanced in at least four ways:

- *Narrowly define the population* you are trying to sample from. For example, don't even pretend that you are trying to generalize to all ESL students in US universities (or even to all EFL students in Japanese universities). Instead, define the population narrowly as in the population of all students in the ELI at UHM. Then and only then will it be reasonable to say that a sample selected randomly or in a stratified manner represents that population of students in the ELI at UHM.

- *Choose participants with random or stratified selection* into the study and then into whatever groups you may want to compare (e.g., treatment and control groups). Those strategies will definitely help to improve the representativeness of the sample(s) and thus the generalizability of the study (see Brown, 2006b [Chapter 28]).

- *Control for self-selection and mortality of participants* (a) by avoiding the use of volunteers whenever possible (i.e., *self-selection*) and (b) by minimizing as much as possible all attrition (i.e., participants dropping out of the study, also known as, *mortality*) by keeping the study short in duration and by encouraging participants to stay in the study. The reasoning here is that people who volunteer tend to be a certain type of gung-ho student not representative of the entire population, and similarly, people who leave a study or drop out may also be a certain type of person who by leaving will make the remaining participants less representative.

- *Use the qualitative concept of transferability* described in Brown (2005b [Chapter 24]), which was described as follows: "Transferability can be enhanced by providing what is often referred to as *thick description* (i.e., giving enough detail so the readers can decide for themselves if the results are transferable to their own contexts)" (p. 32). What I am saying is that providing readers with very clear information about who the participants were and how they were selected will help those readers determine for themselves how much the results can be generalized, or better yet, how much the results may apply to their own teaching/research situations.

Conclusion

In direct answer to your original question, the characteristics of sound quantitative research are generally considered to be: reliability, validity, replicability, and generalizability. These are of course ideals that researchers should strive for and of course may be enhanced, or defended in a variety of different ways depending on the type of study, the research questions involved, the nature of the variables, the choices of statistical analysis techniques, and so forth. Because these characteristics are ideals, they can also serve as standards against which you as a reader can judge the quality of quantitative research that you encounter in our ever growing literature. And of course, remember to apply these same standards just as critically to any research that you yourself may produce.

Those readers who find quantitative research methods intriguing may find it useful to read books like Baayen (2008), Brown (1988, 2001e), Brown and Coombe (2015), Brown and Rodgers (2002), Butler (1985), Dörnyei (2003, 2007), Hatch and Lazaraton (1991), Porte (2010), and Scholfield (1995); and, those interested in moving beyond the basic level should consider reading Plonsky (2015) and perhaps even Tabachnick and Fidell (2012).

(updated and reprinted from Brown, 2015b)

CHAPTER 26

CHARACTERISTICS OF SOUND MIXED METHODS RESEARCH

QUESTION: In Brown, 2005b [Chapter 24], you described the characteristics of sound qualitative research by describing the importance of dependability, credibility, confirmability, and transferability. I think it would also be useful to know about the characteristics of sound quantitative and even mixed methods research. Could you address these research paradigms as well?

ANSWER: You are absolutely right, Brown (2005b [Chapter 24]) reviewed the characteristics of good quality qualitative research. Since then, the first part of your question was answered in Brown (2015b [Chapter 25]), which covered the characteristics of sound quantitative research. Here, I will address the second part of your question by examining the characteristics of sound mixed methods research. I will begin by reviewing once again my definition of what I think *research* is, as well as the key concepts in qualitative and quantitative research. Then I will turn to the issues that researchers need to address in order to produce sound mixed methods research. I will do so by explaining nine forms of legitimation and six techniques that can be applied. As I proceed through these explanations, you will see how mixed methods research includes both quantitative and qualitative methods, but creates a research paradigm that is unique in its own right.

What is research?

In the two related chapters on this topic (listed in the previous paragraph), I showed how I came to settle (in Brown, 1992a and 2004d) on a single definition for research that was broad enough to include all the definitions listed in Brown (1992a): research is "any systematic and principled inquiry." I also showed how quantitative and qualitative research can be systematic and principled in different, but similar ways. Generally speaking, *quantitative research* can be defended by the researcher and judged by the reader in terms of its reliability, validity, replicability, and generalizability. In contrast, *qualitative research* can be defended or judged in term of its dependability, credibility, confirmability, and transferability. Naturally, because mixed methods research systematically combines both quantitative and qualitative methods, mixed methods researchers should consider all of the issues raised in the previous two sentences for each of the research types, but should also consider the characteristics of properly combining the two types of research in such a way that it is not just a hodge-podge of quantitative and qualitative methods (sometimes referred to snidely as *multi-methods research*), but rather is a systematic and principled combination of the two research paradigms that results in a third paradigm—one that can truly be called *mixed methods research* (MMR).

How can we know if mixed methods research is systematic and principled?

We can enhance, defend, and judge the quality of MMR based on a concept called *legitimation* (Onwuegbuzie & Johnson, 2006). Brown (2014b) defined legitimation as:

> the degree to which MMR integration of qualitative and quantitative research strengthen and provide legitimacy, fidelity, authority, weight, soundness, credibility, trustworthiness, and even standing to the results and interpretations in MMR. Clearly, MMR investigators will want to think about legitimation in terms of how they can design their research to enhance it and thereby enhance the resulting *meta-inferences* (i.e., inferences at the MMR or integration level of study) (p. 128).

Brown (2015c) summarized the extensive discussion originally presented by Onwuegbuzie and Johnson (2006, pp. 56-60) of the following nine subtypes of legitimation:

1. *Sample legitimation* – appropriately integrating qualitative and quantitative samples.

2. *Inside-outside legitimation* – adequately using insider and outsider perspectives.

3. *Weakness minimization legitimation* – compensating for the weaknesses in some approaches with the strengths of others.

4. *Sequential legitimation* – minimizing the effects of method sequencing.

5. *Conversion legitimation* – maximizing the effects of using both qualitative and quantitative data.

6. *Paradigmatic mixing legitimation* – combining and blending the traditions, standards, and belief systems that underlie qualitative and quantitative paradigms.

7. *Commensurability legitimation* – maximizing the benefits that accrue from switching and integrating different worldviews.

8. *Multiple validities legitimation* – maximizing the benefits that arise from legitimation of the separate qualitative and quantitative methods based on the use of quantitative, qualitative, and mixed validity types.

9. *Political legitimation* – maximizing the degree to which the consumers of the MMR value the inferences from both qualitative and quantitative methods.

Thus legitimation can be enhanced or defended in an MMR study by systematically combining samples, inside-outside perspectives, and paradigms, as well as by minimizing the effects of the weaknesses in and sequencing of different research methods, and maximizing the degree to which consumers value both qualitative and quantitative inferences, the effects of using both qualitative and quantitative data, integrating different worldviews, using separate qualitative and quantitative methods, and mixing validity types. Using some or all of these strategies to strengthen the legitimation of any particular MMR study will increase the soundness of the meta-inferences that result.

If these nine concepts seem a bit overwhelming, it may help to know that Brown (2015c, pp. 133-135) discusses six key practical techniques that mixed methods researchers can apply when trying to enhance the legitimation of their studies.

1. *Convergence* techniques examine the qualitative and quantitative data for evidence of similar conclusions.

2. *Divergence* techniques look at the data for contradictions, surprises, or anomalies that could lead to new conclusions or to additional new research avenues.

3. *Elaboration* techniques examine the various data sources to see if some of them might amplify or expand on interpretations from other data sources.

4. *Clarification* techniques investigate various data sources to see if they might help understand, explain, or illuminate interpretations from other data sources.

5. *Exemplification* techniques look at various data sources for examples of inferences drawn from other data.

6. *Interaction* techniques move from qualitative to quantitative to qualitative and back to build cyclically on all five of the previous techniques.

Again, using these techniques in an MMR study can enhance its soundness, and as such, readers should look for evidence of these techniques in judging the quality of MMR studies.

Conclusion

In direct answer to your original question, the characteristics that researchers should employ to strengthen the quality of an MMR study and readers should look for in judging the quality of an MMR study are the following *forms of legitimation*: sample, inside-outside, weakness minimization, sequential, conversion, paradigmatic mixing, commensurability, multiple validities, and political forms of legitimation. To accomplish some or all of that, several *techniques* can be applied by the MMR investigator: convergence, divergence, elaboration, clarification, exemplification, and interaction techniques.

However, neither the MMR investigator nor the reader should expect all nine forms of legitimation and all six techniques to be appropriate for a particular study. Instead, any decisions about the quality of MMR should be a matter of degree. More specifically, it would help to ask how many of the forms of legitimation and techniques were applied? To what degree were they used? And, how effectively did they work together?

If you find MMR intriguing, you can explore further in Brown, 2014b and 2015c, or if you are hopelessly fascinated by MMR, some or all of the following general MMR books may prove useful: Bergman (2008); Cresswell (2009); Cresswell and Plano Clark (2007); Greene (2007); Mertens (2010); Plano Clark and Creswell (2008); Tashakkori and Teddlie (1998, 2010); and Teddlie and Tashakkori (2009).

(updated and reprinted from Brown, 2016)

PART II: SECOND LANGUAGE RESEARCH

SECTION E: INTERPRETING RESEARCH

CHAPTER 27

WHAT DO DISTRIBUTIONS, ASSUMPTIONS, SIGNIFICANCE VS. MEANINGFULNESS, MULTIPLE STATISTICAL TESTS, CAUSALITY, AND NULL RESULTS HAVE IN COMMON?

QUESTION: The field of statistics and research design seems so complicated with different assumptions, and problems associated with each form of analysis. Is there anything simple? I mean are there any principles that are worth knowing that apply across the board to many types of statistical analyses?

ANSWER: Fortunately, a number of issues are common to the most frequently reported forms of statistical analysis. In this chapter, I will discuss a number of those issues in the following six categories: distributions underlie everything else, assumptions must be examined, statistical significance does not assure meaningfulness, multiple statistical tests cloud interpretations, causal interpretations are risky, and null results do not mean sameness.

Distributions underlie everything else

Statistical studies investigate variables, and those variables are operationalized (i.e., observed and quantified) into scales that are nominal, ordinal, interval, or ratio (for definitions and examples of these different types of scales, see Brown, 2011a [Chapter 16]). The variables of focus in the majority of language studies are observed or measured as interval or ratio scales (known collectively as continuous scales). For many statistical analyses, such continuous scales need to be normally distributed, or if they are not, the researcher needs to consider what the effect might be of that lack of normality.

As I will explain in the next section, most statistical analyses make certain assumptions, the first of which in many cases is the assumption of normality (i.e., for the statistics to work well, the distributions in the continuous scales must be normal, or approximately normal). This is particularly important for correlational statistics, or statistics that involve correlation (e.g., reliability estimates, regression analysis, factor analysis, structural equation modeling, analysis of covariance, etc.). To ensure that their statistics can function appropriately, researchers always need to check the assumptions that underlie those statistics. Sadly, that is not often the case in second language research. At the very least, researchers should present their descriptive statistics (including means, standard deviations, minimum and maximum values, numbers of people and items, reliability estimates, etc.) so that readers can examine for themselves the degree to which important assumptions like normality, equality of variances, reliability, and so forth have been met. That is why I report descriptive statistics and reliability estimates in my own studies before I do anything else. If all quantitative researchers would do the same, that habit would go a long way toward increasing the quality and interpretability of the quantitative research in our field because the distributions of data (normal or otherwise) underlie everything else in statistical analyses.

Assumptions must be examined

Why do statistical tests have assumptions? The various statistical tests that researchers use were all created and tested for application under certain conditions, and they were found to work under those conditions. If those conditions do not obtain, that is, if the assumptions are not met, researchers cannot be sure if their statistics are being properly applied and accurately doing what they were designed to do. For example, the common Pearson product-moment correlation coefficient assumes that (a) the data for both variables are on a continuous scale, (b) the observations within those scales are independent of each other, (c) the distributions for the scales are normal, and (d) the relationship between the two scales is linear (for explanations of how these assumptions are defined, how they can be checked, and how the results should be interpreted when violations of the assumptions occur, see Brown, 2001e, pp. 140-143). If the assumptions are met, all is well, and the researcher can interpret the results within the limits of probability that the statistics indicate. However, if the assumptions are not met, the researcher cannot be sure of the interpretations. For example, in the case of the correlation coefficient, if the distribution for one of the scales (or both) is skewed (i.e., non-normal with values *scrunched up*[1] at one or the other end of the scale), it may not be appropriate to use a correlation coefficient at all, or it may be wise to adjust for the violation of the assumption by normalizing the variables. Alternatively, it may be necessary to interpret the resulting correlation coefficient very cautiously, while recognizing the likely effects of the skewing. In my experience, the likely effect when one (or both) variables is skewed is that the magnitude of any resulting correlation coefficient will tend to be depressed (i.e., will tend to provide an underestimate of the actual state of affairs). In any case, ignoring the assumptions of the seemingly simple correlation coefficient is ill-advised.

I don't want to get down in the weeds here by discussing the assumptions of every statistical procedure. The point is that for virtually every form of statistical analysis, two things are true: there is a standard error for that statistic (see Brown, 2011b [Chapter 33]), and there are assumptions that should be considered in setting up, conducting, and interpreting the analysis of that statistic (for an overview of the assumptions underlying a wide variety of statistical analyses, see Brown, 1992b).

Statistical significance does not assure meaningfulness

One of the biggest problems in second language quantitative research occurs when researchers treat statistical significance as though it indicates meaningfulness. I have spent 35 years chanting that statistical significance and meaningfulness are different things, yet nothing seems to change. It is a fact that a study with a sufficiently large sample size can produce statistics (e.g., correlation coefficients, t-tests, etc.) that are statistically significant for even small degrees of relationship or small mean differences. Those p-values that lead to interpretations of statistical significance (e.g., $p < .05$ for a particular correlation coefficient) only reveal the probability that the statistic occurred by chance alone (e.g., $p < .05$ for a correlation coefficient means that there is only a 5% chance that correlation coefficient of this magnitude would occur by chance alone).

---

[1] Yes, *scrunched up* is far from the technical terminology for this phenomenon, but this phrase really captures the spirit of skewing, so please bear with me.

That *p*-value does not mean that the correlation or mean difference or whatever is being tested is large, interesting, noteworthy, or meaningful. These characteristics can only be determined by looking at things like the magnitude of the correlation within the particular research context or the size of the mean difference in the context. For instance, it is perfectly valid to ask if a significant (with $p < .01$) correlation of .40 found in a particular study is also meaningful and interesting. But, the researcher cannot answer that question without considering the magnitude of the statistical results within the context of the specific research situation. Sometimes, a small correlation is very interesting because the researcher is looking for any sign of relationship. In such a situation, .40 would be meaningful. Other times (e.g., when costs or other stakes are very high), only a strong correlation of say .90 or higher will be meaningful. Similarly, a mean difference of 10 points on a 20 point scale might seem very interesting, but on a 1000 point scale 10 points might be far from interesting, especially if it took 300 hours of instruction to produce that one percent difference. So clearly, interpreting the meaningfulness of any statistic is different from, and additional to, first deciding whether that result has a high probability of being a non-chance statistical finding. In other words, while significance is a precondition for interpreting a statistic result at all (after all nobody wants to interpret a result that is due to chance alone), the degree to which the same statistic is interesting or meaningful will depend on the magnitude of the results and the context in which they were found. That is why statistical significance, though a precondition for meaningfulness, does not assure meaningfulness.

Multiple statistical tests cloud interpretations

Multiple statistical tests are another big problem in our research that my chanting does not seem to have affected. This phenomenon occurs when researchers perform multiple statistical tests without adjusting their *p*-values for that fact. During the last 35 years, I have observed multiple statistical tests in so many second language research studies that I can't even guess how many there are out there. Yet, I continue to staunchly believe (because of my training and experience with statistics) that multiple statistical tests create important problems in interpreting statistical results. I have explained this issue elsewhere in more detail (e.g., Brown, 1990c, 2001e, pp. 169-171, 2008a [Chapter 34], and I am not alone in holding this view (e.g., Dayton, 1970, pp. 37-49; Kirk, 1968, pp. 69-98; Shavelson, 1981, pp. 447-448; and so forth).

In brief, the problem is that conducting multiple statistical tests seriously clouds the interpretation of resulting statistical tests, usually by increasing the probability of finding spuriously significant results (i.e., results that are not really significant, popularly known as "false positives"). This problem is amplified by the fact that researchers who produce spuriously significant results do not know which of their results are spuriously significant, so even results that might actually be significant cannot be trusted. The kindest way to put this problem is that multiple statistical tests cloud interpretations. Fortunately, with proper use of the analysis of variance (ANOVA) family of statistics, the effects of such multiple comparisons can be controlled (by including all of the comparisons in one omnibus ANOVA design) or minimized (by using the Bonferroni adjustments when multiple comparisons cannot be avoided). (For more on the latter topic, see Brown, 2001e, pp. 169-171, 2008a [Chapter 34].)

Causal interpretations are risky

Another axiom that I live by is that it is irresponsible to interpret significant statistics, even ones that appear to be meaningful, especially correlation coefficients, as indicating causality. Just because two sets of numbers seem to be related does not mean that either variable is causing the other. There are many reasons for two sets of numbers to be correlated without either causing the other. Most notably a third factor may be causing both of the variables of interest to be related. For example, when I was young and stupid, I smoked and drank coffee like my life depended on it. In fact, the numbers of cigarettes per hour and the number of cups of coffee per hour were probably significantly correlated (at say $p < .01$). Does that mean that the coffee was causing the cigarettes or vice versa? No, of course not. There was simply a relationship. A third variable was probably causing both (e.g., fatigue, or need for stimulation, or social pressures, or advertising, or some combination of these factors). The message should be clear: be very careful if you are tempted to interpret causation based on any statistic. There may always be an alternative explanation that you overlooked for your result. That is why causal interpretations are so risky.

Null results do not mean sameness

Researchers are often tempted to interpret a lack of statistical significance (e.g., the probability is greater than 5%, or $p > .05$) as showing statistical sameness. For example, a researcher may use two ESL classes as experimental groups with one group getting some specific instructional treatment and the other group serving as a control group that gets some unrelated *placebo* treatment. Since the two groups were *samples of convenience* (i.e., not randomly assigned), the teacher/researcher will be tempted to compare the two groups on some form of pretest to see if they are the same at the beginning of the experiment. Naturally, they are never exactly the same, so the researcher performs a *t*-test to see if the difference is significant and infers (or counts on the reader to infer) from a non-significant result (i.e., $p > .05$) that the two groups were therefore statistically the same at the beginning of the study. This is not a correct inference. That is, the $p > .05$ *does not indicate* the probability that the two groups were the same on average. It *does indicate* that the researcher was unable to establish that the mean difference was statistically significant. Such a result can easily occur simply because the research design lacked sufficient power to detect a statistically significant result. Many factors can contribute to a lack of power: a sample size that is too small, measurement that lacks reliability, limited variation in ability levels for the construct being measured, and so forth. To determine if this is the case, procedures known as power analysis need to be included to defend any conclusion about the probability of sameness for the means of two groups. The bottom line is that a finding of no statistically significant mean difference indicates that the study was unable to establish significance, not that the two means are the same. (For further explanation of this issue, see Brown, 2007a [Chapter 29], 2007b [Chapter 30].)

Conclusion

In the title of this chapter, I asked the following question: What do distributions, assumptions, significance vs. meaningfulness, multiple statistical tests, causality, and null results have in common? The simple answer is that these are six of my pet statistical peeves. To recap briefly, my pet statistical peeves are that researchers in our field often:

1. Forget to consider the potential effects of their data distributions on their statistical results (and foolishly forget to report descriptive statistics)

2. Fail to check the assumptions for the statistics they use, much less consider what violations of those assumptions mean for the interpretation of their results

3. Act as if statistical significance means that the results of their study are interesting and meaningful, which is flat out not true

4. Let multiple statistical tests cloud their interpretations

5. Make unjustified causal interpretations of their results
6. And, treat non-significant results as though they indicate the sameness of two groups

Why should anyone care about my pet statistical peeves? These peeves have developed over 35 years of experience in the ESL/EFL/Applied Linguistics field, and they are based on reading thousands of statistical studies in which I have witnessed researchers overinterpreting, underinterpreting, and/or misinterpreting their statistical results because they were either ignorant of these six sets of issues or willfully ignored them. Such overinterpretation, underinterpretation, and/or misinterpretation of statistical results means that the interpretations were wrong in important ways. And yet, they serve as the knowledge base of our field.

In direct answer to your question, the six sets of issues covered in this chapter serve as principles that are worth knowing because they are important to the quality of the statistical research in our field and because they "apply across the board to many types of statistical analyses," as you put it. As a consumer of statistical studies, you can help improve the quality of the research in our field by paying attention to these issues whenever you pick up a professional journal and read quantitative research studies. My guess is that you already read such studies critically in terms of their content, but you might now want to also read them critically in terms of their statistical research methods. You can help increase the quality of the quantitative research in our field by being a critical reader, by spreading the word about these problems to your colleagues, and by complaining in letters to the editors of professional journals where you see researchers ignore these six sets of issues. Together we can help improve the statistical research methods used in the research of our field by refusing to tolerate shoddy work. How can that help but be good for the field, and good for our knowledge about second language learning and teaching?

(updated and reprinted from Brown, 2012a)

CHAPTER 28

GENERALIZABILITY FROM SECOND LANGUAGE RESEARCH SAMPLES

QUESTION: It seems one of the most common mistakes by novice researchers is making statements about a large population on the basis of a small sample. Is there any rigorous way to compute how a classroom research sample of 40 might actually be able to generalize to a Japanese undergraduate university population of 2,809,000? What precautions should novice researchers take when attempting to generalize their studies to larger populations?

ANSWER: You seem to be asking several different questions simultaneously: one about sampling and generalizability, and the others about sample size and statistical precision and power. I will deal with the first (generalizability) question in this chapter and the others (precision & power) in Chapters 29 and 30.

Generalizability is usually defined as the degree to which the results of a study based on a sample can be said to represent the results that would be obtained from the entire population from which the sample was drawn. In other words, generalizability depends on the degree to which the particular sample in question can be said to be representative of the population. To explain that, I will first have to define and discuss (a) samples and populations, (b) random samples, (c) stratified samples, and then come back to the issue of (d) what constitutes adequate generalizability to a population.

Samples and populations

A *population* is the entire group of people that a particular study is interested in. For example, political polls in the US are often focused on the entire voting population of the country. Such polls are typically based on samples taken from that population, but the polls would not be very useful if inferences about the entire voting population were not possible. In second language studies, we are often interested in the population of all ESL students in the US, or all university-level EFL students in Japan, or some such population. However, few language researchers have the resources to study these entire populations. So researchers use *samples*, that is, subgroups of the students are drawn from the population to represent the whole population. Researchers use samples for a variety of reasons: usually some combination of making the data collection and analysis cheaper, more practical, efficient, and/or effective. Properly sampled data should represent what would result if data for the entire population were used. In other words, the results of the study should be representative of results that would occur if the researcher were able to investigate the entire population. A number of strategies are used to accomplish this *representativeness*, but the two most common are called random samples and stratified random samples.

Random samples

Random samples are created by making sure that each person in the population has an equal chance of being selected into the sample. This can be achieved by clearly defining the population that is the focus of the study, listing all the members of that population, assigning a separate ID number for each member of the population, and randomly selecting the members of the sample on the basis of random numbers generated in a spreadsheet or taken from random numbers tables (which are found in the back of many statistics books). By using random numbers to decide who should be in the sample, the selection is made dispassionately, thereby minimizing any conscious or unconscious biases in the results of the study. It is assumed that a sample made up of a large number of randomly selected people drawn from the population (i.e., a *random sample*) will probably represent the population from which it was drawn. Researchers widely accept this assumption that random samples are representative (for more information on random sampling, see Brown, 1988, pp. 111-113; Brown, 2001e, pp. 72-74, Thompson, 2006, pp. 12-13).

Stratified samples

Stratified samples are created in a slightly different way: by clearly defining the population that is the focus of the study, identifying *strata* (i.e., salient characteristics of the population and/or particular characteristics of interest to the researcher), selecting members from each of the strata in the population (perhaps using random numbers as described above) so that the resulting sample has about the same proportions of each characteristic as the whole population. For instance, in the population of students studying English at Tokyo University, a researcher might choose to use strata within the population for: gender (male, or female), home prefecture, academic status (graduate or undergraduate), and type of major (e.g., science and humanities). With correct information about how many students fall into each of these categories, the stratified sample would be created by selecting students from each of the strata in proportion to those same strata in the total population.

As I point out in Brown (2001e, p. 73), three factors influence whether random or stratified sampling procedure is more appropriate.

1. If the population is comparatively heterogeneous, a stratified sampling strategy may be more appropriate, since a random sample might not supply an adequate variety of people from each stratum.

2. If the sample will be small or the groups formed within the study will have unequal sizes, a stratified sampling may be more appropriate.

3. If the researcher wants to use the strata as variables in the study, stratified random sampling may be more appropriate.

However, if the opposite is true, that is, the sample is relatively homogeneous and large with equal sized groups, and the strata are not important to the analysis, a random sample may prove better because it removes the need to define the strata in the population and sample proportionately from each stratum.

What constitutes adequate generalizability?

In most of the second language studies I have read, the sampling has been neither random nor stratified. The samples have instead typically been *samples of convenience* (i.e., made up of *the students at our university who took the placement examination* or students in *my class and my friend's class*. This can be problematic when language professionals think of such *samples of convenience* as representing a larger population.

There are two problems with this way of thinking. The first problem is that the "some larger population" cannot be defined. What is the population of ESL students in the US or university EFL students in Japan? In the first case, there are literally hundreds of nationalities and language background students studying ESL in the US. At each language center in the US, I'm willing to bet that there is a different balance of language backgrounds (not to mention differences in the balance for genders, educational backgrounds, IQs, socio-economic status, etc.). In order to sample from such a population we would need to define it. We could do so by tracking down and listing every ESL student in the US. Unfortunately, even if we could find them all, by the time we had our list, the population would have changed. Thus defining such a population is nearly impossible. Similar problems would arise in trying to define the population of all EFL students in Japanese universities (even if we could get permission to do such a study).

The second problem with samples of convenience is that often they should not be thought of as samples at all, but rather should be viewed as intact populations, perhaps as *populations of convenience*. That is, since these groups of students are so poorly selected that they cannot be said to represent anything larger than themselves, they should be considered populations of convenience that represent themselves.

The mistake that researchers make is in generalizing from such populations of convenience to larger populations. For instance, a researcher might do a study of 40 undergraduate students at Tokyo University and then try to generalize the findings to "a Japanese undergraduate university population of 2,809,000" (as you put it). The problem, of course, is that students from Tokyo University (or those from any other university) can in no way be said to serve as a sample that represents the population of all Japanese university students. Another team of researchers might do a large scale study of the trends in EFL scores for high school students in Ibaraki prefecture and then make the mistake of generalizing from that population to the larger population of all high school students in Japan. The problem of course is that even using the population of all the high school students in Ibaraki prefecture does not justify saying that they constitute a random, stratified, or any other sort of representative sample of all the high school students in Japan. It would be much better to simply discuss such a study in terms of it representing the population of all high school students in Ibaraki prefecture (during such-and-such a period of time).

Given the fact that many of the sets of students used in second language studies are samples of convenience and the fact that samples of convenience themselves are typically the populations beyond which it is irresponsible to generalize, perhaps we should be less concerned with generalizability and more concerned with the transferability of the results of a study (as suggested by the discussion in Lazaraton, 1995, p. 465). *Transferability* is the demonstration of the "applicability of the results of a study in one setting to another context, or other contexts" (Brown, 2001e, p. 226). In other words, given that we very often cannot generalize our results beyond the population of convenience, perhaps we should abandon the notion of generalizability and, instead, describe the groups of students in these populations of convenience *thickly* (i.e., in considerable detail) so other researchers and the readers of our studies can decide for themselves if the results are *transferable* to the settings that they are dealing with.

(updated and reprinted from Brown, 2006b)

CHAPTER 29

SAMPLE SIZE AND POWER

QUESTION: One topic I think many people would be interested in is something about sampling sizes and calculating sampling errors. It seems many teachers just randomly select a number between 20-50 when determining the size of their samples without knowing *why* (or how) a sample size for a survey should be estimated—or how to calculate the error of measurement that is probably due to sampling error. Since most of the research studies language teachers in Japan conduct involve small samples, some information about calculating sampling errors is probably needed.

ANSWER: As I pointed out in Brown (2006b [Chapter 28]), you seem to be asking several questions simultaneously: one about sampling and generalizability, and at least two others about sample size and statistical precision and power. I addressed the first question (sampling and generalizability) in Brown (2006b [Chapter 28]). In this one, I will discuss sample size as it relates to power. However, I will kick the can of precision a bit further down the road, by discussing it in Brown (2007b [Chapter 30]).

Null hypotheses

To lay some groundwork, I must first define the notion of the null hypothesis (H_0), which is "the hypothesis that the phenomenon to be demonstrated is in fact absent" (Fisher, 1971, p. 13). For example, it is the hypothesis that there is no correlation ($r = 0$), or that there is no difference between the means ($M_1 = i$) in a t-test, or that there is no difference between the observed and expected frequencies ($f_o = f_e$) in a X^2 test. The null hypothesis is important because it is what L2 researchers are most often testing in their studies. If they can reject the null hypothesis at a certain alpha level (e.g., $p < .05$), then they can accept as probable whatever alternative hypothesis makes sense, for example, that the correlation is a non-chance occurrence (e.g., $r < 0$ at $p < .05$), or that the first mean is greater than the second mean for reasons other than chance (e.g., $M_1 < M_2$ at $p < .05$) in a t-test, or that the observed frequency is greater than the expected frequency due to factors other than chance (e.g., $f_o < f_e$ at $p < .05$). Once again, focusing on rejecting the null hypothesis and declaring a significant (at $p < .05$)

correlation, mean difference, or difference between observed and expected frequencies is how L2 researchers typically proceed.

Type I vs. Type II errors

Most often, the probability statements in the above examples are taken to indicate the probability that the researcher will accept the alternative hypothesis when in reality the null hypothesis is true (see α in lower-left corner of Figure 29.1). That seems to be the primary concern of most researchers in L2 studies. However, there is another way to look at these issues that involves what are called Type I and Type II errors. From this perspective, α is the probability of making a Type I error (accepting the alternative hypothesis when in reality the null hypothesis is true), and β is the probability of making a Type II error (accepting the null hypothesis when in reality the alternative hypothesis is true). By extension, $1 - \alpha$ is the probability of not making a Type I error, and $1 - \beta$ is the probability of not making a Type II error.

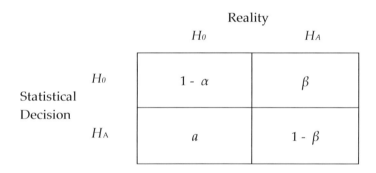

Figure 29.1. Four Ways of Looking at the Probabilities in Statistical Tests

As I mentioned above, the primary concern of most researchers in L2 studies (indeed in most social sciences) is to guard against Type I errors, errors that would lead to interpreting observed correlations, mean differences, frequency differences, etc. as non-chance (or probably real) when they are in reality due to chance fluctuations. However, researchers in our field seldom think about Type II errors and their importance. Recall that Type II errors are those that might lead us to accept that a set of results is null (i.e., there is nothing in the data but chance fluctuations) when in reality the alternative hypothesis is true. L2 researchers may be making Type II errors every time they accept the null hypothesis because they are so tenaciously focused on Type I errors (α) while completely ignoring Type II errors (β). What is the solution to this problem? We should calculate β every time we do an analysis. But this is difficult, right? No, with programs like SPSS, we can easily calculate power (1 - β) for many analyses (see explanation below). Then, once we know 1 - β, we can also calculate β by subtracting the power statistic from 1. Thus results like those shown in Figure 29.2 can easily be obtained for many analyses.

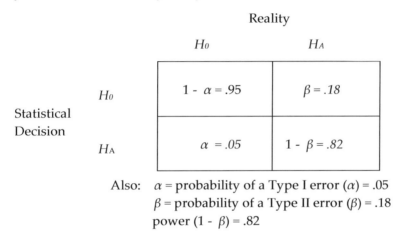

Figure 29.2. Four Probabilities Worth Thinking About in a Hypothetical Study

What is power?

In the simplest terms, the power of a statistical test is "the probability that it [i.e., the statistical test] will lead to the rejection of the null hypothesis, i.e., the probability that it will result in the conclusion that the phenomenon exists" (Cohen, 1988, p. 4). Thus power is the $1 - \beta$ in Figures 1 and 2, which turned out to be .82. But is that high enough? How much power is enough? Cohen (1988, p. 56, and elsewhere) discussed this issue and proposed that, "…when the investigator has no other basis for setting the desired power value, the value .80 [should] be used. This means that β is set at .20." Thus in the same sense that researchers conventionally set the cut-point for α at .05 or .01, the cut-point for β can reasonably be set at less than .20 (or greater than .80 for power). As a result, we can say that the power of .82 shown in Figure 29.2 indicates that the study had sufficient statistical power for the researcher to accept the alternative hypothesis with a fair amount of confidence. By extension, we can say that power of .82

indicates that β = .18 (1.00 - β = 1.00 - .82 = .18) and that the probability of accepting the null hypothesis when in reality the alternative hypothesis is true is only .18.

What sorts of errors do L2 researchers make by ignoring power?

The two most common Type II errors that L2 researchers make are those that have to do with (a) establishing the equivalence of groups at the beginning of a study and (b) not knowing what to do with null results when they arise in the main analyses of a study. I will use examples from papers published by Mason (2004) and Kondo-Brown (2001) because they illustrate the issues involved and because they are both Japan-related studies.

Errors related to the equivalence of groups at the beginning of a study. Mason (2004, p. 8) implies that the groups in her study were the same at the beginning of her study when she writes, "A one-way ANOVA showed that there was no significant difference among the groups on the pretest $F(2, 93)$ = 1.514, p = .225." The problem of course is that a non-significant difference like this one indicates that α (or the probability of accepting the alterative hypothesis when in reality the null hypothesis is true) is .225. It does not indicate β (the probability of accepting the null hypothesis when in reality the alternative hypothesis is true). The alternative hypothesis that the means are different could still be true in Mason's study, but remain undetected because of weak research design (too small a sample size, low reliability in the measurements, etc.). This is a common Type II error made in L2 research. She is accepting the null hypothesis when in reality the alternative hypothesis could be true. If she had calculated 1 - β (power) and it had turned out to be .80 or higher (with a corresponding β of .20 or lower), she would then have been in a position to make the interpretation that she did. But she didn't do that and so she will never know what the most probable cause is of the null result. Many L2 researchers have made this mistake. That needs to change.

Errors resulting from not knowing what to do with null results. As good researchers often do in our field nowadays, Mason (2004, p. 8) set her alpha level low at .01 in her main analysis because she recognized a potential for Type I errors: "The alpha level was set at .01, as multiple ANOVAs were used for the analyses." However, she did not recognize the potential threat from Type II errors in the same analysis, when she wrote: "All three groups in this study improved significantly, but there were no significant differences among the groups in gains. The group that wrote summaries in Japanese, their first language, was the most efficient, making the greatest gains in terms of points gained for the time devoted to English" (Mason, 2003, p. 15). Mason seems to be having trouble with the fact that she did not find statistically significant differences in her study between the groups. In effect, she chooses to accept the null between-groups results without justification. She then ignores the null results and proceeds to interpret the analysis in terms of efficiency.

If, instead, she had calculated power (1 - β), and it had turned out to be .80 or higher (with a corresponding β of .20 or lower), she would have had to acknowledge that her study had sufficient power to reject the null hypothesis, but had not done so, and that her observed differences could only be interpreted as chance fluctuations. If, on the other hand, the power had turned out to be .79 or lower, she could have discussed the design issues that might have caused the lack of power to detect significant differences. Either way her interpretation would have been clearer and more accurate than falling back on interpreting the lack of a statistically significant difference in terms of efficiency (after discovering that those null differences may have simply resulted from chance fluctuations).

Another example from Japan shows how knowing what to do with null results (i.e., knowing how power statistics can be effectively used to understand null results) can help a researcher grasp the meaning of the results of her statistical tests. Kondo-Brown (2001, p. 101) clearly did use power statistics and did so successfully in my view[1] when she wrote the following:

> In fact, in a follow-up power analysis on the production tests, the observed power (1 - β), which is the probability of correctly rejecting the null hypothesis (Tabachnick & Fidell, 1996: 36-37), was 0.50 for the immediate posttest and 0.11 for the delayed posttest, both of which were fairly low (for more information about power analysis, see Cohen, 1988; Lipsey, 1990). This suggests that the design (i.e., *n*-size, distributions, and treatment magnitude) may not have been strong enough to detect significant differences.

---

[1] In the interest of full disclosure, I must confess that this top-notch researcher is in fact my wife, so I may be a bit biased in my assessment of her phenomenal abilities. That does not change the value of this example.

The bottom line with regard to power analysis is that there is much to be gained in our understanding of the statistical results of our studies if only we will ask our statistical programs to calculate power.

How can we calculate power?

In many SPSS analyses, we can calculate power by asking for it as an option. For example, Figure 29.3 shows the Options window available in the GLM analyses for univariate ANOVA (in this case a 2 x 2 two-way ANOVA with anxiety and tension as the independent variables and trial 3 as the dependent variable using the Anxiety 2.sav example file that comes with SPSS v. 14). Notice that getting the power statistics was no more difficult than checking a box (see the results in Table 29.1 below).

Figure 29.3. Example of Asking for Power Analysis in the Options Window in SPSS

Notice in Table 29.1 that the *p* values (0.90, 0.55, & 0.10) indicate that there were no significant differences (i.e., no *p* values below .05) for Anxiety, Tension, or their interaction, but also that there was not sufficient power to detect such effects (i.e., the power statistics of 0.05, 0.09, & 0.37 were not above .80 in any case). All of this leads to the quite reasonable conclusion that the study lacked sufficient power to detect any significant effects even if they exist in reality, in this case, it is probably because the sample size was very small (*n* = 12) in a relatively complex 2 x 2 two-way ANOVA design.

Table 29.1. *Results of the Analysis Shown in Figure 29.3*

Source	SS	df	MS	F	p	Power
Anxiety	0.08	1	0.08	0.02	0.90	0.05
Tension	2.08	1	2.08	0.38	0.55	0.09
Anxiety x Tension	18.75	1	18.75	3.46	0.10	0.37
Error	43.33	8	5.42			
Total	785.00	12				

Conclusion

Clearly, L2 researchers would benefit from considering both Type I and Type II errors. Naturally, this will necessitate discussing not only α but also β and 1-β (power) in our studies so we can correctly accept the null hypotheses or alternative hypothesis in our various statistical tests. Equally important, power statistics can help us to better understand Type II threats in our studies, in particular, the degree to which the sample size, reliability of measurement, strength of treatment, etc. provide adequate power for finding a statistically significant result if in fact it exists. When you are doing your statistics, why not click on that observed power box while you are at it?

In a more direct answer to the original question, if the power of a statistical test is sufficient (i.e., is .80 or higher), the sample size is probably sufficient for the common research purposes discussed here. If the power statistic is not large enough (i.e., .79 or lower), the researcher might want to consider increasing the sample size and thereby just possibly raise the power of the study. Indeed, it is even possible to use the power statistic to estimate how much larger the sample should be. For an example of this use of power, see Gorsuch (1999, pp. 189-196). [For more on this and related topics, see Cohen, 1988; Kline, 2005; Kraemer & Thiemann, 1987; Lipsey, 1990; Murphy & Myors, 2004; Rosenthal, Rosnow, & Rubin, 2000; and Thompson, 2006.]

(updated and reprinted from Brown, 2007a)

CHAPTER 30

SAMPLE SIZE AND STATISTICAL PRECISION

QUESTION: One topic I think many people would be interested in is something about sampling sizes and calculating sampling errors. It seems many teachers just randomly select a number between 20-50 when determining the size of their samples without knowing *why* (or how) a sample size for a survey should be estimated—or how to calculate the error of measurement that is probably due to sampling error. Since most of the research studies language teachers conduct involve small samples, some information about calculating sampling errors is probably needed.

ANSWER: As I pointed out in the previous two chapters, you seem to be asking several questions simultaneously: one about *sampling* and *generalizability*, a second about sample *size* and *power*, and a third about *sample size* and *statistical precision*. I addressed sample size and generalizability in Brown (2006b [Chapter 28]), and I addressed sample size and power in Brown (2007a [Chapter 29]). I will attempt to address the issues involved in sample size and statistical precision in the present chapter.

What are samples and populations, statistics and parameters?

As I pointed out in Brown, (2006b, p. 24 [Chapter 28]), a *population* is "the entire group of people that a particular study is interested in." For instance, we might be interested in the population of all university EFL students in Japan. Given that few language researchers have the resources to study such a large population in its entirety, they typically use samples (i.e., subgroups drawn from the population to represent the population). In samples, we calculate *statistics* like the sample mean and standard deviation, commonly symbolized as M and SD (or S). But these sample statistics represent the population *parameters* for the population mean and standard deviation (commonly symbolized by the Greek letters μ and σ). One way of thinking about the relationship between such statistics and the parameters they represent is *statistical precision*, that is, how precisely the statistics from a sample represent the parameters in a population.

What is statistical precision?

Cohen (1988, p. 6) defines the *statistical precision* of a sample statistic as "the closeness with which it can be expected to approximate the relevant population value. It is necessarily an estimated value in practice, since the population value is generally unknown" (Cohen, 1988, p. 6). This precision is usually estimated using a standard error, that is, the amount of chance fluctuation (or lack of precision) we can expect in sample estimates. We can use the *standard error* as an estimate of the precision of a statistic in two ways: descriptively or inferentially (for more on these two ways of looking at the standard error, see Thompson, 2006, pp. 154-155).

How is precision used descriptively?

Descriptively, when precision is estimated using a *standard error*, it is thought of as the amount of fluctuation from the population parameter that we can expect by chance alone in sample estimates. For example, for a sample mean (M), we can calculate the standard error of the mean (SE_M), which provides an estimate of how much fluctuation from the population parameter we can expect in sample estimates of M. Since standard errors are distributed normally, we can expect sample means to vary by chance ±1 SE_M 68% of the time, ±2 SE_M 95% of the time, and ±3 SE_M 98% of the time (for a review of how these percentages work, see Brown, 1988, pp. 80-85; or 2005c, pp. 116-123). For example, if the mean for a sample turned out to be 78 with a conveniently round SE_M of 2, we would expect such sample means to vary by chance between 76 and 80 (68% of the time), between 74 and 82 (95% of the time), and between 72 and 84 (98% of the time). The following equation can be used to calculate the standard error of the mean (SE_M):

$$SE_M = \sqrt{\frac{S^2}{n}}$$

Where:

SE_M = standard error of the mean; S = standard deviation; n = group size

So, the SE_M for a group of 30 students with a mean of 50 and a standard deviation of 10 would be 1.83, as follows:

$$SE_M = \sqrt{\frac{S^2}{n}} = \sqrt{\frac{10^2}{30}} = \sqrt{\frac{100}{30}} = \sqrt{3.3333} = 1.8257418 \approx 1.83$$

The standard error for a Pearson product-moment correlation coefficient (*r*), or the *SEr*, is calculated as follows:

$$SE_r = \frac{1-r^2}{\sqrt{n-1}}$$

So, the *SEr* for a group of 30 students whose scores on two different tests correlate at .80 would be .067, as follows:

$$SE_r = \frac{1-r^2}{\sqrt{n-1}} = \frac{1-.80^2}{\sqrt{30-1}} = \frac{1-.64}{\sqrt{29}} = \frac{.36}{5.3851648} = .0668503 \approx .067$$

Such standard errors can be calculated for all statistical estimates of parameters and can all be interpreted the same way: as the degree to which the statistical estimates are likely to fluctuate, or put another way, as the degree to which the statistical estimates are precise.

How is precision used inferentially?

Inferentially, the standard error is also commonly used in estimating the statistical significance of differences between or among parameter estimates. For example, a *t*-test can be used to estimate the probability that an observed difference between two means, say between treatment-group and control-group means, is statistically significant (i.e., that the difference is due to other than chance factors). One formula for the *t*-test where the two samples are independent and are the same size, is as follows:

$$t = \frac{M_t - M_c}{\sqrt{\frac{S_t^2}{n_t} + \frac{S_c^2}{n_c}}}$$

Notice that the numerator represents the difference between the treatment-group mean and the control-group mean ($M_t - M_c$), and that the denominator contains the two standard errors for the treatment and control groups. Thus the *t*-test is simply a ratio of the mean difference to the square root of the sum of their standard errors, or put another way, the *t*-test is the mean difference in relation to the precision with which the two means were estimated.

What is the relationship between sample size and precision?

Though several factors *can* affect the precision of a parameter estimate, sample size is always a factor. As Cohen (1988, p. 6), put it,

> depending upon the statistics in question, and the specific statistical model on which the test is based, reliability [i.e., precision] may or may not be directly dependent upon the unit of measurement, the population value, and the shape of the population distribution. However, it is *always* dependent upon the size of the sample.

Look at any of the equations above for various permutations of standard error, and notice that all of them have the *n*-size in the denominator. Hence, with all other factors held steady, as sample size increases, the standard error decreases, or gets more precise. Put another way, as the sample size increases so does the statistical precision of the parameter estimate. This has ramifications for both the descriptive and inferential uses of the standard error. Descriptively, as sample size goes up, parameter estimates become more precise. Inferentially, as sample sizes go up, parameter estimates are more precise, so differences between or among parameter estimates can be smaller and still turn out to be statistically significant.

Conclusion

As you put it in your question, "since most of the research studies language teachers in Japan conduct involve small samples, some information about calculating sampling errors is probably needed." I would extend this notion beyond your intended meaning to suggest that studies would benefit greatly from having more precision and this can be achieved most directly by increasing sample sizes. I would also argue that, when small sample sizes are absolutely unavoidable, standard errors ought to be calculated, reported, and included in the researcher's thinking about any statistical results.

(updated and reprinted from Brown, 2007b)

CHAPTER 31

SKEWNESS AND KURTOSIS

QUESTION: My computer program has a function that provides what it calls "basic statistics." Among those are Skew and Kurtosis. Your book on testing says that abnormally skewed and peaked distributions may be signs of trouble and that problems may then arise in applying testing statistics. What are the acceptable ranges for these two statistics and how will they affect the testing statistics if they are outside those limits?

ANSWER: Probably the most commonly used *number crunching* software program on Windows and Mac computers is *Excel*® (Microsoft, 1996). In my Windows version of that program, I simply select Tools, then select Data Analysis, then select Descriptive Statistics and hit enter. Then I fill in the input range (the numbers I want to analyze), and the output range (where I want to put the resulting statistics) and check Summary Statistics. When I hit return, the *Excel* program puts a number of useful descriptive statistics into my spreadsheet, including all of the following: mean, standard error of the mean, median, mode, standard deviation variance, kurtosis, skewness, range, minimum, maximum, sum, count, largest, smallest, and confidence level. But, your question focuses in on the skew and kurtosis statistics. So I'll narrow the discussion to only those two statistics.

Skewness

Let me begin by talking about skewness. In its help screens, *Excel*® defines SKEW as a function that "returns the skewness of a distribution. Skewness characterizes the degree of asymmetry of a distribution around its mean. Positive skewness indicates a distribution with an asymmetric tail extending towards more positive values. Negative skewness indicates a distribution with an asymmetric tail extending towards more negative values" (Microsoft, 1996). While that definition is accurate, it isn't 100 percent helpful because it doesn't explain what the resulting number actually means.

The skewness statistic is sometimes also called the skewedness statistic. Normal distributions produce a skewness statistic of about zero. (I say "about" because small variations can occur by chance alone). So a skewness statistic of -0.01819 would be an acceptable skewness value for a normally distributed set of test scores because it is very close to zero and is probably just a chance fluctuation from zero. As the skewness statistic departs further from zero, a positive value indicates the possibility of a positively skewed distribution (that is, with scores bunched up on the low end of the score scale) or a negative value indicates the possibility of a negatively skewed distribution (that is, with scores bunched up on the high end of the scale). Values of 2 standard errors of skewness (*SES*) or more (regardless of sign) are probably skewed to a significant degree.

The *SES* can be estimated roughly using the following formula (after Tabachnick & Fidell, 1996):

$$SES = \sqrt{\frac{6}{N}}$$

Thus, *SES* is simply square root of 6 divided by *N*. For example, let's say you are using *Excel*® and calculate a skewness statistic of -.9814 for a particular test administered to 30 students. An approximate estimate of the *SES* for that skewness statistic for this example would be:

$$SES = \sqrt{\frac{6}{N}} = \sqrt{\frac{6}{30}} = \sqrt{.20} = .4472$$

Since two times the standard error of the skewness is .8944 and the absolute value of the skewness statistic is .9814, which is greater than .8944, you can assume that the distribution is significantly skewed. Since the sign of the skewness statistic is negative, you know that the distribution is negatively skewed. Alternatively, if the skewness statistic had been positive, you would have known that the distribution was positively skewed. Yet another alternative interpretation would be that the skew statistic fell outside the range between -.8944 and +.8944, so you can assume that the skewness was outside the expected range of chance fluctuations in that statistic, which would further indicate a distribution has a statistically significant skew.

On a norm-referenced test, the existence of positively or negatively skewed distributions as indicated by the skewness statistic is important for you to recognize as a language tester because skewing, one way or the other, will tend to reduce the reliability of the test. Perhaps more importantly, from a decision-making point of view, if the scores are scrunched up around any of your cut-points, making a decision will be difficult because many students will be near that cut-point. Skewed distributions will also create problems insofar as they indicate violations of the assumption of normality that underlies many of the other statistics like correlation coefficients, *t*-tests, etc. used to study test validity.

However, violations of that assumption of normality are only problematic if the test is norm-referenced and being used for norm-referenced purposes. As I have discussed elsewhere (see for instance, Brown, 1996a, pp. 138-142), a skewed distribution may actually be a desirable outcome on a criterion-referenced test. For example, a negatively skewed distribution with students all scoring very high on an achievement test at the end of a course may simply indicate that the teaching, materials, and student learning are all functioning very well. This would be especially true if the students had previously scored poorly in a positively skewed distribution (with students generally scoring very low) at the beginning of the course on the same or a similar test. In fact, the difference between the positively skewed distribution at the beginning of the course and the negatively skewed distribution at the end of the course would be an indication of how well the course fits the students' abilities as well as how much the students learned in the course.

You should also note that, when reporting central tendency for skewed distributions, it is a good idea to report the median in addition to the mean. A few very skewed scores (representing only a few students) can dramatically affect the mean, but will have less effect on the median. This is why we rarely read about the average family income (or mean salary) in the United States. Just a few billionaires like Bill Gates would make the average family income very high, higher than most people actually make. I guess that means that most of us, even those U.S. citizens working for good salaries in Japan, would be below average in terms of family incomes in the United States. However, in terms of median income, most of us working in Japan would be above the median income in the United States. Hence, median income is reported and makes a lot more sense to most people. The same is true in any skewed distributions of test scores as well. So reporting the median along with the mean in skewed distributions is a generally good idea.

Kurtosis

The *Excel* help screens tell us that "kurtosis characterizes the relative peakedness or flatness of a distribution compared to the normal distribution. Positive kurtosis indicates a relatively peaked distribution. Negative kurtosis indicates a relatively flat distribution" (Microsoft, 1996). And, once again, that definition doesn't really help us understand the meaning of the numbers resulting from this statistic.

Normal distributions produce a kurtosis statistic of about zero (again, I say *about* because small variations can occur by chance alone). So a kurtosis statistic of 0.09581 would be an acceptable kurtosis value for a mesokurtic (that is, normally high) distribution because it is close to zero. As the kurtosis statistic departs further from zero, a positive value indicates the possibility of a leptokurtic distribution (that is, too tall) or a negative value indicates the possibility of a platykurtic distribution (that is, too flat, or even concave if the value is large enough). Values of 2 standard errors of kurtosis (*SEK*) or more (regardless of sign) probably differ from mesokurtic to a significant degree.

The *SEK* can be estimated roughly using the following formula (again after Tabachnick & Fidell, 1996):

$$SEK = \sqrt{\frac{24}{N}}$$

For example, let's say you are using *Excel*® and calculate a kurtosis statistic of + 1.9142 for a particular test administered to 30 students. An approximate estimate of the *SEK* for this example would be:

$$SEK = \sqrt{\frac{24}{N}} = \sqrt{\frac{24}{30}} = \sqrt{.80} = .8944$$

Since two times the standard error of the kurtosis is 1.7888 and the absolute value of the kurtosis statistic was 1.9142, which is greater than 1.7888, you can assume that the distribution has statistically significant kurtosis. Since the sign of the kurtosis statistic is positive, you know that the distribution is leptokurtic (too tall). Alternatively, if the kurtosis statistic had been negative, you would have known that the distribution was platykurtic (too flat). Yet another alternative interpretation would be that the kurtosis statistic fell outside the range between - 1.7888 and + 1.7888, so you can assume that the kurtosis was outside the expected range of chance fluctuations in that statistic.

The existence of flat or peaked distributions as indicated by the kurtosis statistic is important to you as a language tester insofar as it indicates violations of the assumption of normality that underlies many of the other statistics like correlation coefficients, *t*-tests, etc. used to study the validity of a test.

Another practical implication should also be noted. If a distribution of test scores is very leptokurtic, that is, very tall, it may indicate a problem with the validity of your decision making processes. For instance, at the University of Hawai'i at Mānoa, we give a writing placement test for all incoming native-speaker freshmen (or should that be freshpersons?) that produces scores on a scale of 0-20 (each student's score is based on four raters' scores, which each range from 0-5). Yearly, we test about 3400 students. You can imagine how tall the distribution must look when it is plotted out as a histogram: 20 points wide and hundreds of students high. The decision that we are making is a four-way decision about the level of instruction that students should take: remedial writing; regular writing with an extra lab tutorial; regular writing; or honors writing. The problem that arises is that very few points separate these four classifications and that hundreds of students are on the borderlines. So a wider distribution would help us to spread the students out and make more responsible decisions, especially if the revisions resulted in a more reliable measure with fewer students near each cut point.

Conclusion

One last point I would like to make: the skewness and kurtosis statistics, like all the descriptive statistics, are designed to help us think about the distributions of scores that our tests create. Unfortunately, I can give you no hard-and-fast rules about these or any other descriptive statistics because interpreting them depends heavily on the type and purpose of the test being analyzed. Nonetheless, I have tried to provide some basic guidelines here that I hope will serve you well in interpreting the skewness and kurtosis statistics when you encounter them in analyzing your tests. But, please keep in mind that all statistics must be interpreted in terms of the types and purposes of your tests.

(updated and reprinted from Brown, 1997a)

CHAPTER 32

EFFECT SIZE AND ETA SQUARED

QUESTION: In Chapter 6 of the 2008 book on heritage language learning that you co-edited with Kimi Kondo-Brown, a study by Kondo-Brown & Fukuda (2008) comparing how three different groups of informants use intersentential referencing is outlined. On page 147 of that book, a MANOVA with a partial eta² of .29 is outlined. There are several questions about this statistic. What does a "partial eta²" measure? Are there other forms of eta that readers should know about? And how should one interpret a partial eta² value of .29?

ANSWER: I will answer your question about partial eta² in two parts. I will start by defining and explaining *eta²*. Then I will circle back and do the same for *partial eta²*.

Eta²

Eta² can be defined as the proportion of variance associated with or accounted for by each of the main effects, interactions, and error in an ANOVA study (see Tabachnick & Fidell, 2001, pp. 54-55, and Thompson, 2006, pp. 317-319). Formulaically, *eta²*, or η^2, is defined as follows:

$$\eta^2 = \frac{SS_{effect}}{SS_{total}}$$

Where:
SS_{effect} = the sums of squares for whatever effect is of interest
SS_{total} = the total sums of squares for all effects, interactions, and errors in the ANOVA

Eta² is most often reported for straightforward ANOVA designs that (a) are balanced (i.e., have equal cell sizes) and (b) have independent cells (i.e., different people appear in each cell). For example, in Chapter 29, I used an example ANOVA to demonstrate how to calculate power with SPSS. That was a 2 x 2 two-way ANOVA with *anxiety* and *tension* as the independent variables and *trial 3* as the dependent variable (using the *Anxiety 2.sav* example file that comes with recent versions of the *SPSS* software). There were three people in each cell and the cells were independent.

Notice in Table 32.1 that the *p* values (0.90, 0.55, & 0.10) indicate that there were no significant effects (i.e., no *p* values below .05) for Anxiety, Tension, or their interaction. Note also that there was not sufficient power to detect such effects (i.e., the power statistics of 0.05, 0.09, & 0.37 were not above .80 in any case). All of this led me to conclude that "the study lacked sufficient power to detect any significant effects even if they exist in reality," which is reasonable given the very small sample size of 12.

Table 32.1. *Results of the Analysis of Anxiety 2.sav example file included with SPSS*

Source	SS	df	MS	F	p	eta^2	Power
Anxiety	0.08	1	0.08	0.02	0.90	0.001	0.05
Tension	2.08	1	2.08	0.38	0.55	0.032	0.09
Anxiety x Tension	18.75	1	18.75	3.46	0.10	0.291	0.37
Error	43.33	8	5.42			0.674	
Total	64.24	12					

Table 32.2. *Descriptive Statistics for Anxiety 2.sav* *

Anxiety	Tension	M	SD	N
1	1	8.67	3.06	3
	2	7.00	2.65	3
2	1	6.00	2.00	3
	2	9.33	1.16	3

*Dependent Variable: Trial 3

Nonetheless, even a cursory look at the means shown in Table 32.2 indicates that fairly large differences exist between means and something noteworthy is going on, so a better designed replication study with a larger sample size might be justified. Eta^2 can help in interpreting the results by indicating the relative degree to which the variance that was found in the ANOVA was associated with each of the main effects (Anxiety and Tension) and their interaction.

Eta² values are easy to calculate. Simply add up all the sums of squares (*SS*), the total of which is 64.24 in the example; then, divide the *SS* for each of the main effects, the interaction, and the error term by that total. The results will be as follows:

$$\eta^2_{Anxiety} = \frac{SS_{Anxiety}}{SS_{Total}} = \frac{0.08}{64.24} = 0.00124533 \approx 0.0012$$

$$\eta^2_{Tension} = \frac{SS_{Tension}}{SS_{Total}} = \frac{2.08}{64.24} = 0.03237858 \approx 0.0324$$

$$\eta^2_{AxT} = \frac{SS_{AxT}}{SS_{Total}} = \frac{18.75}{64.24} = 0.291874221 \approx 0.2919$$

$$\eta^2_{Error} = \frac{SS_{Error}}{SS_{Total}} = \frac{43.33}{64.24} = 0.674501867 \approx 0.6745$$

Interpretation of these values is easiest if the decimal point is moved two places to the right in each case, the result of which can be interpreted as percentages of variance associated with each of the main effects, the interaction, and error.

Starting with Anxiety, the value of 0.0012 indicates that a mere 0.12% of the variance is accounted for by Anxiety, whereas Tension accounts for 3.24%, the Anxiety x Tension (A x T) interaction accounts for a much larger 29.19%, and a whopping 67.45% is accounted for by Error. Now let's consider the A x T interaction and Error separately in more detail.

The 29.19% accounted for by the A x T interaction should lead the researcher to understand that this interaction effect is much more important than either of the individual main effects for Anxiety or Tension, a fact that, even though there are no significant effects, may help in designing future studies and understanding why the present one did not detect significant differences. Such an important interaction effect should lead the researcher to want to plot out that relationship as shown in Figure 32.1, where we see that the Tension groups 1 (dotted line) and 2 (plain black line) do indeed have different means but in opposite relationships for Anxiety 1 and 2. That is, the Tension 1 group is higher than the Tension 2 group when Anxiety is 1, but the Tension 1 group is lower than the Tension 2 group when Anxiety is 2.

Thus there is a strong pattern, but it is not consistent across Anxiety 1 and 2 conditions. If it were consistent, the lines would be parallel. Thus, even with a non-significant interaction (where $p = .10$), the eta^2 value of .2919 drew our attention to an important interaction effect that is revealing in itself, and which may help to understand why there were no significant main effects for Tension or Anxiety (i.e., because the interaction cancels out any such differences).

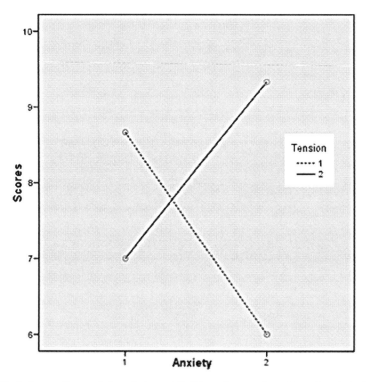

Figure 32.1. Interaction of Anxiety with Tension using the *Anxiety 2.sav* example

The whopping 67.45% accounted for by *Error* in Table 32.1 indicates that more than two-thirds of the variance was not accounted for at all in this design. This error variance may be due to unreliable variance in the study due to poor measurement or design, other systematic variables that might be of interest (if they were operationalized and included in the study), and so forth. All in all, eta^2 values indicate not only that the interaction effect and error are causing almost 97% of the variance in the study (67.45 + 29.19 = 96.64), but also ways to redesign the study so it will be more powerful and meaningful.

One problem with eta² is that the magnitude of eta² for each particular effect depends to some degree on the significance and number of other effects in the design (Tabachnick & Fidell, 2001, p. 54). One statistic that minimizes the effects of this issue is *partial eta²*.

Partial eta²

Partial eta² can be defined as the ratio of variance accounted for by an effect and that effect plus its associated error variance within an ANOVA study. Formulaically,

$$\eta^2_{partial} = \frac{SS_{effect}}{SS_{effect} + SS_{error}}$$

Where:

SS_{effect} = the sums of squares for whatever effect is of interest

SS_{error} = the total sums of squares for whatever error term is associated with that effect

In applied linguistics studies, partial eta² is most often reported for ANOVA designs that have non-independent cells (i.e., the same people appear in more than one cell). For example, in Brown, Hilgers, and Marsella (1991), students wrote compositions on two different types of topics (a narrative topic and an analytic topic) which were organized into ten prompt sets. The people who wrote on each of the ten prompt sets were different from each other (so this is also known as a *between subjects effect*). In contrast, every student wrote on each of the two topic types, so these were treated as repeated measures (also known as a *within subjects effect*). The cell sizes *within subjects* were exactly the same (which makes sense because they were the same people), whereas the cell sizes *between subjects* were different to small degrees. The original results of this 10 x 2 two-way repeated-measures ANOVA for prompt sets and topic types are shown in Table 32.3.

Table 32.3. *Two-Way Repeated-Measures ANOVA for 1989 Prompt Sets and Topic Types (As presented in Brown et al., 1991)*

Source	SS'	df	MS	F	p
Between Subjects					
Prompt Set	158.372	9	17.597	9.703	0.00
Error	3068.553	1692	1.814		
Within Subjects					
Topic Type	0.344	1	0.344	0.194	0.66
Prompt Set by Topic Type	137.572	9	15.286	8.611	0.00
Error	3003.548	1692	1.775		

Table 32.4. *Two-Way Repeated-Measures ANOVA for 1989 Prompt Sets and Topic Types (Adapted from Brown et al., 1991 with Partial Eta^2 Added)*

Source	SS	df	MS	F	p	Partial Eta^2
Between Subjects						
PromptSet (PS)	158.372	9	17.597	9.703	0.00	0.0490
Error BS	3068.553	1692	1.814			
Within Subjects						
Topic Type (TT)	0.344	1	0.344	0.194	0.66	0.0001
Prompt Set by Topic Type	137.572	9	15.286	8.611	0.00	0.0438
Error WS	3003.548	1692	1.775			

From my present perspective (many years later), the 1991 Brown et al. study would have been strengthened by clearly labeling the error effects and adding partial eta^2 values to the two-way repeated-measures ANOVA source table as shown in Table 32.4. These partial eta^2 values are easy to calculate. Simply divide the SS for each effect by the SS of that effect plus the SS for the error associated with that effect. The results will be as follows:

$$\text{Partial } \eta^2_{PS} = \frac{SS_{PS}}{SS_{PS} + SS_{Error\ BS}} = \frac{158.372}{158.372 + 3068.553} = 0.049078302 \approx 0.0491$$

$$\text{Partial } \eta^2_{TT} = \frac{SS_{TT}}{SS_{TT} + SS_{Error\ WS}} = \frac{0.344}{0.344 + 3003.548} = 0.000114518 \approx 0.0001$$

$$\text{Partial } \eta^2_{PSxTT} = \frac{SS_{PSxTT}}{SS_{PSxTT} + SS_{Error\ WS}} = \frac{137.572}{137.572 + 3003.548} = 0.043797116 \approx 0.0438$$

The interpretation of these partial eta² values is similar to what we did above for eta² in that we need to move the decimal point two places to the right in each case, and interpret the results as percentages of variance. However, this time the results indicate the percentage of variance in each of the effects (or interaction) and its associated error that is accounted for by that effect (or interaction). Starting with Prompt Sets, the value of 0.0490 indicates that 4.90% of the between subjects variance (PS + Error BS) is accounted for by Prompt Sets, whereas Topic Types accounts for nearly none (0.01%) of the within subtexts variance (TT plus Error WS), though the Prompt Sets by Topic Types interaction (PSxTT) accounts for a somewhat larger 4.38% of the within subjects variance (PSxTT plus Error WS).

Conclusion

In direct answer to your question, Kondo-Brown and Fukuda (2008) correctly chose to use partial eta² because their design was a MANOVA, which by definition involves non-independent or repeated measures. When they reported that partial eta² was .29, it meant that the effect for group differences in their MANOVA accounted for 29% of the group-differences plus associated error variance, as explained above. This percentage was sufficient to lead them to do univariate follow-up ANOVAs that helped them to further isolate exactly where the significant and interesting means differences were to be found.

In a number of chapters, I have covered a number of issues related to the ANOVA sorts of studies including: sampling and generalizability, sampling errors, sample size and power, and effect size and eta squared. All of these are ways to expand your thinking about ANOVA—ways that are often ignored in applied linguistics. They have long been important to understanding ANOVA results in psychology, education, and other fields, and we ignore them to our detriment. To paraphrase something one of my stats teachers said back in the late 1970s: Reporting the traditional ANOVA source table (with *SS*, *df*, *MS*, *F*, and *p*) and discussing the associated significance levels isn't the *end* of the study; it's just the *beginning* because we can learn much more by carefully plotting and considering the interaction effects and doing follow up analyses like planned or post-hoc comparisons, power and effect size analyses, and so forth. I hope I have delivered that message loud and clear.

(updated and reprinted from Brown, 2008b)

CHAPTER 33

CONFIDENCE INTERVALS, LIMITS, AND LEVELS

QUESTION: Could you explain the difference between these three terms: confidence intervals, confidence limits, and confidence levels? I am not entirely confident I understand the distinction. How are these statistics calculated? When are they generally used? When are they used in language testing?

ANSWER: Once again, in preparing to answer this seemingly easy question, I discovered that the answer is a bit more complex than I at first thought. To explain what I found, I will have to address the following sub-questions:

1. What are standard errors?
2. How are these standard error statistics calculated?
3. What are confidence intervals, confidence limits, confidence levels, etc.?
4. When are these statistics used in language testing?

What are standard errors?

To understand these various confidence concepts, it is necessary to first understand that, when we calculate any *statistic* based on a sample, it is an estimate of something else. Thus when we calculate the sample mean (*M*), that statistic is an estimate of the population mean (μ); when we calculate a reliability estimate for a set of test scores, it is an estimate of the proportion of true score variance accounted for by those scores; and when we use regression to predict one student's score on Test Y from their score on Test X, it is simply an estimate of what their actual score might be. However, estimates are just that, estimates. Thus they are not 100% accurate. The issues of standard errors and confidence are our statistical attempts to examine the inaccuracy of our estimates; this inaccuracy is also known as *error*. All statistics are estimates and all statistics have associated errors. The mean of a sample on some measured variable is an estimate, as are the standard deviation, the variance, any correlations between that variable and others, means comparisons statistics (e.g., *t*-test, *F*-ratio, etc.), observed and expected frequency comparisons (e.g., chi-square), and so forth. We can estimate the magnitude of the errors for any of these statistics by calculating the standard error for whatever statistic is involved. We then interpret the standard error in probability terms, which is where confidence intervals, limits, and levels come in.

How are these standard error statistics calculated?

In my experience in language testing, we most often encounter the standard error of the mean, the standard error of measurement, and the standard error of estimate.[1] All three are explained in more detail in Brown (1999a [Chapter 19]). However, I will briefly cover the calculations here and supply examples for each.

Standard error of the mean. One simple way to look at the mean of a set of scores is to think about it as a sample-based estimate of the mean of the population from which the sample was drawn. Since that estimate is never perfect, it is reasonable to want to know how much error there may be in that estimate of the population mean. The magnitude of this error can be calculated using the standard error of the mean (SE_M) as follows:

$$SE_M = \frac{S}{\sqrt{N}}$$

Where the SE_M = the standard error of the mean, S = the standard deviation of the scores on a test, and N = the number of examinees who took the test. Consider a test that has a mean of 51, $S = 12.11$, and $N = 64$. The SE_M would be:

$$SE_M = \frac{S}{\sqrt{N}} = \frac{12.11}{\sqrt{64}} = \frac{12.11}{8} = 1.51375 \approx 1.51$$

---

[1] Interestingly perhaps, given that the various standard error statistics are themselves estimates, it must be possible to estimate the standard errors of standard error statistics. For example, it should be possible to estimate the error involved (i.e., the standard error) in estimating the standard error of the mean. But ultimately, who would care?

This SE_M is an estimate of the amount of variation due to error that we can expect in sample means. For more information on interpreting the SE_M, see the discussion below of confidence intervals, limits, and levels.

Standard error of measurement (SEM). Language testers use reliability estimates to investigate the proportion of consistent variation in scores on a test (for more on this topic see Bachman, 2004; Brown, 1997b [Chapter 23], 1998a [Chapter 18], 2002a [Chapter 17], 2005c). Another more useful way to look at the consistency of test scores is to estimate the magnitude of the error by calculating the *SEM* as follows:

$$SEM = S\sqrt{1 - r_{xx'}}$$

Where S = the standard deviation of the scores on a test and $r_{xx'}$ = the reliability estimate for those scores (e.g., Cronbach alpha, K-R20, etc.). Consider a test that has a mean of 31, S of 5.15, and $r_{xx'}$ of .93. The *SEM* would be:

$$SEM = S\sqrt{1 - r_{xx'}} = 5.15\sqrt{1 - .93} = 5.15\sqrt{.07} = 5.15(.2646) = 1.36269 \approx 1.36$$

This *SEM* is an estimate of the amount of variation in the scores that is due to error in the sample score estimates of the examinees' true scores. For more information on interpreting the *SEM*, see the discussion below of confidence intervals, limits, and levels.

Standard error of estimate (see). Language testers use regression to predict scores on one test (usually labeled Test Y) from scores on another (usually labeled Test X). One useful way to think about those predictions of Y scores is to estimate how much error there is in the Test Y predictions by calculating the *see* as follows:

$$see = S_y\sqrt{1 - r_{xy}^2}$$

Where S_y = the standard deviation of the scores on Test Y and r_{xy} = the correlation coefficient for the degree of relationship between the Test X scores and those on Test Y. Consider a regression analysis where S_y = 9.54 and r_{xy} = .80. The *see* would be:

$$see = S_y\sqrt{1 - r_{xy}^2} = 9.54\sqrt{1 - .80^2} = 9.54\sqrt{1 - .64} = 9.54\sqrt{.36} = 9.54(.60) = 5.724 \approx 5.72$$

This *see* is an estimate of the amount of variation due to error that we can expect in the predicted Test Y scores based on scores on Test X in a particular regression analysis.

For more information on interpreting the *se*, go to the discussion below of confidence intervals, limits, and levels.

What are confidence intervals, confidence limits, confidence levels, etc.?

The confidence intervals, limits, and levels that you asked about in your question, all have to do with the next step after you have the standard error calculated. This next step is to interpret the standard error. In order to do so, we need to understand the differences among confidence intervals, limits, and levels so we can clearly think, talk, and write about our interpretations of standard errors.

Before we turn to using any of the types of standard errors (*se*) described above to help us interpret our sample statistics, we need to understand that errors are typically assumed to be normally distributed. Since all of the error estimates that we are talking about are *standard* errors, they are standardized and can be described as shown in Figure 33.1.

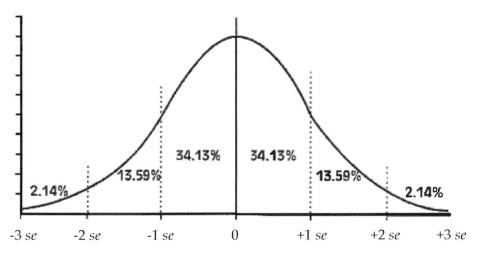

Figure 33.1. The distribution assumed for standard errors.

Notice in Figure 33.1 that I have provided the percentages that we would expect in each area. For instance, we expect 34.13% of the errors to fall between zero and +1 *se*. We can also expect about 68% of the errors to fall in the range between -1 *se* and +1 *se* (34.13 + 34.13 = 68.26 ≈ 68); similarly, we can expect about 95% of the errors to fall in the range between -2 *se* and +2 *se* (13.59 + 34.13 + 34.13 + 13.59 = 95.44 ≈ 95); and we can expect about 99% of the errors to fall in the range between -3 *se* and +3 *se* (2.14 + 13.59 + 34.13 + 34.13 + 13.59 + 2.14= 99.72 ≈ 99; note that this last one is rounded to 99% because theoretically we can never account for 100% of error). We use these percents under the distribution to help in establishing confidence intervals.

Coming back to the terminology, a *confidence interval* is the "range of values of a sample statistic that is likely, at a given level of probability called a confidence level, to contain a population parameter.[2]" It is the "interval that will include the population parameter a certain percentage of the time in the long run (over repeated sampling)" (Vogt & Johnson, 2011, p. 67).

In contrast, a *confidence level* is the degree of confidence, or certainty, that the researcher wants to be able to place in the confidence interval. Put another way, the confidence level is the probability that whatever is being estimated by the statistic falls within the confidence interval. The confidence level is usually expressed as a percentage, but it can also take the form of a proportion (which is also sometimes called a *confidence coefficient*). The confidence levels cited above were 68%, 95% or 99%. Since the 68% confidence level is only about two-thirds certainty, most researchers in the social sciences select either 95%, which is very confident, or 99%, which is about as confident as we would ever need to be. APA (2010, p. 34) suggests "As a rule, it is best to use a single confidence level, specified on an *a priori* basis (e.g., a 95% or 99% confidence interval), throughout the manuscript."

And finally, the *confidence limits* (also known as *confidence bounds*), are simply "the upper and lower values of a confidence interval, that is, the values defining the range of a confidence interval" (Vogt & Johnson, 2011, p. 68). So in a case where the ±2 *se* confidence interval turns out to be 47.98 to 54.02 for the 95% confidence level, the confidence limits are 47.98 and 54.02.

---

[2] About this term *parameter*, note that *statistics* are used in samples to estimate analogous *parameters* in the population from which the sample was drawn. For example, a sample mean statistic, M, is often calculated to estimate the analogous population parameter μ.

When are these statistics used in language testing?

Why should we care? Consider what the latest APA Manual (APA, 2010) says: "the inclusion of confidence intervals (for estimates of parameters, for functions of parameters such as differences in means, and for effect sizes) can be an extremely effective way of reporting results. Because confidence intervals combine information on location and precision and can often be directly used to infer significance levels, they are, in general, the best reporting strategy. *The use of confidence intervals is therefore strongly recommended*" (p. 34, italics added).

In language testing, we use confidence intervals to interpret at least the standard error of the mean (SE_M), standard error of measurement (*SEM*), and standard error of the estimate (*see*), as I will explain in three separate subsections.

Confidence and the **SE_M**. Let's begin by considering the example used above for the SE_M, where the mean was 51 and the SE_M turned out to be 1.51. The mean (*M*) for the sample, which turned out to be 51, is the best estimate that we have of the parameter μ. However, the SE_M of 1.51 tells us that there is error in that estimate and how big the error is. Since we assume that error is normally distributed, we can estimate the range within which the population mean is likely to exist in probability terms. In this case, we know that the population mean is likely to fall within ±1 SE_M 68% of the time (34.13 + 34.13 = 68.26 ≈ 68), ±2 SE_M 95% of the time (34.13 + 34.13 + 13.59 + 13.59 = 95.44 ≈ 95), and ±3 SE_M 99% of the time (34.13 + 34.13 + 13.59 + 13.59 + 2.14 + 2.14 = 98.58 ≈ 99).

Hence, we can say that the population μ in our example will fall within plus or minus one confidence interval of the sample mean of 51, that is, from 49.49 to 52.51 about 68% of the time (±1 *se* in this case = ±1.51; 51 − 1.51 = 49.49; 51 + 1.51 = 52.51). Using the same reasoning, we can say that the population μ in our example will fall within plus or minus two confidence intervals of the sample mean, that is, from 47.98 to 54.02 with 95% probability (±2 *se* in this case = ±3.02; 51 − 3.02 = 47.98; 51 + 3.02 = 54.02), and that the population μ in our example will fall within plus or minus three confidence intervals of the sample mean, that is, from 46.47 to 55.53 with 99% probability (±3 *se* in this case = ±4.53; 51 − 4.53 = 46.47; 51 + 4.53 = 55.53).

Confidence and the **SEM**. The *SEM* calculated in the example above turned out to be 1.36, which can be used to further estimate confidence intervals that indicate how many score points of variation can reasonably be expected with 68%, 95%, or 99% probability around any given point (e.g., a score or a cut-point). Let's say a student scored 32; that student (or any student with that same score) has a 68% probability of getting a score between 30.64 and 33.36 (32 – 1.36 = 30.64; 32 + 1.36 = 33.36) by chance alone if the test were administered repeatedly. Similarly, any examinee with a score of 32 is likely to fall within two *SEMs* (1.36 + 1.36 = 2.72) plus or minus (32 - 2.72 = 29.28; 32 + 2.72 = 34.72), or a band from 29.28 to 34.72, 95% of the time by chance alone. And finally, an examinee falling within three *SEMs* (3 x 1.36 = 4.08) plus or minus (32 – 4.08 = 27.92; 32 + 4.08 = 36.08), or a band from 27.92 to 36.08, is likely to fluctuate within that band 99% of the time. In practical terms, language testers most often use the *SEM* in cut-point decision making, where they may want to at minimum consider gathering additional information about any examinees who have scores within the band of plus or minus one *SEM* of a given cut-point in order to increase the reliability of that decision making. However, whether the tester chooses a 68%, 95%, or 99% confidence level is a judgment call. For additional information on *SEM*, see Bachman (2004, pp. 171-174), or Brown (2005c, pp. 188-190, 193-195).

Confidence and the see. The *see* calculated in the example above turned out to be 5.72, which can be used to further estimate *confidence intervals* (*CIs*) that indicate how many score points of variation can reasonably be expected with 68%, 95%, or 99% probability around any given predicted Test Y score in a regression analysis. Test users need to know that the actual Test Y score for any examinee is likely to fall within one *see*, plus or minus, of the Test Y score predicted from Test X 68% of the time. Let's say a student's predicted Test Y score is 50; that student (or any student with that same score) has a 68% probability of actually getting a score between 44.28 and 55.72 (50 – 5.72 = 44.28; 50 + 5.72 = 55.72) by chance alone. Similarly, any examinee with a score of 50 is likely to fall within two *sees* (5.72 + 5.72 = 11.44), plus or minus (50 - 11.44 = 38.56; 50 + 11.44 = 61.44), for a band from 38.56 to 61.44, 95% of the time by chance alone. And finally, an examinee falling within three *sees* (3 x 5.72 = 17.16) plus or minus (50 – 17.16 = 32.24; 50 + 17.16 = 67.16), or a band from 32.24 to 67.16, is likely to fluctuate within that band 99% of the time. In practical terms, language testers may want to use this information to examine the degree to which the prediction is accurate (e.g., the *see* of 5.72 in the example here does not seem to indicate a terribly accurate prediction; a glance at the correlation coefficient of .80 above further supports this conclusion), or to make their predictions fairer by at least taking into account the fact that examinees' actual scores on Test Y would likely be within the band of plus or minus one *see* in order to increase the accuracy of the prediction making. Whether the tester chooses to use the 68%, 95%, or 99% confidence level is once again a judgment call.

Conclusion

In direct answer to the original questions above: *I defined* confidence intervals, confidence limits, and confidence levels above, and I also explained that we must begin by calculating standard errors of various kinds. I pointed out that we can calculate standard errors for virtually any statistic, but I focused on the SE_M, SEM, and *see* because they are the ones that I've often used in my language testing research (note that I have also found myself using standard errors of skewness and kurtosis, standard errors of effect sizes, and others).

Once we have a standard error value in hand (for whatever statistic), we can then use the confidence intervals, limits, and levels to help us interpret those standard errors. I hope the explanations and examples I have provided here have helped you understand how all of this works and will help you to interpret the standard errors of your own statistics in the future.

(updated and reprinted from Brown, 2011b)

CHAPTER 34

THE BONFERRONI ADJUSTMENT

QUESTION: An interesting paper discussing how science and non-science majors respond differently to a reading test is now online at:

www.jalt.org/pansig/2007/HTML/Weaver.htm (Weaver, 2007)

The author mentions using a "Bonferroni adjustment" to compare science majors with non-science majors and reduce the likelihood of a Type I error. What is a Bonferroni adjustment? When should it be used? Whereas some authors contend it is useful, at least one other author contends "… Bonferroni adjustments are, at best, unnecessary and, at worst, deleterious to sound statistical inference" (Perneger, 1998).

ANSWER: In order to answer your various questions, I will have to address a number of sub-questions of my own: (a) What's the problem with interpreting multiple statistical comparisons? (b) What's the probability of one or more t-tests being spuriously significant? (c) How can we solve this problem of spuriously significant differences? (d) How does the Bonferroni adjustment help with this problem? And, (e) does everybody agree that the Bonferroni adjustment should be used?

What's the problem with interpreting multiple statistical comparisons?

Let me begin by stating that I am not, by any means, the first researcher to notice that the results of multiple t-tests present a set of problems (see Brown, 1988, p. 170; Dayton, 1970, pp. 37-49; Kirk, 1968, pp. 69-98; Shavelson, 1981, pp. 447-448). Essentially, the problem is that an inferential statistic like the two-sample t-test is designed to tell us the probability that the means of the two samples are significantly different at a certain significance level. For example, if two samples of 17 men and 17 women had means of 18.5 and 14.5, respectively, and standard deviations of 2.5 and 3.5, respectively, we might want to find out if the observed difference is just a chance fluctuation or is a significant difference at say $p < .05$ (i.e., with a probability of 5%). In this case, we might use an independent samples t-test to investigate this issue, and it would turn out that t = 3.83, which is indeed significant at $p < .05$. Thus we can say there is only a 5%

probability that the difference between the means for men and women reported here occurred by chance (for more on this calculation, see Brown & Rodgers, 2002, pp. 205-210).

So far, so good. However, a problem arises if we decide we want to do another *t*-test in the same study (say between Japanese and Americans), or two *t*-tests, or ten *t*-tests, or fifty *t*-tests. For the sake of argument, let's consider an extreme example where we want to compare two groups of 100 students on each of 100 different tests (Test T001 to Test T100) using 100 *t*-tests. Table 34.1 shows the results for such a hypothetical study. Notice that Table 34.1 gives the means on each test for groups 1 and 2, as well as the absolute difference (i.e., regardless of sign) between those means and the absolute *t*-test (i.e., regardless of sign) for each comparison. Notice also that the asterisks next to some of the Abs. *t* values indicate that those comparisons are significant at $p < .05$. It turns out that six out of the 100 comparisons are significant at $p < .05$. So what is the problem?

The problem is that Table 34.1 shows that six out of 100 comparisons are significant at .05 even though these analyses are based on data that are 100% random. I produced the data for each pair of groups to be a set of random normal standardized *T* scores. Yet, six of the *t*-tests turned out to be significant at .05. This is approximately what we would expect from random numbers. If I were to repeat the procedures with new random normal data, there might be four or three or seven or five significant *t*-tests, but on average over many such pseudo-studies based on random numbers, I would expect about 5% to be significant at $p < .05$. These are called spuriously significant results (i.e., significant differences that occur by chance alone). Such findings are completely reasonable because $p < .05$ indicates that there is a five percent probability of such findings by chance alone, and indeed we found that approximately five percent (actually 6% in this particular instance) were indeed significant when based on random normal data.

Could such patterns occur in real data? Consider a study by Politzer and McGroarty (1985) published in the *TESOL Quarterly*. These authors reported 228 *t*-tests in their study, of which 11 were significant. In other words, their results were that 4.8% of their 228 *t*-tests were significant at $p < .05$ (11 / 228 = .048). Thus their results are no different from what we would expect if the numbers they used in their study had been randomly generated rather than based on real-life data. In short, despite the fact that they found "significant differences," because those differences are based on multiple comparisons (i.e., 228 *t*-tests), their results were no different from what we would expect by chance alone. Yet the authors of that article, who apparently did not notice this problem, went on to interpret their results and publish them in *TESOL Quarterly*, and other researchers continue to cite those results. That's the problem.

Is the Politzer and McGroarty study the only one with multiple statistical comparisons? No, I have noticed many such studies during my 38 years in applied linguistics. A few examples that jump immediately to mind are Anisfeld, Bogo, and Lambert (1962), who reported a total of 223 *t*-tests, Carrell, Pharis, and Liberto (1989), who conducted 12 *t*-tests, and Fotos and Ellis (1991), who included 21 *t*-tests.

Table 34.1. *Study of 100 pairs of means based on 100 random normal data points for each group*

Test	Group 1	Group 2	Abs. Diff.	Abs. T		Test	Group 1	Group 2	Abs. Diff.	Abs. T	
T001	50.39	48.43	1.96	1.29		T051	49.95	50.78	0.83	0.62	
T002	51.68	49.62	2.06	1.40		T052	50.53	49.60	0.93	0.64	
T003	52.29	50.78	1.50	1.15		T053	49.69	49.64	0.05	0.04	
T004	50.25	48.56	1.69	1.16		T054	50.45	51.63	1.18	0.85	
T005	48.77	48.82	0.05	0.04		T055	49.53	49.48	0.06	0.04	
T006	51.72	50.75	0.96	0.74		T056	51.35	50.00	1.35	0.96	
T007	48.41	51.39	2.98	2.40	*	T057	49.53	50.32	0.80	0.56	
T008	50.65	49.90	0.75	0.52		T058	48.13	50.04	1.92	1.33	
T009	50.71	49.99	0.72	0.54		T059	49.99	50.03	0.05	0.03	
T010	50.60	49.31	1.29	1.01		T060	51.89	50.11	1.78	1.28	
T011	50.34	49.31	0.86	0.64		T061	50.80	47.18	3.62	2.91	*
T012	50.78	48.98	1.79	1.20		T062	51.61	49.99	1.61	1.10	
T013	49.54	49.87	0.33	0.24		T063	49.82	50.82	1.00	0.71	
T014	50.37	51.07	0.70	0.52		T064	50.94	49.90	1.04	0.73	
T015	50.52	48.80	1.72	1.30		T065	49.68	52.19	2.52	1.72	
T016	52.13	49.68	2.46	1.82		T066	50.75	51.75	1.00	0.66	
T017	49.63	49.27	0.36	0.28		T067	49.08	49.32	0.24	0.14	
T018	48.95	51.45	2.50	1.62		T068	49.19	50.76	1.56	1.09	
T019	51.48	48.89	2.59	1.78		T069	51.01	50.61	0.39	0.27	
T020	50.80	48.82	1.97	1.34		T070	49.99	50.67	0.68	0.48	
T021	48.93	48.5	0.43	0.43		T071	51.09	49.69	1.40	1.02	
T022	51.26	49.79	1.47	1.01		T072	49.46	49.01	0.45	0.32	
T023	50.55	49.83	0.72	0.48		T073	51.1	50.38	0.78	0.56	
T024	49.65	51.33	1.68	1.19		T074	50.47	49.37	1.10	0.78	
T025	51.60	48.80	2.79	2.07	*	T075	50.17	51.33	1.16	0.82	
T026	51.07	51.39	0.32	0.23		T076	49.72	49.88	0.16	0.11	
T027	48.58	50.43	1.85	1.31		T077	50.57	50.27	0.30	0.21	
T028	51.10	50.72	0.39	0.28		T078	48.72	46.85	1.87	1.41	
T029	48.63	51.40	2.77	1.95		T079	50.62	49.90	0.72	0.49	
T030	50.35	49.73	0.62	0.43		T080	50.98	49.15	1.84	1.42	
T031	48.93	49.13	0.20	0.14		T081	49.45	48.93	0.52	0.39	
T032	49.80	51.16	1.36	0.93		T082	51.10	51.10	0.00	0.00	
T033	51.11	51.16	0.05	0.04		T083	49.52	50.44	0.92	0.64	
T034	50.45	49.40	1.05	0.74		T084	49.87	50.18	0.30	0.22	
T035	48.95	50.06	1.11	0.82		T085	51.89	50.87	1.01	0.71	

Test	Group 1	Group 2	Abs. Diff.	Abs. T		Test	Group 1	Group 2	Abs. Diff.	Abs. T	
T036	52.09	49.87	2.22	1.50		T086	49.31	49.72	0.41	0.32	
T037	49.55	51.48	1.93	1.50		T087	52.24	50.28	1.96	1.27	
T038	49.03	50.05	1.02	0.67		T088	49.92	51.34	1.42	1.05	
T039	50.59	48.40	2.19	1.53		T089	49.66	49.44	0.22	0.15	
T040	49.45	49.32	0.13	0.08		T090	49.76	49.28	0.49	0.33	
T041	49.06	49.51	0.44	0.31		T091	50.69	51.51	0.83	0.57	
T042	50.70	49.01	1.69	1.16		T092	52.07	48.40	3.67	2.77	*
T043	50.53	49.46	1.07	0.77		T093	48.42	50.04	1.62	1.17	
T044	49.66	50.96	1.30	0.89		T094	47.99	50.81	2.83	2.01	*
T045	46.84	50.12	3.28	2.24	*	T095	51.33	49.80	1.52	1.04	
T046	49.02	49.78	0.77	0.55		T096	50.47	49.69	0.79	0.59	
T047	49.88	50.04	0.16	0.11		T097	49.21	50.07	0.86	0.60	
T048	49.82	49.17	0.66	0.44		T098	48.74	49.13	0.39	0.26	
T049	49.32	49.02	0.30	0.20		T099	50.86	50.37	0.49	0.37	
T050	49.58	50.28	0.71	0.52		T100	49.01	49.10	0.09	0.06	

*$p < .05$, two-tailed

What's the probability of one or more *t*-tests being spuriously significant?

The problem with multiple *t*-tests then, is that a certain, but unknown, probability exists that one or more significant differences will be found by chance alone. As the number of *t*-tests increases in a given study, the probability that one or more spuriously significant differences will be detected increases. The gravity of this problem depends to some degree on whether the means are independent (i.e., the groups are made up of different participants, as in a comparison of males and females, where they cannot be the same people) or non-independent (i.e., the same participants are measured under different circumstances, as in a comparison of the pretest and posttest scores where there are two scores for each person, one for the pretest and one for the posttest).

For *independent means*, the probability of one or more *t*-tests being spuriously significant (i.e., the probability of committing a Type I error), can be calculated using $1 - (1 - \alpha)^c$, where α is the predetermined acceptable significance level (e.g., .05) and c is the number of comparisons (see Chapter 29 for an explanation of Type I error). For example, with α set at .05, the probability of a Type I error for one comparison is $1 - (1 - .05)^1 = 1 - .95 = .05$, or 5 percent, as we would expect. For six comparisons, it is $1 - (1 - .05)^6 = 1 - .7351 = .2649$, or 26 percent. For ten comparisons it is 40 percent, for fifteen comparisons it is 54 percent, for twenty comparisons it is 64 percent, and so forth.

For non-independent means, the probabilities are even higher: Cochran and Cox (1957) estimated that the probability of a spuriously significant difference occurring for six *t*-tests is approximately 40%, for 10 *t*-tests it's about 60%, for 20 *t*-tests it's 90%, and so forth.

Whether the means are independent or non-independent, then, the problem is that one (or more) of the observed significant differences may be spuriously significant. We can calculate the probability of this occurring, but because we cannot determine which of the "significant" differences are spurious, the interpretation of results for studies using multiple comparisons becomes very tricky, if not impossible. That's where the Bonferroni adjustment comes in.

How can we solve this problem of spuriously significant differences?

Well trained researchers in our field design their studies to include one relatively complex analysis drawn from the analysis-of-variance family of inferential statistics (e.g., ANCOVA, MANOVA, MANCOVA, etc.) that maintains an experimentwise alpha level of .05 or .01, yet allows a posteriori multiple comparison tests like the Duncan, Newman-Keuls, Dunnett, Tukey HSD, or Scheffé test (see Kirk, 1968, pp. 87-97; Jaccard, Becker, & Wood, 1984 for more on these methods). The issue of multiple comparisons is one reason that such analyses are so useful. Indeed, we must ask ourselves why these more complex analyses would exist at all if we can simply go ahead and do as many *t*-tests as we want.

Unfortunately, using these more complex ANOVA-family designs requires a fair amount of training (e.g., when I was at UCLA, ANOVA was a course in educational statistics requiring three prerequisite statistics courses). Also unfortunately, most of the people doing statistical research in our field do not have that much training.

What can researchers who are not so well trained do? One thing they can do is to go ahead and do multiple *t*-tests, but then use the Bonferroni adjustment to at least roughly compensate for the mess they are making with their *p* values.

How does the Bonferroni adjustment help with this problem?

One version of the Bonferroni adjustment that is commonly used is as follows: $\alpha_{adjusted} = \alpha / c$ (where α is the overall experimentwise alpha; c is the number of comparisons made; and $\alpha_{adjusted}$ is the adjusted alpha level at which each of c comparisons must be tested for significance).

For example, we might want to apply the Bonferroni adjustment to the data in Table 34.1 in order to maintain an experimentwise alpha of .05. Given that we have 100 comparisons, the adjusted alpha would be $\alpha_{adjusted} = \alpha / c = .05 / 100 = .0005$. Checking to see if any of the *t*-tests in Table 34.1 reached $p < .0005$, it turns out that none of the results are significant. Thus, all six spuriously significant differences have been removed with the result that no significant differences have been found for the randomly generated data in Table 34.1, which is just as it should be. Another example of using the Bonferroni adjustment is provided in Sasaki (1996) who did 25 *t*-tests and found (after the adjustment) that 24 of those *t*-tests were significant. And, of course, the Weaver (2007) article that you mentioned in your question used the same strategy for the same purpose.

Increasingly, researchers in applied linguistics are using this Bonferroni adjustment strategy as one of their many statistical tools. However, because the Bonferroni adjustment is a rough approximation, it is not always the best solution for the problem of multiple comparisons. Often the best way to proceed is to use the ANOVA family of statistical tools. Nevertheless, if there is no other solution, the Bonferroni adjustment is better than nothing.

I should also point out that the Bonferroni adjustment is not restricted to use with multiple *t*-tests. It is also used by researchers to account for spurious significances that might occur in multiple ANOVAs, multiple chi-square tests, multiple correlation coefficients, and so forth.

Does everybody agree that the Bonferroni adjustment should be used?

As Perneger (1998) points out, application of the Bonferroni adjustment is increasingly widespread in the social sciences. Does everybody agree that this adjustment should be used? No. But then, does everybody agree on anything in the social sciences? The answer to this question is also no. Maybe in the social sciences, as in the sciences, we should take the safe route and follow whatever the consensus is. If so, the consensus seems to be that using the Bonferroni adjustment is all right if you use it cautiously. But then, following the herd is not always the correct way to go. So what are you to do?

Perhaps the clearest way to think about the differences in views on any issue in statistics is to recognize that there are many points of view on this issue, ranging from the relatively liberal points of view of some people (like Perneger, 1998; Siegel, 1990), who seem to be saying that multiple *t*-tests are okay, to very conservative views expressed by other researchers (like myself in Brown, 1990c & 2001e; Sasaki, 1996; Tabachnick & Fidell, 2001, 2012; and Weaver, 2007), who advocate that care be taken in interpreting multiple *t*-tests and that the Bonferroni is one way of being careful. One problem I see with the views of people on the liberal end of this issue is that they tend to assume that researchers (and readers of research) have more knowledge about statistics than they actually have. Certainly in applied linguistics, we should probably never assume much statistical sophistication on the part of readers or researchers.

As I have pointed out elsewhere, "The position taken by this author is based on the 'conservative' philosophy that, in applying statistics, great care and caution must always be practiced in order to minimize the possibility of publishing 'significant' results that may have occurred by chance alone" (Brown, 1990c, p. 770). In short, I know enough about statistics and research to be very distrustful of the numbers and statistics involved. As a result, I take a conservative and careful position on the issue of multiple comparisons, one that sometimes involves the Bonferroni adjustment.

(updated and reprinted from Brown, 2008a)

Part II: Second Language Research

Section F: Research Analyses

CHAPTER 35

THE COEFFICIENT OF DETERMINATION

QUESTION: In a recent paper on cloze tests (Brown, Yamashiro, & Ogane, 2001, p. 143), you mentioned that the coefficients of determination for cloze tests vary from .19 to .83. Can you explain what coefficients of determination are? How are they calculated?

ANSWER: The central issue underlying your question is: how can we interpret correlation coefficients? To answer that question, I must deal with three sub-questions: (a) What does a correlation coefficient mean? (b) What does a coefficient of determination mean? And, (c) how does the coefficient of determination help put the interpretation of correlation coefficients into perspective?

What does a correlation coefficient mean?

Correlation was once defined for me by one of my professors at UCLA as the "go-togetherness" of two sets of numbers. That definition has always made sense to me. The degree to which two sets of numbers go together can be calculated using a statistic called the *correlation coefficient*.[1] Correlation coefficients (often symbolized by r, or r_{xy}) can turn out to be as high in a positive direction as +1.00 if the relationship between the two sets of numbers is perfect and in the same direction (as is the case in Table 35.1 below for Tests A and B). A correlation coefficient can also turn out to be as high in a negative direction, that is -1.00, if the relationship is perfect and in opposite directions

---

[1] Throughout this explanation, I am referring to the most commonly reported correlation coefficient, the Pearson product-moment correlation coefficient, which is appropriate when the two sets of numbers are on continuous scales. The coefficient of determination is only appropriate for use with the Pearson coefficient, not with other non-parametric coefficients like the Spearman rank-order coefficient.

(as is the case in Table 35.1 for Tests A and C, or B and C). A correlation coefficient can also turn out to be zero if no relationship at all exists between the two sets of numbers (as would be the case between two sets of random numbers). Basically, this is what a correlation coefficient represents. However, this coverage of the topic has necessarily been brief because the focus here is on the *coefficient of determination*. [For much more on calculating and interpreting correlation coefficients, see Brown 1996a, or any other good applied statistics or testing book.]

Table 35.1. *Example Data for Tests A, B, and C*

Test A	Test B	Test C
9	8	1
8	7	2
7	6	3
6	5	4
5	4	5
4	3	6
3	2	7
2	1	8
1	0	9

One problem that arises in interpreting correlation coefficients is that their relative magnitudes are not proportional. That is to say, a correlation coefficient of .80 cannot be said to be accounting for twice as much "go-togetherness" as a coefficient of .40. Thus it is difficult to interpret and understand correlation coefficients, especially relative to each other.

What does a coefficient of determination mean?

The *coefficient of determination* makes interpreting correlation coefficients easier. Notwithstanding its impressive name, calculating this coefficient is simple. The coefficient of determination is simply the squared value of the correlation coefficient. That is why the symbol for this statistic is r_{xy}^2. The resulting coefficient of determination provides an estimate of the *proportion* of overlapping variance between two sets of numbers (i.e., the degree to which the two sets of numbers vary together).

By simply moving the decimal point two places to the right, you can interpret a coefficient of determination as the *percentage* of variance shared by the two sets of numbers. So, a coefficient of determination of .81 can be interpreted as a proportion, or as 81%. For example, if you have two sets of scores on Tests X and Y, and they correlate at .90, you could square that value to get the coefficient of determination of .81 and interpret that result as meaning that 81% of the variance in Test X is shared with Test Y, or for that matter, that 81% of the variance on Test Y is shared with Test X. By extension, you should recognize that you don't know what the remaining 19% (100% - 81% = 19%) on each test is related to.

How does the coefficient of determination put the interpretation of correlation coefficients into perspective?

Why bother calculating the coefficient of determination? Well, as explained in the previous section, it is worthwhile because the proportions (or percentages) represented by the coefficient of determination are easier for most people to understand and because you can truly say that the ratios represented by various values of this coefficient have meaning. In other words, a coefficient of determination of .80 can be said to represent twice as much overlapping variance between two sets of numbers as a coefficient of .40.

In addition, Table 35.2 illustrates how sharply the coefficients of determination decline in magnitude when compared with their respective correlation coefficients. For example (as shown in Table 35.2), a correlation of:

.90 squared equals .81 (i.e., 81%) or about four-fifths overlap,
.80 squared equals .64 (i.e., 64%) or about two-thirds overlap,
.70 squared equals .49 (i.e., 49%) or about one-half overlap,
.60 squared equals .36 (i.e., 36%) or about one-third overlap,
.50 squared equals .25 (i.e., 25%) or about one-quarter overlap,
.40 squared equals .16 (i.e., 16%) or about one-fifth overlap,
.30 squared equals .09 (i.e., 9%) or about one-tenth overlap,
.20 squared equals .04 (i.e., 4%) or about one-twenty-fifth overlap (almost nothing)
.10 squared equals .01, or less than one-hundredth overlap (definitely nothing)

Table 35.2. *Some Example Correlation Coefficients and Corresponding Coefficients of Determination*

Correlation Coefficient (r_{xy})	Coefficient of Determination (r_{xy}^2)
1.00	1.00
0.90	0.81
0.80	0.64
0.70	0.49
0.60	0.36
0.50	0.25
0.40	0.16
0.30	0.09
0.20	0.04
0.10	0.01

Notice how much more rapidly the coefficients of determination drop as you scan down Table 2 than do the correlation coefficients. This should help you recognize that correlation coefficients can be misleading. For example, I have seen a correlation coefficient of .60 called a "moderate" correlation. After all, .60 on a scale from .00 to 1.00 *appears* to represent about three-fifths overlap. But when you square that value to find the coefficient of determination, you quickly realize that the proportion of relationship is .36, or 36%, which is only about one-third overlap. How can that be said to represent a moderate relationship? Even a "moderate" correlation of .70 is only .49 when squared, and thus represents less than one-half overlap between whatever two sets of numbers are involved. The bottom line is that the coefficient of determination transforms a correlation coefficient into a statistic that you can more readily interpret and compare to other coefficients.

Conclusion

Your original question asked about our statement (Brown, Yamashiro, & Ogane, 2001, p. 143) that the coefficients of determination for cloze tests have varied from .19 to .83. You should now understand that these values of .19 to .83 would result from squaring correlation coefficients ranging from .44 ($.44^2$ = .1936 or about .19) to .91 ($.91^2$ = .8281 or about .83), and that each of these coefficients of determination represent the proportion of overlap between two sets of numbers (in this case, between cloze test scores and some other measure of overall English language proficiency such as the TOEFL).

For more on coefficients of determination, see Brown (1996a) or any other good applied statistics or testing book.

(updated and reprinted from Brown, 2003a)

CHAPTER 36

PRINCIPAL COMPONENTS ANALYSIS AND EXPLORATORY FACTOR ANALYSIS: DEFINITIONS, DIFFERENCES, AND CHOICES

QUESTION: In Chapter 7 of the 2008 book on heritage language learning that you co-edited with Kimi Kondo-Brown, there is a study (Lee & Kim, 2008) comparing the attitudes of 111 Korean heritage language learners. On page 167 of that book, a principal components analysis (with varimax rotation) describes the relationships among 16 purported reasons for studying Korean with four broader factors. Several questions come to mind. What is a principal components analysis? How does principal components analysis differ from factor analysis? What guidelines do researchers need to bear in mind when selecting "factors"? And finally, what is a varimax rotation, and why is it applied?

ANSWER: This is an interesting question, but a big one, made up of at least three sets of sub-questions: (a) what are principal components analysis (PCA) and exploratory factor analysis (EFA), how are they different, and how do researchers decide which to use? (b) How do investigators determine the number of components or factors to include in the analysis? (c) What is rotation, what are the different types, and how do researchers decide which to use? And, (d) how are PCA and EFA used in language test and questionnaire development? I will address the first one (a) in this chapter. And, I'll turn to the other three in subsequent chapters.

What are principal components analysis and exploratory factor analysis?

Principal components analysis (PCA) and exploratory factor analysis (EFA) are often referred to collectively as factor analysis (FA). The general notion of FA includes "a variety of statistical techniques whose common objective is to represent a set of variables in terms of a smaller number of hypothetical variables" (Kim & Mueller, 1978, p. 9). A more elaborate definition is provided by Tabachnick and Fidell (2012, p. 612):

… statistical techniques applied to a single set of variables when the researcher is interested in discovering which variables in the set form coherent subsets that are relatively independent of one another. Variables that are correlated with one another but largely independent of other subsets of variables are combined into factors.

In the study you mentioned, Lee and Kim (2008) looked at the attitudes expressed by 111 heritage and traditional learners of Korean, and then performed a PCA (with varimax rotation) on the results. The participants answered a 34-item questionnaire with both Likert and open-ended items. The PCA was used to analyze the results for 16 of the Likert items on motivations for studying Korean. The researchers found that four broad factors underlay the relationships among the participants' responses to these items. How researchers go about deciding on the number of factors and why they decide to use a particular kind of rotation will be addressed in subsequent chapters. However, that these researchers did find four components is evident in Table 36.1.

Notice in Table 36.1 that the wording of each of the Likert items is given in the first column. The next four columns are labeled Components 1, 2, 3, and 4, and each column shows values that look suspiciously like correlation coefficients (positive and negative); that's because they are correlation coefficients. The analysis has actually generated a set of four new predicted values for each participant—one value for each of the four components (in essence these are four new hypothetical variables, Components 1, 2, 3, and 4). These values are called component scores, and they can be saved as data if the researcher so wishes. The correlation coefficients in Table 36.1 are the correlations between all participants' Likert answers for each item (or *variable*, as they are called in FA), and these component scores. For example, the correlation between their Likert answers to the "I learn Korean to transfer credits to college" item and their component 1 scores is 0.83—a fairly high correlation, wouldn't you say? In contrast, the correlations of those same Likert answers and the Component 2, 3, and 4 scores are very low. Is that clear? The remaining correlation coefficients can be interpreted in similar manner.

Some of the correlation coefficients in Table 36.1 are in bold-faced italics to emphasize them. For example, in the Component 1 column, the first six correlations (by convention, these are called *loadings*) of .63 to .83 are emphasized because they are much higher than the other loadings in that same column. Similarly, the Component 2 loadings of .48 to .80 are highlighted, the Component 3 loadings of .44 to .71 are accentuated, and the

Principal Components Analysis and Exploratory Factor Analysis 239

Table 36.1. *Principal Components Analysis (with Varimax Rotation) Loadings of Motivation Items (adapted from Lee & Kim, 2008)*

	Instrumental		Integrative		
	Comp 1 School-related	Comp 2 Career-related	Comp 3 Personal fulfillment	Comp 4 Heritage ties	h^2
I learn Korean to transfer credits to college.	**0.83**	0.01	0.17	-0.11	**0.72**
I learn Korean because my friend recommended it.	**0.82**	0.14	0.06	0.22	**0.74**
I learn Korean because my advisor recommended it.	**0.80**	0.10	0.36	0.04	**0.78**
I learn Korean because of the reputation of the program and instructor.	**0.77**	0.12	0.12	0.22	**0.67**
I learn Korean for an easy A.	**0.69**	0.18	-0.29	0.16	**0.61**
I learn Korean to fulfill a graduation requirement.	**0.63**	0.11	0.19	-0.18	**0.47**
I learn Korean to get a better job.	0.04	**0.80**	0.20	0.11	**0.69**
I learn Korean because I plan to work overseas.	0.26	**0.80**	0.11	0.10	**0.75**
I learn Korean because of the status of Korean in the world.	0.10	**0.73**	0.20	0.22	**0.63**
I learn Korean to use it for my research.	0.38	**0.48**	**0.44**	0.10	**0.58**
I learn Korean to further my global understanding.	0.16	0.33	**0.71**	0.08	**0.65**
I learn Korean because I have an interest in Korean literature.	0.18	0.04	**0.64**	0.13	**0.56**
I learn Korean because it is fun and challenging.	0.04	0.04	**0.63**	**0.46**	**0.63**
I learn Korean because I have a general interest in languages.	0.11	0.03	**0.57**	**0.51**	**0.59**
I learn Korean because it is the language of my family heritage.	-0.01	0.26	0.05	**0.80**	**0.71**
I learn Korean because of my acquaintances with Korean speakers.	0.10	0.21	0.20	**0.70**	**0.58**
% of variance explained by each factor	0.23	0.15	0.14	0.12	0.64

Note. Extraction Method: Principal Component Analysis. Rotation Method: Varimax; Eigenvalue > 1.0

Component 4 loadings from .46 to .80 are emphasized. For each of the four components, the variables with loadings that are much higher than the others in the same column are of particular interest because they are for the variables that are most highly related to the component scores.

How high is a high loading? Well, obviously, as correlation coefficients, they can range from 0.00 to 1.00 and 0.00 to -1.00, with the sign depending on the direction of the relationship. The reader can decide whether the values reported in a particular study are adequate. However, loadings below 0.30 are typically ignored in such analyses. In the study reported in Table 36.1, it appears that the researchers decided that a better cut-point would be 0.40 (i.e., there are values above 0.30 but below 0.40, which are not emphasized) for deciding which loadings should be interpreted. It is up to the researcher to decide on the cut point and up to the readers to decide whether they buy that cut point. The researcher also interprets the patterns found in such analyses—a fact that can become a problem. Researchers risk seeing only those patterns they want to see because they are free to interpret the results any way they like. As a result, it is particularly important that researchers be transparent in explaining how they made their decisions, and that readers carefully examine the researchers' interpretations to make sure those interpretations make sense and are believable.

Consider Component 1 in Table 36.1, which is labeled "school-related." Have a look at the first six items on the questionnaire (i.e., those loading heaviest on Component 1). Are those questions really school-related? I suppose if the "friend" is a school friend, those six questions can truly be said to all be school-related? Now, what do you think of the four items for "career-related" Component 2? Are the five items for Component 3 all related to "personal fulfillment"? Are those loading heavily on Component 4 related to "heritage ties"? I think these interpretations are pretty good, but what do you think? That's important too.

There are additional numbers around the edges of Table 36.1 that are also worth considering. In the column furthest to the right, there are *communalities* (h^2). These values indicate the proportion of variance found in each item that can be accounted for by the four components in this analysis. For instance, the 0.72 at the top right indicates that 72% of the variance in the "I learn Korean to transfer credits to college" variable is accounted for by the four components in this analysis. Clearly, this analysis is much better at accounting for the variance in some variables than in others. Which variable has the highest communality? Which has the lowest? Why is the relative value of these communalities important? It's important because those variables with relatively high communalities are being accounted for fairly well, while those with low ones are not. Across the bottom of Table 36.1, the following numbers represent the proportion of variance accounted for by each component: 0.23, 0.15, 0.14, and 0.12. These indicate that

Component 1 accounts for 23% of the variance, Component 2 accounts for 15%, Component 3 accounts for 14%, and Component 4 accounts for 12% of the variance. The last number at the bottom right of Table 36.1 (0.64) indicates the total proportion of variance accounted for by the analysis as a whole. In other words, 64% (or just shy of two-thirds of the variance) was accounted for by this analysis. This total proportion of variance can be calculated by either adding up the individual proportions of variance accounted for by each of the four components, or by averaging the communalities.

How are PCA and EFA different?

Calculations for both PCA and EFA involve matrix algebra, as well as matrices of eigenvectors and eigenvalues. Any explanation of this would be quite involved and not particularly enlightening for most readers of this chapter, so suffice it to say that both PCA and EFA depend on calculating and using matrices of eigenvectors and values in conjunction with a matrix of the correlation coefficients, all of which are based on the variables being studied.

The difference between PCA and EFA in mathematical terms is found in the values that are put in the diagonal of the correlation matrix. In PCA, 1.00s are put in the diagonal, meaning that all of the variance in the matrix is to be accounted for (including variance unique to each variable, variance common among variables, and error variance). That would, therefore, by definition, include all of the variance in the variables. In contrast, in EFA, the communalities are put in the diagonal, meaning that only the variance shared with other variables is to be accounted for (excluding variance unique to each variable and error variance). That would, therefore, by definition, include only variance that is common among the variables.

How do researchers decide whether to use PCA or EFA?

The difference between PCA and EFA in conceptual terms is that PCA analyzes variance and EFA analyzes covariance (Tabachnick & Fidell, 2012, pp. 639-640). Thus when researchers want to analyze only the variance that is accounted for in an analysis (as in situations where they have a theory drawn from previous research about the relationships among the variables), they should probably use EFA to exclude unique and error variances, in order to see what is going on in the covariance, or common variance. When researchers are just exploring without a theory to see what patterns emerge in their data, it makes more sense to perform PCA (and thereby include unique and error variances), just to see what patterns emerge in all of the variance.

For purposes of illustration, I will use data based on the 12 subtests of the *Y/G Personality Inventory* (Y/GPI) (Guilford & Yatabe, 1957), which are: social extraversion, ascendance, thinking extraversion, rhathymia, general activity, lack of agreeableness, lack of cooperativeness, lack of objectivity, nervousness, inferiority feelings, cyclic tendencies, and depression. The first six scales have been shown to be extraversion measures; the last six scales have been shown to be neuroticism measures (for definitions and more information on the Y/GPI, see Robson, 1994; Brown, Robson, & Rosenkjar, 2001). The data used for this illustration are based on an English language version administered to 259 students at two universities in Brazil. The descriptive statistics for this sample are shown in Table 36.2.

Table 36.2. *Descriptive Statistics for the 12 Y/GPI Scales Administered to University Students in Brazil*

Trait	M	SD	N
Social extraversion	6.56	3.62	259
Ascendance	10.10	3.71	259
Thinking extraversion	12.33	2.72	259
Rhathymia	10.33	3.73	259
General activity	5.42	3.79	259
Lack of agreeableness	7.06	2.72	259
Lack of cooperativeness	10.47	3.43	259
Lack of objectivity	9.45	3.41	259
Nervousness	11.65	4.96	259
Inferiority feelings	9.52	3.85	259
Cyclic tendencies	11.38	3.93	259
Depression	12.99	4.63	259

Table 36.3 shows PCA and EFA analyses (with varimax rotation) and the resulting loadings for the Y/GPI administered in Brazil. Notice that the first column contains labels for the 12 scales. Then the next four columns show the results for a PCA of the data, and the last four columns show analogous results for an EFA of the same data. Notice that the patterns are very clear in both cases, but that the actual loadings differ for the PCA and EFA. Note also that the patterns of relatively strong loadings are the same for both analyses, so in that sense, it made little difference which analysis was used. However, notice also that including all of the variance in the PCA produced generally higher loadings, higher communalities, and ultimately accounted for more

variance overall (61.3% as opposed to 47.8%) than the EFA (which excluded the unique and error variances). The comparison of these two analyses indicates that the unique variances (and perhaps error variances) of the variables, which are used in the PCA, are contributing to higher loadings with the components in ways that are not present in the EFA. That is, of course, worth thinking about.

Table 36.3. *PCA and EFA (with Varimax Rotation) Loadings for the 12 Y/GPI Scales Administered in Brazil*

Variables	Rotated PCA Eigenvalues ≥ 1.00				Rotated EFA Eigenvalues ≥ 1.00			
	Comp 1	Comp 2	Comp 3	h^2	Factor 1	Factor 2	Factor 3	h^2
Social extraversion	-0.139	**0.744**	-0.140	0.592	-0.135	**0.665**	-0.118	0.474
Ascendance	-0.109	**0.658**	-0.099	0.455	-0.109	**0.548**	-0.098	0.321
Thinking extraversion	-0.091	-0.053	**0.916**	0.851	-0.072	-0.026	**0.530**	0.287
Rhathymia	0.419	**0.644**	0.221	0.639	0.391	**0.606**	0.206	0.562
General activity	-0.227	**0.746**	-0.068	0.613	-0.219	**0.680**	-0.070	0.515
Lack of agreeableness	0.150	**0.638**	0.304	0.522	0.119	**0.540**	0.197	0.345
Lack of cooperativeness	**0.562**	0.054	0.171	0.348	**0.466**	0.029	0.060	0.221
Lack of objectivity	**0.693**	0.067	-0.247	0.546	**0.614**	0.044	-0.187	0.415
Nervousness	**0.798**	-0.177	-0.022	0.669	**0.759**	-0.171	-0.021	0.606
Inferiority feelings	**0.695**	-0.481	0.085	0.722	**0.677**	-0.469	0.101	0.689
Cyclic tendencies	**0.820**	0.110	-0.014	0.685	**0.785**	0.106	-0.005	0.627
Depression	**0.812**	-0.232	-0.058	0.716	**0.784**	-0.227	-0.076	0.672
Proportion of Variance	0.295	0.225	0.093	0.613	0.259	0.182	0.037	0.478

In sum, the primary differences between PCA and EFA are that: (a) PCA is appropriate when researchers are just exploring for patterns in their data without a theory and therefore want to include unique and error variances in the analysis, and (b) EFA is appropriate when researchers are working from a theory drawn from previous research about the relationships among the variables and therefore want to include only the variance that is accounted for in an analysis (thereby excluding unique and error variances) in order to see what is going on in the covariance, or common variance.

Basically, researchers tend to: (a) use PCA if they are on a fishing expedition trying to find patterns in their data and have no theory on which to base the analysis, or (b) use EFA if they have a well-grounded theory on which to base their analysis. Generally, the second strategy is considered the stronger form of analysis.

Conclusion

I have shown what PCA and EFA (collectively known as factor analysis or FA) are, and in part, how they should be presented and interpreted. In the process, I have defined and exemplified loadings, communalities, proportions of variance, components, factors, PCA, and EFA. I have also explored the basic mathematical and conceptual differences between PCA and EFA, and discussed how researchers decide on whether to use PCA or EFA. However, much about FA has been left unexplained. How do researchers decide the number of components or factors to include in the analysis? For instance, how did I decide on the three components and factors shown in Table 36.3? Also, what is rotation, what are the different types, and how do researchers choose which type to use? For instance, what is the varimax rotation mentioned in Tables 36.1 and 36.3 (and the associated text), and why did the researchers choose it? As I mentioned above, I will address these issues in two subsequent chapters.

(updated and reprinted from Brown, 2009a)

CHAPTER 37

CHOOSING THE RIGHT NUMBER OF COMPONENTS OR FACTORS IN PCA AND EFA

QUESTION: In Chapter 7 of the 2008 book on heritage language learning that you co-edited with Kimi Kondo-Brown, a study (Lee & Kim, 2008) compares the attitudes of 111 Korean heritage language learners. On page 167 of that book, a principal components analysis (with varimax rotation) describes the relation of examining 16 purported reasons for studying Korean with four broader factors. Several questions come to mind. What is a principal components analysis? How does principal components analysis differ from factor analysis? What guidelines do researchers need to bear in mind when selecting "factors"? And finally, what is a varimax rotation and why is it applied?

ANSWER: This inquiry has four sub-questions: (a) what are principal components analysis (PCA) and exploratory factor analysis (EFA), how are they different, and how do researchers decide which to use? (b) How do investigators determine the number of components or factors to include in the analysis? (c) What is rotation, what are the different types, and how do researchers decide which to use? And, (d) how are PCA and EFA used in language test and questionnaire development? I have addressed the first question (a) in the previous chapter. I'll attend to the second one (b) here, and answer the other two in subsequent chapters).

Choosing the Number of Components or Factors to Include in a PCA or EFA

So, how do researchers decide on the number of components or factors to include in a PCA or EFA? If the researcher erroneously includes the same number of PCA components as there are variables (say 12 components in the 12-variable Y/GPI Brazilian university student example used in the previous chapter), each factor will represent one variable, as shown in Table 37.1. Such situations, where only one variable loads heavily in each column, indicate that the factor scores for each factor essentially represent a single variable; the researcher already knew about the single variable, so such single loading "components" or "factors" do not represent any underlying combinations of variables that provide new or interesting information (see the discussion of trivial factors below).

Table 37.1. *PCA Results for the 12 Y/GPI Scales Administered in Brazil with 12 Components Based on 12 Variables*

Variables	1	2	3	4	5	6	7	8	9	10	11	12
S	-0.042	-0.003	0.191	-0.085	0.132	**0.924**	-0.048	0.159	0.196	-0.014	-0.104	-0.074
A	-0.006	0.029	**0.952**	-0.044	0.090	0.175	0.010	0.076	0.157	0.008	-0.134	-0.056
T	0.017	-0.069	0.008	-0.021	0.033	-0.039	**0.992**	0.047	-0.047	-0.029	0.014	-0.039
R	0.054	0.119	0.083	0.061	0.202	0.160	0.059	**0.922**	0.143	0.163	-0.005	0.066
G	0.052	-0.077	0.186	-0.075	0.149	0.213	-0.063	0.154	**0.900**	-0.056	-0.152	-0.138
AG	0.056	0.009	0.089	-0.005	**0.958**	0.119	0.037	0.180	0.124	0.069	-0.059	-0.018
CO	**0.961**	0.103	-0.005	0.107	0.057	-0.035	0.020	0.048	0.044	0.088	0.114	0.154
O	0.112	**0.934**	0.031	0.151	0.010	-0.002	-0.082	0.113	-0.068	0.180	0.108	0.153
N	0.136	0.180	-0.053	**0.870**	-0.005	-0.097	-0.029	0.067	-0.076	0.262	0.233	0.216
I	0.183	0.156	-0.213	0.292	-0.092	-0.146	0.026	-0.010	-0.203	0.201	**0.814**	0.191
C	0.116	0.226	0.012	0.271	0.096	-0.013	-0.043	0.199	-0.060	**0.862**	0.170	0.186
D	0.253	0.225	-0.085	0.267	-0.027	-0.103	-0.068	0.091	-0.183	0.220	0.190	**0.815**

What researchers need instead is some way to determine a smaller number of factors or components (hereafter referred to collectively as *factors*) that account for large amounts of the overall variance without creating any bloated specifics. To that end, a number of "stopping rules" have been proposed to determine when the researcher should stop adding factors (see Bryant & Yarnold, 1995, pp. 102-104; Gorsuch, 1983, pp. 164-174). How does a researcher know how many factors to use? When should the researcher stop? There are various statistical tests to determine the optimum number of variables (Gorsuch, 1983, pp. 143-164), but more commonly these non-statistical strategies are used:

1. Kaiser's stopping rule
2. Scree test
3. Number of non-trivial factors
4. A priori criterion

5. Percentage of cumulative variance

Each of these topics will now be explained and exemplified in turn.

Examples illustrating the five stopping rules

I will base this discussion on the same example used in the previous chapter. Recall that the data were based on the 12 subtests of the *Y/G Personality Inventory* (Y/GPI) (Guilford & Yatabe, 1957) which were: social extraversion, ascendance, thinking extraversion, rhathymia, general activity, lack of agreeableness, lack of cooperativeness, lack of objectivity, nervousness, inferiority feelings, cyclic tendencies, and depression. The data were based on an English language version of the Y/GPI administered to 259 students at two universities in Brazil for comparative purposes. The descriptive results for these data were shown in Table 36.2 of the previous chapter.

Because ample theory and research indicate that the first six subtests are extraversion scales and the remaining six pertain to neuroticism (for more on the Y/GPI, see Guilford & Yatabe, 1957; Robson, 1994; Brown, Robson, & Rosenkjar, 2001), it would probably make sense to perform the EFA instead of PCA (as discussed in the last chapter). Let's consider each of the five ways of deciding on the appropriate number of factors when they are applied to the example data.

Kaiser's stopping rule. Kaiser's stopping rule states that only the number of factors with eigenvalues over 1.00 should be considered in the analysis. The initial analysis of the example data indicated that three factors had an eigenvalue of 1.00 or higher (see Table 37.2 which is taken directly from the initial analysis SPSS output). Notice in Table 37.2 that the Factors 1, 2, and 3 (labeled in the first column) have eigenvalues of 3.751, 2.492, and 1.115, respectively. Thus all three are above Kaiser's cut-point of 1.00. Factors 4 to 12 are below that cut-point with values of .851 down to .250.

Table 37.2. *Initial EFA for the 12 Y/GPI Scales Administered in Brazil*

Factor	Initial Eigenvalues		
	Total	% of Variance	Cumulative %
1	3.751	31.257	31.257
2	2.492	20.768	52.025
3	1.115	9.293	61.318
4	.851	7.088	68.407
5	.770	6.413	74.819
6	.605	5.043	79.862
7	.577	4.808	84.670
8	.497	4.144	88.814
9	.444	3.696	92.510
10	.341	2.839	95.349
11	.309	2.571	97.920
12	.250	2.080	100.000

Now consider the results shown in Table 37.3 for a three-factor EFA of the example data (with varimax rotation). Notice that the first column contains labels for the 12 scales. Then the next four columns show the results for the EFA including loadings, communalities (on the right), and proportions of variance (across the bottom). Factor 1 appears to have fairly strong loadings from the six neuroticism scales as expected. Factor 2 also has fairly high loadings from the first, second, fourth, fifth, and sixth extraversion scales. Notice that Rhathymia loads on both factors (such variables are referred to as *complex*. In this case, Rhathymia has a poor positive correlation with Factor 1 and a higher positive correlation with Factor 2). Inferiority feelings also loads on both factors (this variable is also *complex*, but in this case, it has a respectable positive correlation with Factor 1 and a fair negative one with Factor 2). Also, surprisingly, the third extraversion scale (Thinking extraversion) does not load on Factor 1 or 2. Thus this variable does not seem to fit the theory developed in previous research. This result does not mean that the theory was wrong for the types of respondents that participated in the previous research. It does mean, however, that Thinking extraversion does not load on either Factor 1 or 2 for the types of Brazilian university students included in the data analyzed here. Indeed, Thinking extraversion has only one loading worth noting at 0.530, and that loading is just sitting there by itself and not forming a factor that is useful in any way. We will consider this situation further in the ensuing discussion.

Table 37.3. *EFA Loadings for the 12 Y/GPI Scales Administered in Brazil (with Varimax Rotation & Eigenvalues over 1.00)*

Variables	Factor 1	Factor 2	Factor 3	h^2
Social extraversion	-0.135	**0.665**	-0.118	0.474
Ascendance	-0.109	**0.548**	-0.098	0.321
Thinking extraversion	-0.072	-0.026	**0.530**	0.287
Rhathymia	*0.391*	**0.606**	0.206	0.562
General activity	-0.219	**0.680**	-0.070	0.515
Lack of agreeableness	0.119	**0.540**	0.197	0.345
Lack of cooperativeness	**0.466**	0.029	0.060	0.221
Lack of objectivity	**0.614**	0.044	-0.187	0.415
Nervousness	**0.759**	-0.171	-0.021	0.606
Inferiority feelings	**0.677**	**- 0.469**	0.101	0.689
Cyclic tendencies	**0.785**	0.106	-0.005	0.627
Depression	**0.784**	-0.227	-0.076	0.672
Proportion of Variance	0.259	0.182	0.037	0.478

Scree test. Another strategy for examining the eigenvalues is called the scree test.[1] This strategy involves creating a graphic visualization of the relationship between eigenvalues and number of factors, as shown in Figure 37.1. The scree plot is a graph of the relationship between the relative magnitude of the eigenvalues and the number of factors. The researcher examines the scree plot and decides where the line stops descending precipitously and levels out (for more on scree plot interpretation, see

---

[1] Why is it called a scree test? Take a look at Figure 37.1 and try to visualize rocks and debris at the bottom of a cliff. See it? That stuff at the bottom of the cliff is called scree in geology.

Bryant and Yarnold, 1995, pp. 103-104). In the case shown in Figure 37.1, that would appear to happen at three factors. The researcher then ignores all of the points along the level part of the line including the transition point, and counts the points along the precipitously dropping part of the line. Thus this particular scree plot indicates that a two factor solution would be appropriate.

Table 37.4 presents just such a two-factor analysis—one in which all variables either load clearly on Factor 1 or 2 (or are complex, as explained above, in the case of Rhathymia and Inferiority feelings) except for Thinking extraversion, which loads on neither factor.

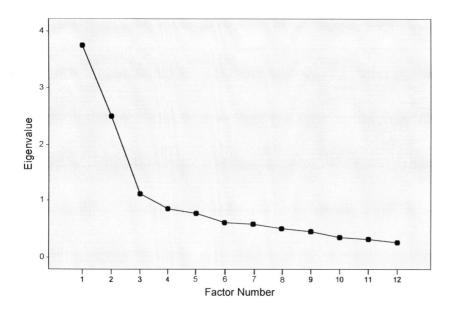

Figure 37.1. Scree Plot for the EFA for the 12 Y/GPI Scales Administered in Brazil

Table 37.4. *EFA (with Varimax Rotation) Loadings for 2 Factors Using the 12 Y/GPI Scales Administered in Brazil*

Variables	Factor 1	Factor 2	h^2
Social extraversion	-0.108	**0.668**	0.458
Ascendance	-0.086	**0.553**	0.314
Thinking extraversion	-0.064	-0.019	0.005
Rhathymia	**0.405**	**0.573**	0.493
General activity	-0.191	**0.692**	0.515
Lack of agreeableness	0.139	**0.527**	0.297
Lack of cooperativeness	**0.468**	0.013	0.219
Lack of objectivity	**0.607**	0.018	0.368
Nervousness	**0.754**	-0.199	0.608
Inferiority feelings	**0.656**	**-0.494**	0.675
Cyclic tendencies	**0.792**	0.077	0.633
Depression	**0.773**	-0.257	0.664
Proportion of Variance	0.255	0.183	0.437

Number of non-trivial factors. Trivial factors are usually defined as those that do not have two or three variables loading above a cut-point, often .30[2]. Table 37.5 shows the loadings from an EFA (with varimax rotation) for an 11-factor solution using the example data. Notice in Table 37.5 that only three factors can be said to have three or more loadings above the cut-point of .30. Factors 5 through 9 are clearly examples of single loading factors, and factors 10 and 11 have no loadings worth considering, while Factor 4 only has two variables loading above the cut-point of .30. All of this would seem to argue for either a three or four-factor solution.

However, there is the possibility that some factors may be trivial. In interpreting trivial and non-trivial factors, it is worth considering that triviality is a matter of degree.

---

[2] Note that Tabachnick and Fidell (2012, p. 651) suggest a cut-point of .32 and above, "then there is 10% or more overlap in variance among factors..."

According to Comrey and Lee (1992), loadings of .71 or higher can be considered "excellent", .63 is "very good", .55 is "good", .45 is "fair", and .32 is "poor". So what magnitude is trivial? Clearly, higher loadings indicate variables that are more highly related to whatever the underlying factor is. Hence, variables with high loadings can be considered purer measures of the underlying factors. This means that two, three, or more loadings higher than .71 are clearly less trivial than say two loadings of .30 or .40.

In Table 37.5, based on the number of loadings and their absolute magnitude, it could be argued that Factors 1 and 2 are less trivial than say Factors 3 and 4. The problem is that triviality may be in the eye of the beholder.

A priori criterion. If the researcher were replicating previous research wherein a specific number of factors were found, it would make sense to set that same number of factors in the replication research. Similarly, if a researcher has created a set of test or questionnaire items to contain a specific number of subtests or scales, it would make sense to set that same number of factors in the factor analysis of those items. These are known as a priori criteria for determining the number of factors. For example, in previous research on the Y/GPI, the 12 subscales were shown to fall into two general categories: extroversion and neuroticism. Thus, a two factor solution for the example data (as shown in Table 37.4) would make theoretical sense based on a priori criteria drawn from previous research.

Percentage of cumulative variance. An approach that is closely related to Kaiser's stopping rule and the scree plot is the percentage of cumulative variance. However, percentages of cumulative variance are harder to interpret than the other two. Clearly, in the example study, a 12 variable solution in a PCA would account for 100% of the variance, but as shown in Table 37.1, that would tell the researcher nothing. So some smaller number of factors should be sought. Looking down the far right column in Table 37.2 reveals the percentages of cumulative variance for various numbers of factors in that analysis. The addition of each factor adds some new variance to the cumulative variance. So where should the researcher stop? It is impossible to say.

Table 37.5. *EFA Loadings for 11 Factors[3] Using the Y/GPI Scales Administered in Brazil (with Varimax Rotation)*

Variables	Factors											
	1	2	3	4	5	6	7	8	9	10	11	h^2
Social extraversion	-0.161	*0.397*	*0.433*	-0.086	0.140	-0.140	-0.008	*0.433*	-0.004	-0.003	0.009	0.606
Ascendance	-0.073	0.176	*0.704*	-0.018	0.106	0.015	0.042	0.044	-0.018	0.006	0.004	0.547
Thinking extraversion	-0.058	0.060	-0.013	0.018	-0.040	*0.620*	-0.045	-0.022	-0.007	-0.001	0.002	0.396
Rhathymia	0.236	*0.688*	0.115	0.007	0.182	0.123	0.237	0.134	0.247	0.103	-0.004	0.736
General activity	-0.238	*0.376*	*0.371*	0.081	*0.637*	-0.157	-0.114	0.079	-0.033	-0.008	-0.006	0.794
Lack of agreeableness	0.008	*0.615*	0.176	0.089	0.044	0.046	-0.049	-0.007	-0.093	-0.033	-0.006	0.433
Lack of cooperativeness	0.256	0.091	-0.025	*0.702*	0.046	0.037	0.064	-0.021	0.009	0.004	0.004	0.575
Lack of objectivity	*0.470*	0.082	0.063	0.180	-0.129	-0.176	*0.501*	-0.007	0.038	0.006	0.006	0.564
Nervousness	*0.820*	-0.020	-0.113	0.164	-0.004	-0.026	0.040	-0.064	0.052	-0.117	-0.044	0.737
Inferiority feelings	*0.675*	-0.209	-0.441	0.266	-0.093	0.103	0.111	0.153	-0.071	0.005	0.199	0.864
Cyclic tendencies	*0.752*	0.286	0.008	0.111	-0.107	-0.081	0.143	-0.067	0.001	0.206	-0.002	0.746
Depression	*0.604*	-0.009	-0.155	*0.439*	-0.294	-0.134	0.121	-0.045	0.399	-0.026	-0.013	0.862
Proportions of Variance	0.208	0.110	0.092	0.071	0.050	0.043	0.032	0.021	0.020	0.006	0.004	0.655

As a result interpreting the percentages of cumulative variance is more a matter of keeping an eye on the amount of cumulative variance being accounted for by various other stopping rules. Close examination of the far right column in Table 37.2 indicates that 61.318% of the variance is accounted for if the three-factor solution (based on Kaiser's stopping rule) is used, but, if the two factor solution is adopted (based on the scree test), only 52.025% of the variance is accounted for.

---

[3] Asking for 12 factors in an EFA with varimax rotation, SPSS warns: "You cannot request as many factors as variables with any extraction method except PC. The number of factors will be reduced by one."

Conclusion

Clearly, there are a number of different ways to look at the issue of deciding how many components or factors to include in a PCA or EFA. I discussed Kaiser's stopping rule, the scree test, number of non-trivial factors, a priori criterion, and percentage of cumulative variance as different ways to make such decisions. Each of these methods indicated that there should be either two or three factors for the example data. But which method is correct? I guess the safest answer is that no method is correct. Instead, some combination of the five sets of issues must be included in making the decision and explaining it to the readers of the resulting research report. The trick is to make the strongest possible set of arguments for why a particular number of factors were selected in a particular analysis. If an a priori criterion argument can be included, that may prove the most convincing and useful, but the point is that the argument for the number of components or factors should be based on a combination of information from the five viewpoints explained here.

In the case of the example data used here, there was indeed a theory-based a priori criterion of two factors. In addition, the scree plot indicated that a two-factor solution was appropriate, and the percentage of variance accounted for by a two-factor solution is about 44% (see bottom right corner of Table 37.4). Finally, three-factor solutions tended to produce a trivial third factor, while two-factor solutions clearly produced two non-trivial factors. Based on all of these considerations, I am most comfortable interpreting the two-factor solution.

Two things should be clear in this discussion of how researchers decide on the number of factors to include in a PCA or EFA. First, the decision must be based on the preponderance of evidence from all five perspectives on the issue. Second, this is not a clear-cut decision based on a set of yes/no questions; there is an art to deciding on and explaining why you decided on a specific number of components or factors. And, third, the abilities needed for making such decisions and explaining them to readers improve over time (though they will never be perfect), so don't be afraid to critically read the explanations provided by researchers in second language studies, and indeed if you have testing, questionnaire, or other appropriate data of your own, don't hesitate to dive in and see what you find with a PCA or EFA.

(updated and reprinted from Brown, 2009b)

CHAPTER 38

CHOOSING THE RIGHT TYPE OF ROTATION IN PCA AND EFA

QUESTION: In Chapter 7 of the 2008 book on heritage language learning that you co-edited with Kimi Kondo-Brown, there is a study (Lee & Kim, 2008) comparing the attitudes of 111 Korean heritage language learners. On page 167 of that book, a principal components analysis (with varimax rotation) describes the relation of examining 16 purported reasons for studying Korean with four broader factors. Several questions come to mind. What is a principal components analysis? How does principal components analysis differ from factor analysis? What guidelines do researchers need to bear in mind when selecting "factors"? And finally, what is a varimax rotation and why is it applied?

ANSWER: This is an interesting question, but a big one, made up of at least four sets of sub-questions: (a) what are principal components analysis (PCA) and exploratory factor analysis (EFA), how are they different, and how do researchers decide which to use? (b) How do investigators determine the number of components or factors to include in the analysis? (c) What is rotation, what are the different types, and how do researchers decide which particular type of rotation to use? And, (d) how are PCA and EFA used in language test and questionnaire development? I addressed the first two questions in previous chapters. I'll attend to the third one here, and address the last one in the next two chapters.

What is rotation?

In the PCA/EFA literature, definitions of *rotation* abound. For example, McDonald (1985, p. 40) defines rotation as "performing arithmetic to obtain a new set of factor loadings (v-f regression weights) from a given set," and Bryant and Yarnold (1995, p. 132) define it as "a procedure in which the eigenvectors (factors) are rotated in an attempt to achieve simple structure." Perhaps a bit more helpful is the definition supplied in Vogt

(1993, p. 91): "Any of several methods in factor analysis by which the researcher attempts to relate the calculated factors to theoretical entities. This is done differently depending upon whether the factors are believed to be correlated (oblique) or uncorrelated (orthogonal)." And even more helpful is Yaremko, Harari, Harrison, and Lynn (1986), who define factor rotation as follows: "In factor or principal-components analysis, rotation of the factor axes (dimensions) identified in the initial extraction of factors, in order to obtain simple and interpretable factors." They then go on to explain and list some of the types of orthogonal and oblique procedures.

How can a concept with a goal of simplification be so complicated? Let me try defining *rotation* from the perspective of a language researcher, while trying to keep it simple. I think of rotation as any of a variety of methods (explained below) used to further analyze initial PCA or EFA results with the goal of making the pattern of loadings clearer, or more pronounced. This process is designed to reveal the simple structure. The choices that researchers make among the orthogonal and oblique varieties of these rotation methods and the notion of simple structure will be the main topics in the rest of this chapter.

What are the different types of rotation?

As mentioned earlier, rotation methods are either orthogonal or oblique. Simply put, *orthogonal rotation* methods assume that the factors in the analysis are *uncorrelated*. Gorsuch (1983, pp. 203-204) lists four different orthogonal methods: equamax, orthomax, quartimax, and varimax. In contrast, *oblique rotation* methods assume that the factors are *correlated*. Gorsuch (1983, pp. 203-204) lists 15 different oblique methods.[1]

Version 16 of SPSS offers five rotation methods: varimax, direct oblimin, quartimax, equamax, and promax, in that order. Three of those are orthogonal (varimax, quartimax, & equamax), and two are oblique (direct oblimin & promax). Factor analysis is not the focus of my life, nor am I eager to learn how to use a new statistical program

---

[1] FYI, the 15 oblique methods are binormamin, biquartimin, covarimin, direct oblimin, indirect oblimin, maxplane, oblinorm, oblimax, obliquimax, optres, orthoblique, orthotran, promax, quartimin, and tandem criteria.

or calculate rotations by hand (though I'm sure I could do it if I had a couple of spare weeks), so those five SPSS options serve as boundaries for the choices I make. But how should I choose which one to use?

Tabachnick and Fiddell (2012, p. 651) argue that "Perhaps the best way to decide between orthogonal and oblique rotation is to request oblique rotation [e.g., direct oblimin or promax from SPSS] with the desired number of factors [see Brown, 2009b [Chapter 37]] and look at the correlations among factors...if factor correlations are not driven by the data, the solution remains nearly orthogonal. Look at the factor correlation matrix for correlations around .32 and above. If correlations exceed .32, then there is 10% (or more) overlap in variance among factors, enough variance to warrant oblique rotation unless there are compelling reasons for orthogonal rotation."

For example, using the same Brazilian data I used for examples in the previous two chapters (based on the 12 subtests of the *Y/G Personality Inventory* from Guilford & Yatabe, 1957), I ran a three-factor EFA followed by a direct oblimin rotation. The resulting correlation matrix for the factors that the analysis produced is shown in Table 38.1. Notice that the highest correlation is .084. Since none of the correlations exceeds the Tabachnick and Fiddell threshold of .32 described in the previous paragraph, "the solution remains nearly orthogonal." Thus, I could just as well run an orthogonal rotation.

Table 38.1. *Correlation Matrix for the Three Factors in an EFA with Direct Oblimin Rotation for the Brazilian Y/GPI Data*

Factor	1	2	3
1	1.000	-0.082	0.084
2	-0.082	1.000	-0.001
3	0.084	-0.001	1.000

Moreover, as Kim and Mueller put it, "Even the issue of whether factors are correlated or not may not make much difference in the exploratory stages of analysis. It even can be argued that employing a method of orthogonal rotation (or maintaining the arbitrary imposition that the factors remain orthogonal) may be preferred over oblique rotation, if for no other reason than that the former is much simpler to understand and interpret" (1978, p. 50).

How do researchers decide which particular type of rotation to use?

We can think of the goal of rotation and of choosing a particular type of rotation as seeking something called simple structure, or put another way, one way we know if we have selected an adequate rotation method is if the results achieve simple structure. But what is simple structure? Bryant and Yarnold (1995, p. 132-133) define *simple structure* as:

> A condition in which variables load at near 1 (in absolute value) or at near 0 on an eigenvector (factor). Variables that load near 1 are clearly important in the interpretation of the factor, and variables that load near 0 are clearly unimportant. Simple structure thus simplifies the task of interpreting the factors.

Using logic like that in the preceding quote, Thurstone (1947) first proposed and argued for five criteria that needed to be met for simple structure to be achieved:

1. Each variable should produce at least one zero loading on some factor.
2. Each factor should have at least as many zero loadings as there are factors.
3. Each pair of factors should have variables with significant loadings on one and zero loadings on the other.
4. Each pair of factors should have a large proportion of zero loadings on both factors (if there are say four or more factors total).
5. Each pair of factors should have only a few complex variables.

In order to understand Thurstone's five criteria, you will need to understand a few more concepts:

1. What's a *zero loading*? One rule of thumb (after Gorsuch, 1983, p. 180) is that zero loadings include any that fall between -.10 and +.10.
2. What's a *significant loading*? With a sample size of say 100 participants, loadings of .30 or higher can be considered significant, or at least salient (see discussion in Kline, 2002, pp. 52-53). With much larger samples, even smaller loadings could be considered salient, but in language research, researchers typically take note of loadings of .30 or higher.
3. And what are *complex variables*? Simply put, these are variables with loadings of .30 or higher on more than one factor.

Now, try going back through Thurstone's five criteria with those three definitions at hand.

Moving towards simplicity . . .

Is achieving simple structure important? Experts in factor analysis seem to think that an abbreviated version of simple structure is important. For example, Kline (2002, p. 66) says, "...I am in agreement with Cattell [1978] and all serious workers in factor analysis that the attainment of simple structure is essential to factor analysis. Where this has not been done there is little reason to take the results seriously." One page earlier, Kline (2002, p. 65) appears considerably more flexible when he says that "Thurstone proposed five criteria for deciding on simple structure, although two of these are of overriding importance, namely that each factor should have a few high loadings with the rest of the loadings being zero or close to zero...Certainly the strict Thurstonian approach is no longer followed." To resolve the apparent contradiction in Kline's views, you need only realize that he is no doubt referring to the less strict definition of simple structure in both statements.

Other experts also appear to use less strict definitions of simple structure, especially when considering what rotation procedure to use in achieving it. For example, Kim and Mueller (1978, p. 50) argue that, "If identification of the basic structuring of variables into theoretically meaningful subdimensions is the primary concern of the researcher, as is often the case in an exploratory factor analysis, almost any readily available method of rotation will do the job." To explore their view, I tried rotating the EFA results for the Brazil data using three orthogonal methods (see Table 38.2) and two oblique methods (see Table 38.3). All of those rotations produced essentially the same pattern of loadings. Put another way, the literature indicates that the choice of rotation may not make much difference; certainly, in language research situations like the one that led to the analyses shown in Tables 38.2 and 38.3, where the factors are not markedly correlated (as demonstrated above), the choice from among those options available in SPSS (whether orthogonal or oblique) appears to make very little difference.

As Gorsuch (1983, p. 205) put it, "If the simple structure is clear, any of the more popular procedures can be expected to lead to the same interpretations." He then recommends rotating with varimax [orthogonal] or promax [oblique]. Kim and Mueller (1978, p. 50) conclude by saying, "We advise that beginners choose one of the commonly available methods of rotation, such as Varimax if orthogonal rotation is sought or Direct Oblimin if oblique rotation is sought. [For more on determining the adequacy of rotation, see Tabachnick & Fiddell, 2012, pp. 651-652]

Table 38.2. *Three Orthogonal Rotations of the Brazil Data*

	Varimax Rotation			Quartimax Rotation			Equamax Rotation		
	Factor			Factor			Factor		
Trait	1	2	3	1	2	3	1	2	3
Social extraversion	-0.135	**0.665**	-0.118	-0.146	**0.662**	-0.122	-0.129	**0.666**	-0.115
Ascendance	-0.109	**0.548**	-0.098	-0.118	**0.545**	-0.100	-0.104	**0.549**	-0.095
Thinking extraversion	-0.072	-0.026	**0.530**	-0.072	-0.024	**0.530**	-0.073	-0.028	**0.530**
Rhathymia	**0.391**	**0.606**	0.206	**0.381**	**0.613**	0.203	**0.396**	**0.602**	0.209
General activity	-0.219	**0.680**	-0.070	-0.230	**0.676**	-0.073	-0.213	**0.682**	-0.067
Lack of agreeableness	0.119	**0.540**	0.197	0.110	**0.543**	0.194	0.124	**0.538**	0.199
Lack of cooperativeness	**0.466**	0.029	0.060	**0.465**	0.037	0.060	**0.466**	0.025	0.060
Lack of objectivity	**0.614**	0.044	-0.187	**0.614**	0.053	-0.188	**0.615**	0.039	-0.187
Nervousness	**0.759**	-0.171	-0.021	**0.762**	-0.158	-0.020	**0.758**	-0.177	-0.021
Inferiority feelings	**0.677**	**-0.469**	0.101	**0.685**	**-0.457**	0.104	**0.673**	-0.476	0.099
Cyclic tendencies	**0.785**	0.106	-0.005	**0.783**	0.119	-0.006	**0.785**	0.099	-0.004
Depression	**0.784**	-0.227	-0.076	**0.788**	-0.214	-0.076	**0.782**	-0.234	-0.077

Table 38.3. *Two Oblique Rotations of the Brazil Data*

	Oblimin Rotation			Promax Rotation		
	Factor			Factor		
Trait	1	2	3	1	2	3
Social extraversion	-0.169	**0.666**	-0.139	-0.200	**0.672**	-0.125
Ascendance	-0.137	**0.549**	-0.115	-0.163	**0.553**	-0.103
Thinking extraversion	-0.070	-0.015	**0.523**	-0.057	-0.014	**0.492**
Rhathymia	**0.360**	**0.597**	0.227	**0.336**	**0.575**	0.322
General activity	-0.254	**0.685**	-0.098	-0.284	**0.695**	-0.100
Lack of agreeableness	0.092	**0.540**	0.198	0.072	**0.531**	0.241
Lack of cooperativeness	**0.464**	0.016	0.097	**0.462**	-0.008	0.180
Lack of objectivity	**0.611**	0.022	-0.138	**0.603**	-0.008	-0.019
Nervousness	**0.767**	-0.194	0.043	**0.771**	-0.231	0.172
Inferiority feelings	**0.700**	**-0.488**	0.163	**0.721**	**-0.521**	0.258
Cyclic tendencies	**0.778**	0.082	0.057	**0.771**	0.042	0.204
Depression	**0.794**	-0.252	-0.010	**0.800**	-0.290	0.123

Conclusion

What should second language researchers do in selecting a rotation method for a PCA or EFA in their research? At minimum, it seems useful to try one oblique rotation method (e.g., direct oblimin or promax, while examining the factor correlation matrix for values over ±0.32, using the criterion explained in Tabachnick & Fiddell, 2012, p. 651) and one orthogonal rotation method (e.g., the ever-popular varimax rotation). Also consider whether there are any theoretical reasons why an orthogonal method might be preferable to an oblique method or vice versa. Above all, the rotated results should be examined for simple structure, at least following Kline's (2002, p. 65) relatively flexible definition: "…that each factor should have a few high loadings with the rest of the loadings being zero or close to zero…" (i.e., less than ±0.10 after Gorsuch, 1983, p. 180).

Coming back to the original question at the top of this chapter (about the Lee & Kim, 2008, study), did they try using at least one oblique and one orthogonal rotation method (while examining oblique rotation factor correlation matrix for values lower than ±0.32)? We have no way of knowing because the researchers did not discuss how or why they chose varimax rotation. Is that a capital crime? Their study would have been clearer if they had provided such an explanation. But no, it is not a capital crime, especially if they successfully achieved a simpler structure in the end. Table 38.4 shows their results. Notice that two to six variables have high loadings on each factor and that most of the rest of the loadings are zero (i.e., below ±0.10) or close to zero. However, it is troubling that five of the variables are complex in the sense that they have loadings above .30 on two or three factors. These indicate that, while the pattern of loadings is strong overall, there is some complexity. More about this in the next chapter.

Table 38.4. *Principal Components Analysis (with Varimax Rotation) for Motivation Items*

	Instrumental		Integrative		
	Factor 1	Factor 2	Factor 3	Factor 4	h^2
	School related	Career related	Personal fulfillment	Ethnic Heritage	
I learn Korean to transfer credits to college.	**0.83**	0.01	0.17	-0.11	**0.72**
I learn Korean because my friend recommended it.	**0.82**	0.14	0.06	0.22	**0.74**
I learn Korean because my advisor recommended it.	**0.80**	0.10	**0.36**	0.04	**0.78**
I learn Korean because of the reputation of the program and instructor.	**0.77**	0.12	0.12	0.22	**0.67**
I learn Korean for an easy A.	**0.69**	0.18	-0.29	0.16	**0.61**
I learn Korean to fulfill a graduation requirement.	**0.63**	0.11	0.19	-0.18	**0.47**
I learn Korean to get a better job.	0.04	**0.80**	0.20	0.11	**0.69**
I learn Korean because I plan to work overseas.	0.26	**0.80**	0.11	0.10	**0.75**
I learn Korean because of the status of Korean in the world.	0.10	**0.73**	0.20	0.22	**0.63**
I learn Korean to use it for my research.	**0.38**	**0.48**	**0.44**	0.10	**0.58**
I learn Korean to further my global understanding.	0.16	**0.33**	**0.71**	0.08	**0.65**
I learn Korean because I have an interest in Korean literature.	0.18	0.04	**0.64**	0.13	**0.56**
I learn Korean because it is fun and challenging.	0.04	0.04	**0.63**	**0.46**	**0.63**
I learn Korean because I have a general interest in languages.	0.11	0.03	**0.57**	**0.51**	**0.59**
I learn Korean because it is the language of my family heritage.	-0.01	0.26	0.05	**0.80**	**0.71**
I learn Korean because of my acquaintances with Korean speakers.	0.10	0.21	0.20	**0.70**	**0.58**
% of variance explained by each factor	**0.23**	**0.15**	**0.14**	**0.12**	**0.64**

Extraction Method: Principal Component Analysis. Rotation Method: Varimax with Kaiser Normalization. Eigenvalue > 1.00.

(updated and reprinted from Brown, 2009c)

CHAPTER 39

HOW ARE PCA AND EFA USED IN LANGUAGE RESEARCH?

QUESTION: In Chapter 7 of the 2008 book on heritage language learning that you co-edited with Kimi Kondo-Brown, there's a study (Lee & Kim, 2008) comparing the attitudes of 111 Korean heritage language learners. On page 167 of that book, a principal components analysis (with varimax rotation) describes the relation of examining 16 purported reasons for studying Korean with four broader factors. Several questions come to mind. What is a principal components analysis? How does principal components analysis differ from factor analysis? What guidelines do researchers need to bear in mind when selecting "factors"? And finally, what is a Varimax rotation and why is it applied?

ANSWER: Those are interesting questions and imply at least five sub-questions: (a) What are principal components analysis (PCA) and exploratory factor analysis (EFA), how do they differ, and how do researchers decide which to use? (b) How do investigators determine the number of components or factors to include? (c) What is rotation, and the most common rotation types, and how do researchers decide which to use? (d) How are PCA and EFA employed in language research? And, (e) how are PCA and EFA used in language test and questionnaire development? I addressed the first three questions (a, b, & c) in previous chapters. I'll attend to the fourth one (d) here, and the fifth one in the next chapter.

So how are PCA and EFA used in language research? I have found at least three uses for these forms of analysis in my research:

1. Reducing the number of variables in a study
2. Exploring patterns in the correlations among variables
3. Supporting a theory of how variables are related

Let's consider each of these issues individually.

Reducing the number of variables in a study

One of the primary uses of factor analyses is to reduce the number of variables in a study. In second language research, we are often dealing with large numbers of variables. Unfortunately, large sets of variables tend to reduce the statistical power of a study (i.e., reduce the possibility of finding statistically significant results even if such results exist in the population). We can often strengthen a study by eliminating redundant variables that are doing pretty much the same thing as other variables.

The fact that PCA and EFA are often used for reducing redundancy among variables is evident in the design of the SPSS statistical software, where PCA and EFA are found in the menu system in version 16 or earlier under **Analyze** then submenus **Data reduction** and **Factor** (or in version 17 under **Analyze** then submenus **Dimension reduction** and **Factor**).

An example of how such data reduction can be applied is found in Brown (1998c), where I used PCA to help reduce 44 variables (various linguistic characteristics of the blanks in 50 cloze passages) to what turned out to be the four most important and relatively orthogonal (i.e., independent, or non-redundant) variables. As I put it in Brown (1998c, pp. 19-20, 24):

> Factor analysis techniques, including principal components analysis and Varimax rotation, were used to investigate the degree to which variables were orthogonal (independent of each other). ... A large number of linguistic variables were also examined for relationship to EFL Difficulty. Four of these variables were selected on the basis of factor analysis as being orthogonal: syllables per sentence, average frequency elsewhere in the passage of the words that had been deleted, the percent of long words of seven letters or more, and the percent of function words. When combined, they proved to be the best predictors of observed EFL Difficulty.

The mechanics of reducing the number of variables in a study can be accomplished in several ways: (a) by going factor-by-factor and using whichever variable loads highest on the first factor to represent all the other variables that load heavily on that factor, then turning to the second factor and doing the same thing, and then turning to the third factor, etc., or (b) by saving and using the component or factor scores (that are produced during the PCA or EFA analyses) as variables to represent the components or factors in the study. Clearly then, one way to use factor analyses is for reducing the number of variables in a study and thereby increasing the power of the study.

Exploring patterns in the correlations among variables

Correlational analysis is very common in second language studies. Research articles often present correlation matrices of all intercorrelations among 5, 10, 20, or more variables, replete with asterisks showing which were significant at $p < .05$, or $p < .01$, or both. Interpreting overall patterns in such matrices by simply eye-balling them is difficult for at least three reasons: (a) each correlation coefficient only represents the degree of relationship between two variables, (b) the p values in large sets of correlation coefficients are accurate for any one pair of variables, but not for the entire set, (c) the underlying sample sizes, distributions, and reliabilities can differ substantially among variables and sometimes dramatically affect the magnitude of the resulting correlation coefficients.

PCA and EFA provide tools that can help explore a correlation matrix and find overall patterns that may exist among the correlations. For example, in Brown (2001g), I analyzed (based on data first gathered and analyzed for Yamashita, 1996, by permission) six types of pragmatics tests: Written Discourse Completion Tasks (WDCT), Multiple-choice DCTs (MDCT), Oral DCTs (ODCT), Discourse Role Play Tasks (DRPT), Discourse Self-Assessment Tasks (DSAT), and Role Play Self Assessments (RPSA). The six tests were all administered in Japan to native-speakers of English learning Japanese as a second language (JSL). All possible correlations for these six pragmatics tests are shown below the diagonal line of 1.00s in Table 39.1. Coefficients of determination, i.e., the squared correlation coefficients, are shown above the diagonal.

Table 39.1. *Correlation Coefficients (Below the Diagonal) and Coefficients of Determination (Above the Diagonal) for the JSL Data*

JSL	WDCT	MDCT	ODCT	DRPT	DSAT	RPSA
WDCT	1.00	0.15	0.45	0.34	0.24	0.16
MDCT	0.39*	1.00	0.14	0.06	0.01	0.03
ODCT	0.67*	0.37*	1.00	0.62	0.31	0.24
DRPT	0.58*	0.24	0.79*	1.00	0.37	0.28
DSAT	0.49*	0.11	0.56*	0.61*	1.00	0.47
RPSA	0.40*	0.18	0.49*	0.53*	0.68*	1.00

*$p < .01$

Notice that the patterns of correlations in Table 39.1 are not very interesting. Sure, 12 of the correlation coefficients in Table 39.1 are significant at $p < .01$. But even with all these significant correlation coefficients, each coefficient only tells us about the degree of relationship between whatever two variables are involved. No amount of staring at Table 39.1 leads to any interesting pattern of overall relationships (except, perhaps, that the MDCT didn't correlate well with any other measure). In addition, there is no way of knowing from Table 39.1 (a) how much differences in the sample sizes, distributions of scores, and test reliabilities of the variables may have affected the relative values of these correlation coefficients, or (b) the degree to which the number of correlation coefficients has distorted the meaning of the p values.

However, a factor analysis of the same data can be much more revealing (see Table 39.2). Notice in Table 39.2 that the highest loadings for each variable (in bold type) indicate that the ODCT, DRPT, DSAT, and RPSA all load most heavily on the first factor, while the WDCT and MDCT load more heavily on the second factor. Because the ODCT, DRPT, DSAT, and RPSA are all tests of oral abilities, the first factor could be labeled as an oral-language factor. In contrast, the WDCT and MDCT can both be considered written-language tests, so factor two might appropriately be labeled a written-language factor. These oral-language and written-language categories were interpreted in the original paper as test method factors. Note, however, that this argument is somewhat undermined by the fact that consideration of all loadings above .30 (i.e., those with asterisks) shows a pattern that was not quite so clear because the WDCT, ODCT, and DRPT are complex, that is, all three load to some meaningful degree on both factors. Nonetheless, the original paper interpreted these patterns as indications of test-method effects—an interpretation that would not have been possible based on the correlation matrix alone.

Clearly then, while it is often difficult to detect patterns in correlation matrices, factor analysis techniques can reveal interesting and interpretable patterns among those same correlation coefficients. However, researchers must take great care in interpreting such patterns, especially insuring that they have looked for complexity and that they only name components or factors very carefully and tentatively based on what they *think* is going on.

Table 39.2. *Factor Analysis of JSL Data (after VARIMAX rotation)*

VARIABLE	FACTOR 1	FACTOR 2	h^2
WDCT	*.56	***.61**	.68
MDCT	-.02	***.90**	.82
ODCT	**.70**	*.54	.78
DRPT	**.78**	*.36	.74
DSAT	**.89**	.03	.79
RPSA	**.82**	.04	.68
Proportion of Variance	.48	.27	.75

*Note. Bold-faced type indicates highest loading for each variable.
Asterisks show all loadings over .30.

Supporting a theory of how variables are related

Sometimes researchers have a theory of how variables should be related to each other. Such was the case in Brown, Rosenkjar, and Robson (2001), where among other things, we examined the *Y/G Personality Inventory* (Y/GPI) (Guilford & Yatabe, 1957), which assesses twelve traits (social extraversion, ascendance, thinking extraversion, rhathymia, general activity, lack of agreeableness, lack of cooperativeness, lack of objectivity, nervousness, inferiority feelings, cyclic tendencies, and depression) with ten items per trait.

Previous research had consistently shown that these twelve traits fall into two general categories labeled neuroticism and extraversion (the first six traits representing extraversion and the last six representing neuroticism). The results shown in Table 39.3 are for Brazilian university students taking the Y/GPI. With the exception of *Thinking extraversion*, the bold-faced italics loadings are in exactly the pattern of relationships that theory would predict.

However, there is also some evidence that these data do not fit the theory. First, *Thinking extraversion* does not load strongly on either factor, perhaps because the participants were Brazilian, or for some other reason. In addition, *Rhathymia* and *Inferiority feelings* load higher than .30 on both factors. So these variables are complex for this data set.

Table 39.3. *Two-Factor Analysis (with Varimax rotation) of the 12 Variables of Question on the Y/G Personality Inventory*

Variables	Rotated 2 Factors		
	Factor 1	Factor 2	h^2
Social extraversion	-0.108	**0.668**	0.458
Ascendance	-0.086	**0.553**	0.314
Thinking extraversion	-0.064	-0.019	0.005
Rhathymia	0.405	**0.573**	0.493
General activity	-0.191	**0.692**	0.515
Lack of agreeableness	0.139	**0.527**	0.297
Lack of cooperativeness	**0.468**	0.013	0.219
Lack of objectivity	**0.607**	0.018	0.368
Nervousness	**0.754**	-0.199	0.608
Inferiority feelings	**0.656**	-0.494	0.675
Cyclic tendencies	**0.792**	0.077	0.633
Depression	**0.773**	-0.257	0.664
Proportion of Variance	0.255	0.183	0.437

Conclusion

Whether or not the patterns found in the data are 100% clear, the underlying complexities, and discrepancies from theory can be very interesting. Such complexities and discrepancies can even serve as the basis for carefully revising or refining the theories that are being examined.

Many researchers use factor analysis for one reason or another without realizing the rich variety of other purposes this form of analysis can serve. I've shown here that EFA and PCA have applications in language research that include at least reducing the number of variables in a study, exploring patterns in the correlations among variables, and supporting a theory of how variables are related. In the next chapter, I will discuss three ways EFA and PCA are often used in test or questionnaire development projects.

If you are currently using EFA and PCA, consider expanding the ways you apply these analyses. If you are *not* currently using EFA and PCA, you might want to ask yourself, why not?

(updated and reprinted from Brown, 2010a)

CHAPTER 40

HOW ARE PCA AND EFA USED IN LANGUAGE TEST AND QUESTIONNAIRE DEVELOPMENT?

QUESTION: In Chapter 7 of the 2008 book on heritage language learning that you co-edited with Kimi Kondo-Brown, there is a study (Lee & Kim, 2008) comparing the attitudes of 111 Korean heritage language learners. On page 167 of that book, a principal components analysis (with varimax rotation) describes the relation of examining 16 purported reasons for studying Korean with four broader factors. Several questions come to mind. What is a principal components analysis? How does principal components analysis differ from factor analysis? What guidelines do researchers need to bear in mind when selecting "factors"? And finally, what is a Varimax rotation and why is it applied?

ANSWER: This is an interesting question, but a big one, made up of at least five sets of sub-questions: (a) What are principal components analysis (PCA) and exploratory factor analysis (EFA), how are they different, and how do researchers decide which to use? (b) How do investigators determine the number of components or factors to include in the analysis? (c) What is rotation, what are the different types, and how do researchers decide which to use? (d) How are PCA and EFA used in language research? And, (e) how are PCA and EFA used in language test and questionnaire development? I addressed the first four questions (a, b, c, & d) in previous chapters. I'll attend to the fifth one (e) here.

So how are PCA and EFA used in language test and questionnaire development? I have found at least three uses for these forms of analysis in developing my tests and questionnaires:

1. Conducting item/subscale analysis to strengthen a test or questionnaire

2. Studying the relative proportions of total, reliable, common, unique, specific, and error variances

3. Providing evidence for convergent and discriminant validity

Let's consider each of these issues individually.

Conducting item/subscale analysis to strengthen a test or questionnaire

One use for PCA or EFA is to conduct item (or subscale) analysis with the goal of revising and strengthening a test or questionnaire. For example, notice in the first three columns of numbers in Table 40.1 (based on a set of data used in the previous chapter) that the *Thinking extraversion* variable is not loading in any meaningful way on either factor even though the questionnaire as a whole was designed to measure two clear sets of factors: extraversion (the first six variables) and neuroticism (the last six variables). Table 40.1 shows what happened when this set of data was analyzed with and without the *Thinking extraversion* variable.

Notice that the analysis with *Thinking extraversion* only accounts for 43.7 percent of the variance (see the bottom of the third column of numbers), while the analysis that left out *Thinking extraversion* accounts for 47.7% (see bottom of the sixth column of numbers). Thus when *Thinking extraversion* is eliminated, the subscales collectively are more clearly measuring extraversion and neuroticism (i.e., all subscales are loading more highly on one or the other of the extraversion factor or neuroticism factor) as predicted by theory. On the basis of this sort of analysis, researchers might choose to revise and improve the questionnaire so that it will work better with the particular group of respondents being studied.

Similarly, *items* can be the objects of this sort of analysis. For example, factor analysis can be used to identify items that are not loading heavily on the subtest into which they were designed to fit. There may be many reasons for such results, but nonetheless, such items are potentially measuring something different from the other items in the same subtest, so getting rid of these items and re-analyzing the data without them may be useful in revising whatever test or questionnaire is involved. In short, factor analysis can be used as a back-and-forth tool for eliminating items that don't work, and/or adding more items like the ones that do work, then re-administering the instrument and examining the degree to which the revised set of items is measuring what it was designed to measure.

Table 40.1. *Two-Factor Factor Analysis (with Varimax rotation) of the Y/G Personality Inventory with and without Thinking Extraversion*

Variables	Rotated 2 Factors (with Thinking extraversion)			Rotated 2 Factors (without Thinking extraversion)		
	Factor 1	Factor 2	h^2	Factor 1	Factor 2	h^2
Social extraversion	-0.108	*0.668*	0.458	-0.142	*0.660*	0.456
Ascendance	-0.086	*0.553*	0.314	-0.113	*0.548*	0.313
Thinking extraversion	-0.064	-0.019	0.005			
Rhathymia	0.405	*0.573*	0.493	0.381	*0.596*	0.501
General activity	-0.191	*0.692*	0.515	-0.225	*0.680*	0.513
Lack of agreeableness	0.139	*0.527*	0.297	0.116	*0.535*	0.299
Lack of cooperativeness	*0.468*	0.013	0.219	*0.468*	0.036	0.220
Lack of objectivity	*0.607*	0.018	0.368	*0.602*	0.045	0.364
Nervousness	*0.754*	-0.199	0.608	*0.762*	-0.164	0.608
Inferiority feelings	*0.656*	-0.494	0.675	*0.681*	-0.462	0.677
Cyclic tendencies	*0.792*	0.077	0.633	*0.786*	0.114	0.632
Depression	*0.773*	-0.257	0.664	*0.783*	-0.221	0.662
Proportion of Variance	0.255	0.183	0.437	0.258	0.179	0.477

Studying the relative proportions of total, reliable, common, unique, specific, and error variances

I'm assuming that everybody reading this chapter understands that test variance can be interpreted as including total variance, true score variance, and error variance (to review, see Brown, 2005c, 169-175). PCA and EFA can help us further understand the proportions of other sorts of variances in collections of variables, subtests, tests, subsections, or questionnaires (all referred to here as variables). More explicitly, PCA and EFA techniques can be used to examine the proportions of *total variance, reliable variance, common variance, unique variance, specific variance,* and *error variance* among variables within a test or questionnaire. Definitions of these concepts follow:

- *total variance* – all the variance in a set of variables; also the reliable + error variances; or common + unique variances; or common + specific + error variances (see Figure 40.1)

- *reliable variance* – the variance in a set of variables that is reproducible, i.e., "that proportion of the data variability that remains constant through replication" (Rummel, 1970, p. 103)
- *common variance* – variance that each variable shares with other variables in "what can be explained by component factors which are real combinations of variables in the scores matrix" (Kline, 2000, p. 131)
- *unique variance* – variance in each variable that is not shared with any of the other variables; or specific + error variance (see Figure 40.1)
- *specific variance* – variance in each variable that is not shared with any other variable minus error variance; or that proportion of the unique variance that is reliable (see Figure 40.1)
- *error variance* – variance not otherwise accounted for in a variable, i.e., random variance

The relationships among total, reliable, common, unique, specific, and error variances *in PCA* are shown in Figure 40.1.

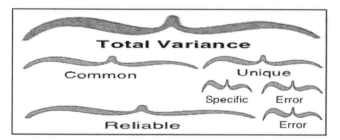

Figure 40.1. Relationships Among Total, Reliable, Common, Unique, Specific, and Error Variances in *PCA* (adapted considerably from Rummel, 1970, p. 103)

PCA techniques can be used to estimate the proportions of common and unique variances within the total variance in set of variables. Let's start with *common variance*, that is, the variance that each variable shares with all the other variables. This common variance is known as the communality (symbolized by h^2). For example, near the bottom of the third column of numbers in the PCA analysis shown in Table 40.2, you will see that the communality for *Depression* in bold italics is .711. That means that 71.1% of the variance in scores for that variable is common variance shared with the other variables in this analysis.

In PCA, *unique variance* is the variance that is due to a particular variable (including the specific variance and error variance associated with that variable), but does not include the variance shared with other variables. So unique variance equals one minus the communality (1 - h^2). In the case of the *Depression* variable, the unique variance = 1 - h^2 = 1 - .711 = .289. So 28.9% of the variance can be said to be unique to the *Depression* variable.

Table 40.2. *Two-Component and Two-Factor Factor Analyses (with Varimax rotation) of the Y/G Personality Inventory without Thinking Extraversion*

Variables	Rotated PCA 2 Components			Rotated EFA 2 Factors		
	Comp 1	Comp 2	h^2	Factor 1	Factor 2	h^2
Social extraversion	-0.150	0.737	0.566	-0.142	0.660	0.456
Ascendance	-0.116	0.654	0.441	-0.113	0.548	0.313
Rhathymia	0.419	0.656	0.605	0.381	0.596	0.501
General activity	-0.238	0.740	0.605	-0.225	0.680	0.513
Lack of agreeableness	0.150	0.649	0.443	0.116	0.535	0.299
Lack of cooperativeness	0.565	0.065	0.323	0.468	0.036	0.220
Lack of objectivity	0.687	0.065	0.476	0.602	0.045	0.364
Nervousness	0.799	-0.170	0.668	0.762	-0.164	0.608
Inferiority feelings	0.703	-0.471	0.715	0.681	-0.462	0.677
Cyclic tendencies	0.819	0.117	0.684	0.786	0.114	0.632
Depression	0.812	-0.226	**0.711**	0.783	-0.221	**0.662**
Proportion of Variance	0.322	0.245	0.567	0.282	0.195	0.477

Because EFA only analyzes reliable variance, it is useful for partitioning the proportions of *reliable* variance in a set of variables. Again, we will begin with common variance, in this case, the proportion of common variance that each variable shares with all the other variables. This common variance is called the communality and is symbolized by h^2. For example, in bottom right corner of the EFA results in Table 40.2, the communality for the *Depression* is .662. That means that 66.2% of the reliable variance for that variable is common variance shared with other variables.

In the case of EFA, the reliable unique variance is the proportion of unique variance that is reliable in a particular variable, but does not include the variance shared with other variables. So the unique proportion of the reliable variance equals one minus the communality (1 - h^2). In the case of the *Depression* variable, the reliable unique variance = 1 - h^2 = 1 - .662 = .338. So 33.8% of the reliable variance can be said to be reliable and unique to the *Depression* variable.

Again, because only reliable variance is analyzed in EFA (in contrast to PCA, which analyzes all the variance), the reliable unique variance and specific variance are the same *in EFA* (Kline, 2000, p. 120) as shown in Figure 40.2 (for more on the differences between PCA and EFA, see Brown, 2009a [Chapter 36]). Therefore, because the reliable unique variance for the Depression variable is 33.8% (and the reliable unique variance = specific variance), the specific variance is also 33.8%. We can therefore say that about 2/3 of the reliable variance in Depression scores is common variance (when this variable is analyzed in this set of variables) and about 1/3 of the reliable variance is reliably unique (or specific) to the *Depression* scores.

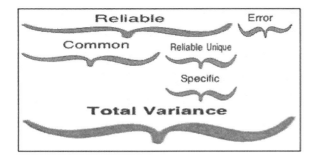

Figure 40.2: Relationships Among Total, Reliable, Common, Reliable Unique, Specific, and Error Variances *in EFA*

Do you see how all of this is useful information for thinking about our tests or questionnaires? We could just derive overall test or questionnaire reliability estimates using Cronbach alpha or other reliability estimates. But PCA can provide additional estimates of the proportions of common variance (71.1% for the Depression variable) and unique variance (28.9% for Depression). In addition, EFA can provide estimates of the proportions of common variance (62.2%) and reliable unique (or specific) variance (33.8%). In other words, we now know that the Depression shares about 2/3 of its reliable variance with the other variables in the analysis, while about 1/3 of the reliable variance in the Depression scale is reliably unique (or specific) to this particular scale.

In the next section, I will explain how language researchers can used PCA or EFA to study the construct validity of their tests or questionnaires. [For more about these concepts and how to estimate each type of variance see Guilford, 1954, pp. 354-357; Magnusson, 1966, pp. 180-182; Gorsuch, 1983, pp. 26-33; or Kline, 2002, pp. 42-43.]

Providing evidence for convergent and discriminant validity

Coming back to the original question at the top of this paper, recall that Lee and Kim (2008) performed a PCA with varimax rotation as shown in Table 40.3. Notice that the first six items load heavily on a Factor 1 (Instrumental School-Related), the next four items on Factor 2 (Instrumental Career-Related), the next five on Factor 3 (Integrative Personal Fulfillment), and the last two on Factor 4 (Heritage Ties). Loadings like these can serve as the basis for a convergent-discriminant validity argument. In this case, we can argue that the instrument is *convergent* (i.e., testing four constructs, or sub-constructs, with certain items converging together on each construct/factor) and *discriminant* (i.e., those same items are not loading as heavily on any other factors). Thus the item loadings provide support in real data for the validity of these four theoretical constructs.

Such an argument is undermined to the degree that there is complexity (i.e., items that load above say .30 on more than one factor) like that found in the 3rd, 10th, 11th, 13th, and 14th items. Indeed, the authors might choose to use this information to do item analysis, (as explained above) by revising, replacing, or deleting the 3rd, 10th, 11th, 13th, and 14th items, administering the questionnaire again and reanalyzing the results in terms of the four sub-constructs.

Conclusion

Many researchers use factor analysis for one purpose or another without realizing the rich variety of other purposes this form of analysis can serve. I showed in the previous chapter (Brown, 2010a [Chapter 39]) that EFA and PCA have applications in research work that include at least reducing the number of variables in a study, exploring patterns in the correlations among variables, and supporting a theory of how variables are related. In this chapter, I expanded the list of uses for EFA and PCA by explaining how they can also be useful: for developing tests and questionnaires by conducting item analysis to strengthen them; for studying the relative proportions of total, reliable, common, unique, specific, and error variances; or for providing evidence for convergent and discriminant validity. If you are currently using EFA and PCA, consider expanding the ways you apply these analyses. If you are *not* currently using EFA and PCA, you might want to ask yourself, why not?

Table 40.3. *Principal Components Analysis (with Varimax Rotation) Loadings of Motivation Items*

	Instrumental		Integrative		
	Factor 1	Factor 2	Factor 3	Factor 4	
	School related	Career related	Personal fulfillment	Ethnic Heritage	h^2
I learn Korean to transfer credits to college.	**0.83**	0.01	0.17	-0.11	**0.72**
I learn Korean because my friend recommended it.	**0.82**	0.14	0.06	0.22	**0.74**
I learn Korean because my advisor recommended it.	**0.80**	0.10	*0.36*	0.04	**0.78**
I learn Korean because of the reputation of the program and instructor.	**0.77**	0.12	0.12	0.22	**0.67**
I learn Korean for an easy A.	**0.69**	0.18	-0.29	0.16	**0.61**
I learn Korean to fulfill a graduation requirement.	**0.63**	0.11	0.19	-0.18	**0.47**
I learn Korean to get a better job.	0.04	**0.80**	0.20	0.11	**0.69**
I learn Korean because I plan to work overseas.	0.26	**0.80**	0.11	0.10	**0.75**
I learn Korean because of the status of Korean in the world.	0.10	**0.73**	0.20	0.22	**0.63**
I learn Korean to use it for my research.	*0.38*	*0.48*	*0.44*	0.10	**0.58**
I learn Korean to further my global understanding.	0.16	*0.33*	**0.71**	0.08	**0.65**
I learn Korean because I have an interest in Korean literature.	0.18	0.04	**0.64**	0.13	**0.56**
I learn Korean because it is fun and challenging.	0.04	0.04	**0.63**	*0.46*	**0.63**
I learn Korean because I have a general interest in languages.	0.11	0.03	**0.57**	*0.51*	**0.59**
I learn Korean because it is the language of my family heritage.	-0.01	0.26	0.05	**0.80**	**0.71**
I learn Korean because of my acquaintances with Korean speakers.	0.10	0.21	0.20	**0.70**	**0.58**
% of variance explained by each factor	**0.23**	**0.15**	**0.14**	**0.12**	**0.64**

(updated and reprinted from Brown, 2010b)

CHAPTER 41

CHI SQUARE AND RELATED STATISTICS FOR 2 X 2 CONTINGENCY TABLES

QUESTION: I used to think that there was only one type of chi-square measure, but more recently, I have become confused by the variety of chi-square measures that exist. Can you explain the difference between a simple chi-square and a (1) likelihood ratio chi-square, (2) a continuity adjusted chi-square, and (3) a Mantel-Haenszel chi-square? Finally, when should each of these statistics be used and what is the difference between a Yates and Pearson correction when used for chi-square data?

ANSWER: Karl Pearson first proposed what we now call chi square in K. Pearson (1900). Generally, *chi square* (also known as *Pearson's goodness of fit chi-square, chi-square test for independence*, or just simply X^2) is a test of the significance of how *observed frequencies* differ from the frequencies that would be expected to occur by chance, cleverly called *expected frequencies*. This test can be applied to many designs, but it is commonly explained in terms of how it applies to 2 x 2 contingency tables like the one shown in Figure 41.1.

In order to tackle your question in more depth, I will address the following topics: calculating simple chi square for a 2 x 2 contingency table (using an example from the literature), calculating statistics for 2 x 2 contingency tables the easy way, checking the assumptions of Pearson's chi square, and using variations on the chi-square theme.

Calculating simple chi square for a 2 x 2 contingency table

In the first study of two reported in Park, Lee, and Song (2005), the authors provide an elegant example of a 2 x 2 contingency table analysis that examined the frequency of whether apologies were present or absent in American and Korean email advertising messages. They describe their results as follows:

> Of 234 American email advertising messages, seven contained some form of apology (e.g., "We are sorry for anything that may cause you inconvenience"),

whereas 74 of 177 Korean email advertising messages contained some form of apology. A chi-square test was conducted to examine the relationship between culture and the presence of apologies. The result showed that the frequency of apologies was significantly associated with culture, $X^2(1) = 95.95$, $p < .01$, $\phi^2 = .23$. A greater number of Korean email advertising messages (41.81%) included apologies than did American email advertising messages (2.99%). (p. 374)

Figure 41.1 shows how the data need to be laid out for the calculations of the X^2 value that Park et al. (2005) found for the two cultures in their study (Korean and American) and the two states of Apology (present or absent).

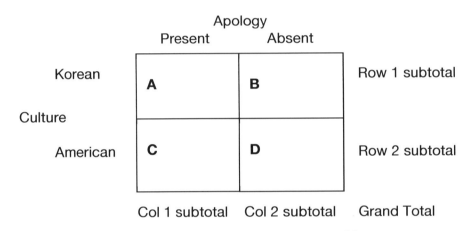

Figure 41.1. Layout for Culture by Apology 2 x 2 Contingency Table

In Figure 41.2, I have filled in the data from the Park et al. (2005) study (the large numbers in italic-bold print) in the appropriate cells. Notice that the row sums on the right side in the first row are for A + B = 74 + 103 = 177 and in the second row are for C + D = 7 + 227 = 234. Similarly, the column sums at the bottom of the first column are for A + C = 74 + 7 = 81 and at the bottom of the second column are for B + D = 103 + 227 = 330. The grand total shown at the bottom right is the sum of all four cells, or A + B + C + D = 74 + 103 + 7 + 227 = 411. Collectively, all of these values around the edges of the contingency table are known as the *marginals*.

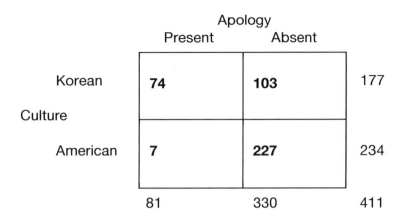

Figure 41.2. Data for Culture by Apology 2 x 2 Contingency Table

Observed frequencies are the frequencies that were actually found in a study and put inside the cells of the contingency table. *Expected frequencies* are estimates of the frequencies that would be found by chance in such a design (based on the marginals). Figure 41.3 shows how the expected frequencies are calculated from the marginals for each cell. For example, the expected frequency for Cell A (Korean-Present) is calculated by multiplying the column 1 marginal times the row 1 marginal and dividing the result by the grade total, or (Col1 x Row1) / Grand Total = (81 x 177) / 411 = 34.882. The expected frequencies for cells B, C, and D are calculated similarly, as shown in Figure 41.3.

Cell	Culture	Apology	Observed	Calculating Expected	(Col. x Row / Total) =	Expected
A	Korean	Present	74	(Col1 x Row1) / Grand Total =	(81 x 177) / 411 =	34.8832
B	Korean	Absent	103	(Col2 x Row1) / Grand Total =	(330 x 177) / 411 =	142.1168
C	American	Present	7	(Col1 x Row2) / Grand Total =	(81 x 234) / 411 =	46.1168
D	American	Absent	227	(Col2 x Row2) / Grand Total =	(330 x 234) / 411 =	187.8832

Figure 41.3. Calculating Expected Frequencies

Notice that Figure 41.4 shows the observed frequencies and marginals once again, but also shows the expected frequencies in parentheses.

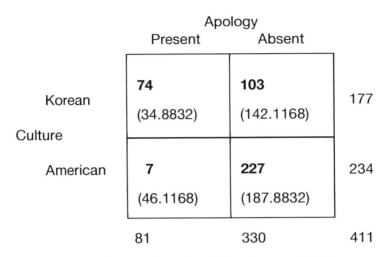

Figure 41.4. Data for Culture by Apology 2 x 2 Contingency Table

Figure 41.5 shows how the *chi-square value* (X^2) is calculated for a 2 x 2 contingency table. Intermediate values are first calculated for each cell based on the observed and expected frequencies in that cell. For example, for Cell A (Korean-Present), the value is calculated by subtracting the observed frequency from the expected frequency and squaring the result, and then dividing the squared result by the expected frequency. In this case, that would be (Observed - Expected)² / Expected = (74 - 34.8832)² / 34.8832 = 43.8642. The same process is repeated for Cells B, C, and D as shown in Figure 41.5. Then the four results are summed and that sum is the chi-squared value. In this case, that would be 43.8642 + 10.7667 + 33.1793 + 8.1440 = 95.9542, or about 95.95, as reported in Park et al. (2005).

Clearly, the chi-square statistic is not difficult to calculate (though the process is a bit tedious). It is also fairly easy to interpret. As Park et al. (2005) put it, "The result showed that the frequency of apologies was significantly associated with culture, $X^2(1)$ = 95.95, $p < .01$, $\phi^2 = .23$" (p. 374). Notice that they symbolize chi-squared as $X^2(1)$ (where the (1) indicates one degree of freedom) and that this chi-square value turns out to be significant at $p < .01$. [To determine the degrees of freedom and whether or not chi-square is significant requires much more information than I can supply in this short chapter; however, further explanations are readily available in Brown, 1988, pp. 182-194, or 2001e, pp. 159-169, or at the *SISA* website referenced in the next section]. Note that the phi-square statistic (ϕ^2) that Park et al. (2005) report will be explained below.

Culture	Apology	Observed	Expected	(Observed − Expected)² / Expected =	
Korean	Present	74	34.8832	(74 - 34.8832)² / 34.8832 =	43.8642
Korean	Absent	103	142.1168	(103 - 142.1168)² / 142.1168 =	10.7667
American	Present	7	46.1168	(7 - 46.1168)² / 46.1168 =	33.1793
American	Absent	227	187.8832	(227 - 187.8832)² / 187.8832 =	8.1440

Sum = *Chi-square value* = 95.9542

Figure 41.5. Calculating Chi square from the Observed and Expected Frequencies

Calculating statistics for 2 x 2 contingency tables the easy way

Now that you understand the basic calculations and interpretation of chi-square analysis for 2 x 2 contingency tables, I will show you an easier way to calculate that statistic and all of the statistics mentioned in your question at the top of this chapter (as well as a few bonus statistics). The first trick is to go to the very handy Simple Interactive Statistical Analysis (or *SISA*) at **www.quantitativeskills.com/sisa/** and explore a bit.

When you are ready to focus on 2 x 2 contingency table analysis go to the following URL: **www.quantitativeskills.com/sisa/statistics/twoby2.htm**. When you arrive at that web page, you will see a screen like the one shown in Figure 41.6. Go ahead and fill in the values from the Park et al. (2005) 2 x 2 contingency table as shown in Figure 41.6. Be sure to also check the boxes next to **Show Tables:** and **Association:** and then click on the **Calculate** button.

A number of tables will appear on your screen including those shown in the first column of Figure 41.7. You will also see numerical output like that extracted into the second column of Figure 41.7 (along with some additional output). Notice that the chi-squared value and its associated probability are shown in the third line of column two, labeled as **Pearson's**.

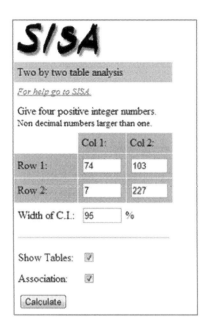

Figure 41.6. Using *SISA* to Calculate Statistics for the Park et al. (2005) Contingency Table

Checking the assumptions of Pearson's chi square

Pearson's chi square for 2 x 2 contingency tables is used to analyze raw frequencies (not percentages or proportions) for two binary variables, or put more precisely, this X^2 statistic is a reasonable test of the significance of the difference between observed and expected raw frequencies if three assumptions are met:

1. The scales are *nominal* (i.e., they are frequencies for categorical variables)
2. Each observation is *independent* of all others
3. As a rule of thumb, the *expected frequencies* are equal to or greater than 5

For example, let's consider these assumptions in the Park et al. (2005) study. First, the scales are clearly *nominal*: culture (American or Korean) and apology (present or absent) are definitely nominal and binary. Second, the observations are *independent*, which means that each observation appears in one and only one cell (i.e., each advertisement is either American or Korean and has an apology present or does not, or put another way, no advertisement appears in more than one cell). Third, the smallest *expected frequency* is 34.8832, which is well over 5. So Park et al. (2005) clearly met the assumptions of Pearson's chi square. [For more on these assumptions, see Brown, 2001e, pp. 168-169.]

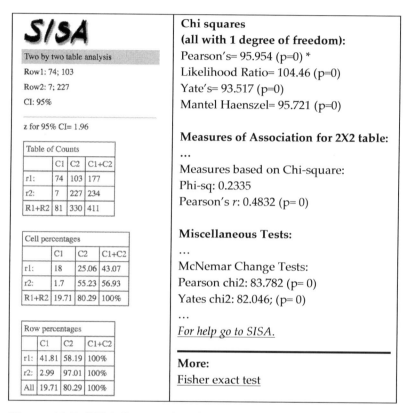

Figure 41.7. *SISA* Output for the Park et al. (2005) 2 x 2 Contingency Table

Using variations on the chi-square theme

Figure 41.7 shows selected statistics from the output that *SISA* provides. Here, I will explain the differences between these statistics, as well as when each would be appropriately applied. When the purpose of the analysis is different or the assumptions are not met, Pearson chi square is not appropriate, but other statistics (most of which are available in the *SISA* output shown in Figure 41.7) have been developed for use in alternative situations as follows:

If the scales are not nominal, other non-parametric statistics (e.g., the *Mantel Haenszel Chi-square* is appropriate if both variables are ordinal—see Conover, 1999. pp. 192-194; Sprent & Smeeton, 2007, pp. 399-403; also see the *SISA* website) or more powerful parametric statistics may be applicable (e.g., Pearson's product-moment correlation coefficient, the *t*-test, ANOVA, regression, etc.—see Brown, 1988, 2001e; Brown & Rodgers, 2002; Hatch & Lazaraton, 1991).

If the observations are not independent, Pearson's chi-square is not applicable. Period. This is a common violation that is ignored in second language research. Indeed, I searched for hours before finding the Park et al. (2005) example that did not violate this assumption. In cases where there is a violation of this assumption, especially sequentially over time (as in a study with a dichotomous nominal variable collected from the same people on two occasions, e.g., before and after instruction), you may want to consider two other statistics: *Cochran's Q test* (see Cochran, 1950; Conover, 1999, pp. 250-258; Sprent & Smeeton, 2007, p. 215) or *McNemar's Q* (see Conover, 1999, pp. 166-170; McNemar, 1947; Sprent & Smeeton, 2007, pp. 133-135; also see *SISA* website; or to calculate this statistic: **vassarstats.net/propcorr.html**). In the 2 x 2 case, the Cochran's Q and McNemar's Q should lead to the same result.

If the design is larger than 2 x 2, the *likelihood ratio* (or G^2) provides an alternative that can readily be used to analyze a table larger than 2 x 2 and then to examine smaller components within the table in more detail (see Sprent & Smeeton, 2007, pp. 362-363; Wickens, 1989; *SISA* website).

If an expected frequency is lower than five, you have three alternatives: Yates correction, the Fisher exact test, or the $N - 1$ chi-square test.

1. *Yates' correction* (Yates, 1934) is equivalent to Pearson's chi-square but with a continuity correction. In cases where an expected frequency is below 5, Yates' correction brings the result more in line with the true probability. In any case, as you can see in the second column of Figure 41.7, the *SISA* website will calculate this statistic for you.

2. *Fisher exact test* (Fisher, 1922) has been shown to perform accurately for 2 x 2 tables with expected frequencies below 5. The Fisher exact test (aka the Fisher-Irwin test) is more difficult to calculate than Yates' correction, but given the power of our personal computers today Yates' correction can easily be replaced by the more exact Fisher exact test. Indeed, as you can see in Figure 41.7, you need only click on Fisher exact test shown in the second column for the *SISA* website to calculate this statistic for you.

3. The *N - 1 chi-square test* is another option. Campbell (2007, p. 3661) compared chi-square analyses of 2 x 2 tables for many different sample sizes and designs and found that a statistic suggested by Karl Pearson's son (E. S. Pearson, 1947) called the *N - 1 chi-square test* provided the best estimates. According to Campbell, as long as the expected frequency is at least 1, this adjusted chi-square (probably the "Pearson correction" referred to in the question at the top of this chapter) provided the most accurate estimates of Type I error levels. However, for expected frequencies below 1, he found that Fisher's exact test performed better.

If the goal is to understand the degree of relationship between two dichotomous variables, *phi-square* (ϕ^2) is calculated by dividing the Pearson chi-square value by the grand total of cases. For example, in Park et al. (2005), ϕ^2 = .2335 as shown in the Figure 41.7 *SISA* Output for the Park et al. (2005) 2 x 2 Contingency Table. To calculate it by hand, use X^2 / *Grand total*, or 95.9542 / 411 = .2335 ≈ .23. This statistic ranges from zero (if there is absolutely no association between the two variables) to 1.00 (if the association between the two variables is perfect). With reference to Figure 41.7, note that the phi square value is equal to the square of the Pearson correlation coefficient reported in Figure 41.7. In other words, squaring Pearson's *r* (.4832) in Figure 41.7 will yield a phi square of .2335.

Conclusion

As the title of this chapter suggested, my purpose here was to explain how chi square and related statistics can be used for analyzing 2 x 2 contingency tables. To do so, I described the processes involved in calculating simple chi square for a 2 x 2 contingency table (using the Park et al., 2005 example from the literature), calculating statistics for 2 x 2 contingency tables the easy way, checking the assumptions of Pearson's chi square, and using variations on the chi-square theme. Along the way, I believe I addressed all parts of the original question at the top of the chapter.

All in all, in my experience, this family of nonparametric statistics has been much abused and misused in our field—perhaps more than any other. Please consider such analyses very carefully when using them and apply them correctly. Be sure, for example, to review the correct procedures as they are described in some of the references listed in this chapter.

(updated and reprinted from Brown, 2013a)

Cross-Reference to Original Columns

The following table provides a cross-reference to the original Statistics Corner columns published in *Shiken* and the *Shiken Research Bulletin*. The originals can be accessed online through the TEVAL website: **teval.jalt.org**.

Chapter Title	Year	Vol	#
Part I: Second Language Testing			
Section A: Testing Strategies			
1. Resources available in language testing	2006	10	1
2. Solutions for problems teachers have with classroom testing	2013	17	2
3. Differences in how norm-referenced and criterion-referenced tests are developed and validated	2014	18	1
4. What is construct validity?	2000	4	2
5. What is two-stage testing?	2001	5	2
6. Testing intercultural pragmatics ability	2015	19	1
7. Test-taker motivations	2004	8	2
8. Extraneous variables and the washback effect	2002	6	2
9. University entrance examinations: Strategies for creating positive washback on English language teaching in Japan	2000	3	2
Section B: Item Analyses			
10. Norm-referenced item analysis (item facility and item discrimination)	2003	7	2
11. Criterion-referenced item analysis (the difference index and B-index)	2003	7	3
12. Point-biserial correlation coefficients	2001	5	3
13. Distractor efficiency analysis on a spreadsheet	2002	6	3
14. Item statistics for weighted items	2000	3	2
15. What issues affect Likert-scale questionnaire formats?	2000	4	1
16. Likert items and scales of measurement	2011	15	1
Section C: Reliability Issues			
17. The Cronbach alpha reliability estimate	2002	6	1
18. Cloze tests and optimum test length	1998	2	1
19. Standard error vs. standard error of measurement	1999	3	1
20. Can we use the Spearman-Brown prophecy formula to defend low reliability?	2001	4	3
21. Generalizability and decision studies	2005	9	1
22. How do we calculate rater/coder agreement and Cohen's kappa?	2013	16	2
23. Reliability of surveys	1997	1	2

Chapter Title	Year	Vol	#
Part II: Second Language Research			
Section D: Planning Research			
24. Characteristics of sound quantitative research	2015	19	2
25. Characteristics of sound qualitative research	2005	9	2
26. Characteristics of sound mixed-methods research	2016	10	1
Section E: Interpreting Research			
27. What do distributions, assumptions, significance vs. meaningfulness, multiple statistical tests, causality, and null results have in common?	2012	16	1
28. Generalizability from second language research samples	2006	10	2
29. Sample size and power	2007	11	1
30. Sample size and statistical precision	2007	11	2
31. Skewness and kurtosis	1997	1	1
32. Effect size and eta squared	2008	12	2
33. Confidence intervals, limits, and levels?	2011	15	2
34. The Bonferroni adjustment	2008	12	1
Section F: Research Analyses			
35. The coefficient of determination	2003	7	1
36. Principal components analysis and exploratory factor analysis--Definitions, differences, and choices	2009	13	1
37. Choosing the right number of components or factors in PCA and EFA	2009	13	2
38. Choosing the right type of rotation in PCA and EFA	2009	13	3
39. How are PCA and EFA used in language research?	2010	14	1
40. How are PCA and EFA used in language test and questionnaire development?	2010	14	2
41. Chi-square and related statistics for 2 x 2 contingency tables	2013	17	1

REFERENCES

Ahn, R.C. (2005). *Five measures of interlanguage pragmatics in KFL (Korean as a foreign language) learners.* Unpublished doctoral dissertation at University of Hawai'i at Mānoa, Honolulu, HI.

Albaum, G. (1997). The Likert scale revisited: An alternate version. *Journal of the Market Research Society, 39,* 331- 349.

Alderson, J. C., & Wall, D. (1993). Does washback exist? *Applied Linguistics, 14,* 115-129.

Allen, E., & Seaman, C. A. (2007). Likert scales and data analyses. *Quality Progress, 40,* 64-65.

Andrich, D. (1978). A rating formulation for ordered response categories. *Psychometrika, 43,* 561-573.

Anisfeld, E., Bogo, N., & Lambert, W. E. (1962). Evaluational reactions to accented English speech. *Journal of Abnormal and Social Psychology, 65,* 223-231.

APA (2010). *The publication manual of the American Psychological Association* (6th ed.). Washington, DC: American Psychological Association.

Baayen, R. H. (2008). *Analyzing linguistic data: A practical introduction to statistics using R.* Cambridge: Cambridge University.

Bachman, L. F. (2004). *Statistical analyses for language assessment.* Cambridge: Cambridge University.

Bachman, L. F., Lynch, B. K., & Mason, M. (1995). Investigating variability in tasks and rater judgments in a performance test of foreign language speaking. *Language Testing, 12*(2), 239-257.

Baggaley, A., & Hull, A. (1983). The effect of nonlinear transformations on a Likert scale. *Evaluation & the Health Professions, 6,* 483-491.

Bailey, K. M. (1996). Working for washback: A review of the washback concept in language testing. *Language Testing, 13,* 257-279.

Bergman, M. (Ed.). (2008). *Advances in mixed methods research.* Thousand Oaks, CA: Sage.

Bolus, R. E., Hinofotis, F. B., & Bailey, K. M. (1982). An introduction to generalizability theory in second language research. *Language Learning, 32,* 245-258.

Brennan, R. L. (1983). *Elements of generalizability theory.* Iowa City, IA: American College Testing Program.

Brennan, R. L. (2001). *Generalizability theory.* New York: Springer-Verlag.

Brown, J. D. (1978). Correlational study of four methods for scoring cloze tests. Unpublished master's thesis at University of California at Los Angeles, Los Angeles, CA.

Brown, J. D. (1980). Relative merits of four methods for scoring cloze tests. *Modern Language Journal, 64*(3), 311-317.

Brown, J. D. (1984a). A cloze is a cloze is a cloze? In J. Handscombe, R. Orem & B. Taylor (Eds.), *On TESOL '83: The question of control. Selected papers from the 17th Annual TESOL Convention, Toronto* (pp. 109-119). Washington, DC: TESOL.

Brown, J. D. (1984b). A norm-referenced engineering reading test. In A. K. Pugh, & J. M. Ulijn (Eds.), *Reading for professional purposes: Studies and practices in native and foreign languages* (pp. 213-222). London: Heinemann Educational Books.

Brown, J. D. (1987). False beginners and false starters: How can we identify them? *The Language Teacher, 11*(4), 9-11.

Brown, J. D. (1988). *Understanding research in second language learning: A teacher's guide to statistics and research design.* Cambridge: Cambridge University.

Brown, J. D. (1989). Improving ESL placement tests using two perspectives. *TESOL Quarterly, 23*(1), 65-83.

Brown, J. D. (1990a). Where do tests fit into language programs? *JALT Journal, 12*(1), 121-140.

Brown, J. D. (1990b). Short-cut estimates of criterion-referenced test consistency. *Language Testing, 7*(1), 77-97.

Brown, J. D. (1990c). The use of multiple *t* tests in language research. *TESOL Quarterly, 24*(4), 770-773.

Brown, J. D. (1991). 1990 Manoa Writing Placement Examination. *Manoa Writing Board Technical Report #14.* Honolulu, HI: Manoa Writing Program, University of Hawai'i at Mānoa.

Brown, J. D. (1992a). What is research? *TESOL Matters, 2*(5), 10.

Brown, J. D. (1992b). Statistics as a foreign language--Part 2: More things to look for in reading statistical language studies. *TESOL Quarterly, 26*(4), 629-664.

Brown, J. D. (1993a). Language test hysteria in Japan? *The Language Teacher, 17*(12), 41-43.

Brown, J. D. (1993b). What are the characteristics of natural cloze tests? *Language Testing, 10*(2), 93-116.

Brown, J. D. (1993c). A comprehensive criterion-referenced language testing project. In D. Douglas & C. Chapelle (Eds.), *A new decade of language testing research* (pp. 163-184). Washington, DC: TESOL.

Brown. J. D. (1995a). English language entrance examinations in Japan: Myths and facts. *The Language Teacher, 19*(10), 21-26.

Brown J. D. (1995b). A gaijin teacher's guide to the vocabulary of entrance examinations. *The Language Teacher, 19*(12), 25.

Brown, J. D. (1995c). Developing norm-referenced language tests for program-level decision making. In J. D. Brown & S. O. Yamashita (Eds.), *Language testing in Japan* (pp. 40-47). Tokyo: Japan Association for Language Teaching.

Brown, J. D. (1995d). Differences between norm-referenced and criterion-referenced tests. In J. D. Brown & S. O. Yamashita (Eds.), *Language testing in Japan* (pp. 12-19). Tokyo: Japan Association for Language Teaching.

Brown, J. D. (1995e). *The elements of language curriculum: A systematic approach to program development.* New York: Heinle & Heinle.

Brown, J. D. (1996a). *Testing in language programs.* Upper Saddle River, NJ: Prentice Hall.

Brown, J. D. (1996b). English language entrance examinations in Japan: Problems and solutions. In G. van Troyer (Ed.), *JALT '95: Curriculum and evaluation* (pp. 272-283). Tokyo: Japan Association for Language Teaching.

Brown, J. D. (1996c). Japanese entrance exams: A measurement problem? *The Daily Yomiuri* (Educational Supplement). February 5, 1996, 15.

Brown, J. D. (1997a). Statistics Corner. Questions and answers about language testing statistics: Skewness and kurtosis. *Shiken: JALT Testing & Evaluation SIG Newsletter*, 1(1), 16-18. Also retrieved from the World Wide Web at

www.jalt.org/test/bro_1.htm; **www.jalt.org/test/PDF/Brown1.pdf**

Brown, J. D. (1997b). Statistics Corner. Questions and answers about language testing statistics: Reliability of surveys. *Shiken: JALT Testing & Evaluation SIG Newsletter*, 1(2), 17-19. Also retrieved from the World Wide Web at

www.jalt.org/test/bro_2.htm; **www.jalt.org/test/PDF/Brown2.pdf**

Brown, J. D. (1997c). Do tests washback on the language classroom? *TESOLANZ Journal*, 5, 63-80.

Brown, J. D. (1998a). Statistics Corner. Questions and answers about language testing statistics: Cloze tests and optimum test length. *Shiken: JALT Testing & Evaluation SIG Newsletter*, 2(2), 19-22. Also retrieved from the World Wide Web at

www.jalt.org/test/bro_3.htm; **www.jalt.org/test/PDF/Brown3.pdf**

Brown, J. D. (1998b). University entrance examinations and their effect on English language teaching in Japan. In J. Kalmy & M. James (Eds.), *Perspectives on secondary EFL education: A publication in commemoration of the 30th anniversary of the Language Institute of Japan* (pp. 20-27). Odawara, Japan: LIOJ.

Brown, J. D. (1998c). An EFL readability index. *JALT Journal*, 20(2), 7-36.

Brown, J. D. (1999a). Statistics Corner. Questions and answers about language testing statistics: Standard error vs. standard error of measurement. *Shiken: JALT Testing & Evaluation SIG Newsletter*, 3(1), 15-19. Also retrieved from the World Wide Web at

www.jalt.org/test/bro_4.htm; **www.jalt.org/test/PDF/Brown4.pdf**

Brown, J. D. (1999b). Relative importance of persons, items, subtests and languages to TOEFL test variance. *Language Testing*, 16(2), 216-237.

Brown, J. D. (1999c). The roles and responsibilities of assessment in foreign language education. *JLTA Journal*, 2, 1-21.

Brown, J. D. (2000a). University entrance examinations: Strategies for creating positive washback on English language teaching in Japan. *Shiken: JALT Testing & Evaluation SIG Newsletter, 3*(2), 4-8. Also retrieved from the World Wide Web at

www.jalt.org/test/bro_5.htm; **www.jalt.org/test/PDF/Brown5.pdf**

Brown, J. D. (2000b). Statistics Corner. Questions and answers about language testing statistics: How can we calculate item statistics for weighted items? *Shiken: JALT Testing & Evaluation SIG Newsletter, 3*(2), 19-21. Also retrieved from the World Wide Web at

www.jalt.org/test/bro_6.htm; **www.jalt.org/test/PDF/Brown6.pdf**

Brown, J. D. (2000c). Statistics Corner. Questions and answers about language testing statistics: What issues affect Likert-scale questionnaire formats? *Shiken: JALT Testing & Evaluation SIG Newsletter, 4*(1), 18-21. Also retrieved from the World Wide Web at

www.jalt.org/test/bro_7.htm; **www.jalt.org/test/PDF/Brown7.pdf**

Brown, J. D. (2000d). Statistics Corner. Questions and answers about language testing statistics: What is construct validity? *Shiken: JALT Testing & Evaluation SIG Newsletter, 4*(2), 7-10. Also retrieved from the World Wide Web at

www.jalt.org/test/bro_8.htm; **www.jalt.org/test/PDF/Brown8.pdf**

Brown, J. D. (2001a). Statistics Corner. Questions and answers about language testing statistics: Can we use the Spearman-Brown prophecy formula to defend low reliability? *Shiken: JALT Testing & Evaluation SIG Newsletter, 4*(3), 7-9. Also retrieved from the World Wide Web at

www.jalt.org/test/bro_9.htm; **www.jalt.org/test/PDF/Brown9.pdf**

Brown, J. D. (2001b). Statistics Corner. Questions and answers about language testing statistics: What is an eigenvalue? *Shiken: JALT Testing & Evaluation SIG Newsletter, 5*(1), 13-16. Retrieved from the World Wide Web at

www.jalt.org/test/bro_10.htm; **www.jalt.org/test/PDF/Brown10.pdf**

Brown, J. D. (2001c). Statistics Corner. Questions and answers about language testing statistics: What is two-stage testing? *Shiken: JALT Testing & Evaluation SIG Newsletter, 5*(2), 13-16. Also retrieved from the World Wide Web at

www.jalt.org/test/bro_11.htm; **www.jalt.org/test/PDF/Brown11.pdf**

Brown, J. D. (2001d). Statistics Corner. Questions and answers about language testing statistics: What is a point-biserial correlation coefficient? *Shiken: JALT Testing & Evaluation SIG Newsletter, 5*(3), 12-15. Also retrieved from the World Wide Web at www.jalt.org/test/bro_12.htm; jalt.org/test/PDF/Brown12.pdf

Brown, J. D. (2001e). *Using surveys in language programs.* Cambridge: Cambridge University.

Brown, J. D. (2001f). Developing and revising criterion-referenced achievement tests for a textbook series. In T. Hudson & J. D. Brown (Eds.). *A focus on language test development: Expanding the language proficiency construct across a variety of tests* (pp. 205-228). Honolulu, HI: University of Hawai'i.

Brown, J. D. (2001g). Six types of pragmatics tests in two different contexts. In K. Rose & G. Kasper (Eds.), *Pragmatics in Language Teaching* (pp. 301-325). Cambridge: Cambridge University.

Brown, J. D. (2002a). Statistics Corner. Questions and answers about language testing statistics: The Cronbach alpha reliability estimate. *Shiken: JALT Testing & Evaluation SIG Newsletter, 6*(1), 14-16. Also retrieved from the World Wide Web at www.jalt.org/test/bro_13.htm; jalt.org/test/PDF/Brown13.pdf

Brown, J. D. (2002b). Statistics Corner. Questions and answers about language testing statistics: Extraneous variables and the washback effect. *Shiken: JALT Testing & Evaluation SIG Newsletter, 6*(2), 12-15. Also retrieved from the World Wide Web at www.jalt.org/test/bro_14.htm; jalt.org/test/PDF/Brown14.pdf

Brown, J. D. (2002c). Statistics Corner. Questions and answers about language testing statistics: Distractor efficiency analysis on a spreadsheet. *Shiken: JALT Testing & Evaluation SIG Newsletter, 6*(3), 20-23. Also retrieved from the World Wide Web at www.jalt.org/test/bro_15.htm; jalt.org/test/PDF/Brown15.pdf

Brown, J. D. (2003a). Statistics Corner. Questions and answers about language testing statistics: The coefficient of determination. *Shiken: JALT Testing & Evaluation SIG Newsletter, 7*(1), 14-16. Also retrieved from the World Wide Web at www.jalt.org/test/bro_16.htm; jalt.org/test/PDF/Brown16.pdf

Brown, J. D. (2003b). Statistics Corner. Questions and answers about language testing statistics: Norm-referenced item analysis (*item facility* and *item discrimination*). *Shiken: JALT Testing & Evaluation SIG Newsletter, 7*(2), 16-19. Also retrieved from the World Wide Web at

www.jalt.org/test/bro_17.htm; www.jalt.org/test/PDF/Brown17.pdf

Brown, J. D. (2003c). Statistics Corner. Questions and answers about language testing statistics: Criterion-referenced item analysis (The *difference index* vs. the *B-index*). *Shiken: JALT Testing & Evaluation SIG Newsletter, 7*(3), 13-17. Also retrieved from the World Wide Web at

www.jalt.org/test/bro_18.htm; jalt.org/test/PDF/Brown18.pdf

Brown, J. D. (2004a). Statistics Corner. Questions and answers about language testing statistics: Yates correction factor. *Shiken: JALT Testing & Evaluation SIG Newsletter, 8*(1), 19-22. Also retrieved from the World Wide Web at

www.jalt.org/test/bro_19.htm

Brown, J. D. (2004b). Statistics Corner. Questions and answers about language testing statistics: Test-taker motivations. *Shiken: JALT Testing & Evaluation SIG Newsletter, 8*(2), 16-20. Also retrieved from the World Wide Web at

www.jalt.org/test/bro_20.htm; jalt.org/test/PDF/Brown20.pdf

Brown, J. D. (2004c). Grade inflation, standardized tests, and the case for on-campus language testing. In D. Douglas (Ed.), *English language testing in U.S. colleges and universities* (2nd ed.) (pp. 37-56). Washington, DC: NAFSA.

Brown, J. D. (2004d). Research methods for applied linguistics: Scope, characteristics, and standards. In A. Davies & C. Elder (Eds.), *The handbook of applied linguistics* (pp. 476-500). Oxford: Blackwell.

Brown, J. D. (2005a). Statistics Corner. Questions and answers about language testing statistics: Generalizability and decision studies. *Shiken: JALT Testing & Evaluation SIG Newsletter, 9*(1), 12-16. Also retrieved from the World Wide Web at

www.jalt.org/test/bro_21.htm; jalt.org/test/PDF/Brown21.pdf

Brown, J. D. (2005b). Statistics Corner. Questions and answers about language testing statistics: Characteristics of sound qualitative research. *Shiken: JALT Testing & Evaluation SIG Newsletter, 9*(2), 31-33. Also retrieved from the World Wide Web at www.jalt.org/test/bro_22.htm

Brown, J. D. (2005c). *Testing in language programs: A comprehensive guide to English language assessment* (New edition). New York: McGraw-Hill.

Brown, J. D. (2006a). Statistics Corner. Questions and answers about language testing statistics: Resources available in language testing. *Shiken: JALT Testing & Evaluation SIG Newsletter, 10*(1), 21-26. Also retrieved from the World Wide Web at

www.jalt.org/test/bro_23.htm

Brown, J. D. (2006b). Statistics Corner. Questions and answers about language testing statistics: Generalizability from second language research samples. *Shiken: JALT Testing & Evaluation SIG Newsletter, 10*(2), 24-27. Also retrieved from the World Wide Web at

www.jalt.org/test/bro_24.htm

Brown, J. D. (2007a). Statistics Corner. Questions and answers about language testing statistics: Sample size and power. *Shiken: JALT Testing & Evaluation SIG Newsletter, 11*(1), 31-35. Also retrieved from the World Wide Web at

www.jalt.org/test/bro_25.htm

Brown, J. D. (2007b). Statistics Corner. Questions and answers about language testing statistics: Sample size and statistical precision. *Shiken: JALT Testing & Evaluation SIG Newsletter, 11*(2), 21-24. Also retrieved from the World Wide Web at

www.jalt.org/test/bro_26.htm

Brown, J. D. (2008a). Statistics Corner. Questions and answers about language testing statistics: The Bonferroni adjustment. *Shiken: JALT Testing & Evaluation SIG Newsletter, 12*(1), 23-28. Also retrieved from the World Wide Web at

www.jalt.org/test/bro_27.htm

Brown, J. D. (2008b). Statistics Corner. Questions and answers about language testing statistics: Effect size and eta squared. *Shiken: JALT Testing & Evaluation SIG Newsletter, 12*(2), 36-41. Also retrieved from the World Wide Web at

www.jalt.org/test/bro_28.htm; jalt.org/test/PDF/Brown28.pdf

Brown, J. D. (2008c). Raters, functions, item types, and the dependability of L2 pragmatic tests. In E. Alcón Soler & A. Martínez-Flor (Eds.), *Investigating pragmatics in foreign language learning, teaching and testing* (pp. 224-248). Clevedon, UK: Multilingual Matters.

Brown, J. D. (2009a). Statistics Corner. Questions and answers about language testing statistics: Principal components analysis and exploratory factor analysis—Definitions, differences, and choices. *Shiken: JALT Testing & Evaluation SIG Newsletter, 13*(1), 26-30. Also retrieved from the World Wide Web at

www.jalt.org/test/bro_29.htm

Brown, J. D. (2009b). Statistics Corner. Questions and answers about language testing statistics: Choosing the right number of components or factors in PCA and EFA. *Shiken: JALT Testing & Evaluation SIG Newsletter, 13*(2), 19-23. Also retrieved from the World Wide Web at

www.jalt.org/test/bro_30.htm

Brown, J. D. (2009c). Statistics Corner. Questions and answers about language testing statistics: Choosing the right type of rotation in PCA and EFA. *Shiken: JALT Testing & Evaluation SIG Newsletter, 13*(3), 20-25. Also retrieved from the World Wide Web at **www.jalt.org/test/bro_31.htm**

Brown, J. D. (2010a). Statistics Corner. Questions and answers about language testing statistics: How are PCA and EFA used in language research? *Shiken: JALT Testing & Evaluation SIG Newsletter, 14*(1), 19-23. Also retrieved from the World Wide Web at **www.jalt.org/test/bro_32.htm**

Brown, J. D. (2010b). Statistics Corner. Questions and answers about language testing statistics: How are PCA and EFA used in language test and questionnaire development? *Shiken: JALT Testing & Evaluation SIG Newsletter, 14*(2), 22-27. Also retrieved from the World Wide Web at

www.jalt.org/test/bro_33.htm

Brown, J. D. (2011a). Statistics Corner. Questions and answers about language testing statistics: Likert items and scales of measurement. *Shiken: JALT Testing & Evaluation SIG Newsletter, 15*(1), 10-14. Also retrieved from the World Wide Web at

www.jalt.org/test/bro_34.htm; jalt.org/test/PDF/Brown34.pdf

Brown, J. D. (2011b). Statistics Corner. Questions and answers about language testing statistics: Confidence intervals, limits, and levels? *Shiken: JALT Testing & Evaluation SIG Newsletter, 15*(2), 23-27. Also retrieved from the World Wide Web at

www.jalt.org/test/bro_35.htm

Brown, J. D. (2012a). Statistics Corner. Questions and answers about language testing statistics: What do distributions, assumptions, significance vs. meaningfulness, multiple statistical tests, causality, and null results have in common? *Shiken Research Bulletin, 16*(1), 28-33. Also retrieved from the World Wide Web at

teval.jalt.org/sites/teval.jalt.org/files/SRB-16-1-Brown-StatCorner.pdf

Brown, J. D. (2012b). Statistics Corner. Questions and answers about language testing statistics: How do we calculate rater/coder agreement and Cohen's kappa? *Shiken Research Bulletin, 16*(2), 30-36. Also retrieved from the World Wide Web at

teval.jalt.org/sites/teval.jalt.org/files/SRB-16-2-Brown-StatCorner.pdf

Brown, J. D. (2012c). What teachers need to know about test analysis. In C. Coombe, S. J. Stoynoff, P. Davidson, & B. O'Sullivan (Eds.), *The Cambridge guide to language assessment* (pp. 105-112). Cambridge: Cambridge University.

Brown, J. D. (2012d). Choosing the right type of assessment. In C. Coombe, S. J. Stoynoff, P. Davidson, & B. O'Sullivan (Eds.), *The Cambridge guide to second language assessment* (pp. 133-139). Cambridge: Cambridge University.

Brown, J. D. (2013a). Statistics Corner. Questions and answers about language testing statistics: Chi-square and related statistics for 2 x 2 contingency tables. *Shiken Research Bulletin, 17*(1), 33-40. Also retrieved from the World Wide Web at

teval.jalt.org/sites/teval.jalt.org/files/SRB-17-1-Brown-StatCorner.pdf

Brown, J. D. (2013b). Statistics Corner. Questions and answers about language testing statistics: Solutions to problems teachers have with classroom testing. *Shiken Research Bulletin, 17*(2), 27-33. Also retrieved from the World Wide Web at

teval.jalt.org/sites/teval.jalt.org/files/SRB-17-2-Full.pdf

Brown, J. D. (2013c). Classical theory reliability. In A. J. Kunnan (Ed.), *The companion to language assessment* (pp. 1165-1181). Oxford: Wiley-Blackwell.

Brown, J. D. (2013d). Score dependability and decision consistency. In A. J. Kunnan (Ed.), *The companion to language assessment* (pp. 1182-1206). Oxford: Wiley-Blackwell.

Brown, J. D. (2014a). Statistics Corner. Questions and answers about language testing statistics: Differences in how norm-referenced and criterion-referenced tests are developed and validated. *Shiken Research Bulletin, 18*(1), 29-33. Also retrieved from the World Wide Web at

teval.jalt.org/sites/teval.jalt.org/files/Shiken%2018-1.pdf

Brown, J. D. (2014b). *Mixed methods research for TESOL.* Edinburgh, UK: University of Edinburgh.

Brown, J. D. (2015a). Statistics Corner. Questions and answers about language testing statistics: Testing intercultural pragmatics ability. *Shiken Research Bulletin, 19*(1), 42-47. Also retrieved from the World Wide Web at

teval.jalt.org/sites/teval.jalt.org/files/19-01-42%20Brown%20Statistics%20Corner.pdf

Brown, J. D. (2015b). Statistics Corner. Questions and answers about language testing statistics: Characteristics of sound quantitative research. *Shiken Research Bulletin, 19*(2), 24-28. Also retrieved from the World Wide Web at

teval.jalt.org/sites/teval.jalt.org/files/19-02-24_Brown.pdf

Brown, J. D. (2015c). Mixed methods research. In J. D. Brown & C. Coombe (Eds.), *The Cambridge guide to research in language teaching and learning* (pp. 78-84). Cambridge: Cambridge University.

Brown, J. D. (2016). Statistics Corner. Questions and answers about language testing statistics: Characteristics of sound mixed-methods research. *Shiken, 20*(1), pp. 21-24. Also retrieved from the World Wide Web at

teval.jalt.org/sites/teval.jalt.org/files/20_01_21_Brown_Statistics_Corner.pdf

Brown, J. D., & Ahn, C. R. (2011). Variables that affect the dependability of L2 pragmatics tests. *Journal of Pragmatics, 43,* 198-217.

Brown, J. D., & Bailey, K. M. (1984). A categorical instrument for scoring second language writing skills. *Language Learning, 34,* 21-42.

Brown. J. D., & Christensen T. (1987). Interview: James D. Brown. *The Language Teacher, 11*(7), 6-10.

Brown, J. D., & Coombe, C. (Eds.) (2015). *The Cambridge guide to research in language teaching and learning.* Cambridge: Cambridge University.

Brown, J. D., Cunha, M. I. A., & Frota, S. de F. N. (2001). The development and validation of a Portuguese version of the Motivated Strategies for Learning Questionnaire. In Z. Dörnyei & R. Schmidt (Eds.), *Motivation and second language acquisition* (pp. 257-280). Honolulu, HI: Second Language Teaching & Curriculum Center, University of Hawai'i.

Brown, J. D., & Gorsuch, G. (1995). An interview with J. D. Brown: Analyzing the value, meaning of entrance examinations. *The Daily Yomiuri.* (Educational Supplement). October, *30*, 15.

Brown, J. D., Hilgers, T., & Marsella, J. (1991). Essay prompts and topics: Minimizing the effect of differences. *Written Communication, 8*(4), 532-555.

Brown, J. D., & Hudson, T. (2002). *Criterion-referenced language testing.* Cambridge: Cambridge University.

Brown, J. D., & Kay, G. S. (1995). English language entrance examinations at Japanese universities: An interview with James Dean Brown. *The Language Teacher, 19*(11), 7-11.

Brown, J. D., Robson, G., & Rosenkjar, P. (2001). Personality, motivation, anxiety, strategies, and language proficiency of Japanese students. In Z. Dörnyei & R. Schmidt (Eds.), *Motivation and second language acquisition* (pp. 361-398). Honolulu, HI: Second Language Teaching & Curriculum Center, University of Hawai'i.

Brown, J. D., & Rodgers, T. (2002). *Doing applied linguistics research.* Oxford: Oxford University.

Brown, J. D., & Ross, J. A. (1996). Decision dependability of item types, sections, tests, and the overall TOEFL test battery. In M. Milanovic & N. Saville (Eds.), *Performance testing, cognition and assessment* (pp. 231- 265). Cambridge: Cambridge University.

Brown, J. D., & Yamashita, S. O. (1995a). English language entrance examinations at Japanese universities: What do we know about them? *JALT Journal, 17*(1), 7-30.

Brown, J. D., & Yamashita, S. O. (1995b). The authors respond to O'Sullivan's letter to JALT Journal: Out of criticism comes knowledge. *JALT Journal, 17*(2), 257-260.

Brown, J. D., & Yamashita S. O. (1995c). English language entrance examinations at Japanese universities: 1993 and 1994. In J. D. Brown & S. O. Yamashita (Eds.), *Language Testing in Japan* (pp. 86-100). Tokyo: Japan Association for Language Teaching.

Brown, J. D., Yamashiro, A. D., & Ogane, E. (2001). The emperor's new cloze: Strategies for revising cloze tests. In T. Hudson & J. D. Brown (Eds.), *A focus on language test development: Expanding the language proficiency construct across a variety of tests* (pp. 143-161). Honolulu, HI: University of Hawai'i.

Bryant, F. B., & Yarnold, P. R. (1995). Principal-components analysis and confirmatory factor analysis. In L. G. Grimm & P. R. Yarnold (Eds.), *Reading and understanding multivariate statistics* (pp. 99-136). Washington, DC: American Psychological Association.

Butler, C. (1985). *Statistics in linguistics*. Oxford: Blackwell.

Campbell, I. (2007). Chi-squared and Fisher-Irwin tests of two-by-two tables with small sample recommendations. *Statistics in Medicine, 26*, 3661-3675.

Canale, M., & Swain, M. (1980). Theoretical bases of communicative approaches to second language teaching and testing. *Applied Linguistics, 1*, 1-47.

Carifio, J., & Perla, R. J. (2007). Ten common misunderstandings, misconceptions, persistent myths and urban legends about Likert scales and Likert response formats and their antidotes. *Journal of Social Sciences, 3*(3), 106-116.

Carr, N. T. (2011). *Designing and analyzing language tests*. Oxford: Oxford University.

Carrell, P. L., Pharis, B. C., & Liberto, J. C. (1989). Metacognitive strategy training for ESL reading. *TESOL Quarterly, 23*, 647-678.

Carroll, J. B., & Sapon, S. M. (1958). *Modern language aptitude test*. New York: The Psychological Corporation.

Cattell, R. B. (1978). *The scientific use of factor analysis*. New York: Plenum.

Cheng, L., & Watanabe, Y. (2004). *Washback in language testing: Research contexts and methods*. Mahwah, NJ: Lawrence Erlbaum Associates.

Cleary, T., Linn, R., & Rock, D. (1968a). An exploratory study of programmed tests. *Educational and Psychological Measurement, 28*, 345-360.

Cleary, T., Linn, R., & Rock, D. (1968b). Reproduction of total test score through the use of sequential programmed tests. *Journal of Educational Measurement, 5*, 183-187.

Cochran W. G. (1950). The comparison of percentages in matched samples. *Biometrika, 37*, 256-266.

Cochran, W. G., & Cox, G. M. (1957). *Experimental designs.* New York: John Wiley.

Cohen, J. (1960). A coefficient of agreement for nominal scales. *Educational and Psychological Measurement. 20*, 37-46.

Cohen, J. (1988). *Statistical power analysis for the behavioral sciences* (2nd ed.). Hillsdale, NJ: Lawrence Erlbaum Associates.

Comrey, A. L., & Lee, H. B. (1992). *A first course in factor analysis* (2nd ed.). Hillsdale, NJ: Lawrence Erlbaum Associates.

Conover, W. J. (1999). *Practical nonparametric statistics* (3rd ed.). New York: Wiley.

Coombs, C. H. (1960). A theory of data. *Psychological Review, 67*, 143-159.

Cornelius, E. T., & Brown, J. D. (1981). *New English course placement tests* (including listening comprehension and grammar subtests with user's manual, test booklets, answer sheets, answer keys, and tapes). Los Angeles: ELS Publications.

Cornelius, E. T., & Brown, J. D. (1982). *New English course progress quizzes* (including items sampled from the points taught in the associated textbook series with user's manual, test booklets, and answer keys). Los Angeles: ELS Publications.

Creswell, J. W. (2009). *Research design: Qualitative, quantitative, and mixed methods approaches.* Thousand Oaks, CA: Sage.

Creswell, J. W., & Plano Clark, V. L. (2007). *Designing and conducting mixed methods research.* Thousand Oaks, CA: Sage.

Cronbach, L. J. (1970). *Essentials of psychological testing* (3rd ed.). New York: Harper & Row.

Cronbach, L. J., Gleser, G. C., Nanda, H., & Rajaratnam, N. (1972). *The dependability of behavioral measurements: Theory of generalizability of scores and profiles.* New York: Wiley.

Cronbach, L. J., Rajaratnam, N., & Gleser, G. C. (1963). Theory of generalizability: A liberalization of reliability theory. *British Journal of Statistical Psychology, 16,* 137-163.

Davis, K. A. (1992). Validity and reliability in qualitative research on second language acquisition and teaching: Another researcher comments... . *TESOL Quarterly, 26,* 605-608.

Davis, K. A. (1995). Qualitative theory and methods in applied linguistics research. *TESOL Quarterly, 29,* 427-453.

Dayton, C. M. (1970). *The design of educational experiments.* New York: McGraw-Hill.

Denzin, N. K. (1994). The art and politics of interpretation. In N. K. Denzin & Y. S. Lincoln (Eds.), *Handbook of qualitative research* (pp. 500-515). Thousand Oaks, CA: Sage.

Denzin, N. K., & Lincoln, Y. S. (Eds.). (1994). *Handbook of qualitative research.* Thousand Oaks, CA: Sage.

Dörnyei, Z. (2003). *Questionnaires in second language research: Construction, administration, and processing.* Mahwah, NJ: Lawrence Erlbaum Associates.

Dörnyei, Z. (2007). *Research methods in applied linguistics.* Oxford: Oxford University.

Enochs, K., & Yoshitake-Strain, S. (1999). Evaluating six measures of EFL learners' pragmatics competence. *JALT Journal, 21,* 29–50.

Fetterman, D. M. (1989). *Ethnography: Step by step.* Newbury Park, CA: Sage.

Fielding, N. G., & Fielding, J. L. (1986). *Linking data.* Beverly Hills, CA: Sage.

Fisher, R. A. (1971). *The design of experiments* (8th ed.). New York: Hafner. Reproduced in J. H. Bennett (Ed.) (1995), *Statistical methods, experimental design, and scientific inference.* Oxford: Oxford University.

Fisher, R. A. (1922). On the interpretation of χ^2 from contingency tables, and the calculation of p. *Journal of the Royal Statistical Society, 85(1),* 87-94.

Fotos, S., & Ellis, R. (1991). Communicating about grammar: A task-based approach. *TESOL Quarterly, 25(4),* 605-628.

Freeman, D. (1998). *Doing teacher research: From inquiry to understanding.* Boston, MA: Heinle & Heinle.

Gates, S. (1995). Exploiting washback from standardized tests. In J. D. Brown & S. O. Yamashita (Eds.), *Language testing in Japan* (pp. 101-106). Tokyo: Japan Association for Language Teaching.

Glesne, C. (1998). *Becoming qualitative researchers: An introduction* (2nd ed.). London: Allyn & Bacon.

Godwin-Jones, B. (2001). Emerging technologies: Language testing tools and technologies. *Language Learning & Technology, 5*(2), 8-12. Also available on the World Wide Web at

llt.msu.edu/vol5num2/emerging/default.html

Gorsuch, G. (1999). *Exploring the relationship between educational policy and instruction in Japanese high school EFL classrooms.* Unpublished doctoral dissertation at Temple University, Philadelphia, PA.

Gorsuch, R. L. (1983). *Factor analysis* (2nd ed.). Hillsdale, NJ: Lawrence Erlbaum Associates.

Grabowski, K. C. (2009). *Investigating the construct validity of a test designed to measure grammatical and pragmatic knowledge in the context of speaking.* Unpublished doctoral dissertation at Columbia University, New York.

Grabowski, K. C. (2013). Investigating the construct validity of a role-play test designed to measure grammatical and pragmatic knowledge at multiple proficiency levels. In S. J. Ross & G. Kasper (Eds.), *Assessing second language pragmatics* (pp. 149-171). London: Palgrave Macmillan.

Green, D. R. (1998). Consequential aspects of the validity of achievement tests: A publisher's point of view. *Educational Measurement, 17*(2), 16-19.

Greene, J. C. (2007). *Mixed methods in social inquiry.* San Francisco: Wiley.

Guilford, J. P. (1954). *Psychometric methods.* New York: McGraw-Hill.

Guilford, J. P., & Fruchter, B. (1973). *Fundamental statistics in psychology and education* (5th ed.). New York: McGraw-Hill.

Guilford, J. P., & Yatabe, T. (1957). *Yatabe-Guilford personality inventory.* Osaka: Institute for Psychological Testing.

Hagquist, C., & Andrich, D. (2004). Is the Sense of Coherence-instrument applicable on adolescents? A latent trait analysis using Rasch-modelling. *Personality and Individual Differences, 36,* 955-968.

Hatch, E., & Lazaraton, A. (1991). *The research manual: Design and statistics for applied linguistics.* Rowley, MA: Newbury House.

Heyneman, S. P., & Ranson, A. W. (1990). Using examinations and testing to improve educational quality. *Educational Policy, 4,* 177-192.

Hirai, A. (1999). The relationship between listening and reading rates of Japanese EFL learners. *Modern Language Journal, 83,* 367-384.

Hodge, D. R., & Gillespie, D. (2003). Phrase completions: An alternative to Likert scales. *Social Work Research, 27,* 45-55.

Huberman, M., & Miles, M. B. (Eds.). (2002). *The qualitative researcher's companion: Classic and contemporary readings.* Beverly Hills, CA: Sage.

Hudson, T., Detmer, E., & Brown, J. D. (1992). *A framework for testing cross-cultural pragmatics.* Honolulu, HI: National Foreign Languages Resource Center.

Hudson, T., Detmer, E., & Brown, J. D. (1995). *Developing prototypic measures of cross-cultural pragmatics.* Honolulu, HI: National Foreign Languages Resource Center.

Hughes, A. (1989). *Testing for language teachers.* Cambridge: Cambridge University.

Itomitsu, M. (2009). *Developing a test of pragmatics of Japanese as a foreign language.* Unpublished doctoral dissertation at Columbia University, New York.

Iwai, T., Kondo, K., Lim, D. S. J., Ray, G., Shimizu, H., & Brown, J. D. (1999). *Japanese language needs assessment 1998-1999* (NFLRC NetWork #13) [HTML document]. Honolulu: University of Hawai'i, Second Language Teaching & Curriculum Center. Retrieved April 30, 1999. Available at

www.lll.hawaii.edu/nflrc/NetWorks/NW13/

Jaccard, J., Becker, M. A., & Wood, G. (1984). Pairwise multiple comparison procedures: A review. *Psychological Bulletin, 96,* 589-596.

Jakobsson, U. (2004). Statistical presentation and analysis of ordinal data in nursing research. *Scandinavian Journal of Caring Sciences, 18,* 437-440.

Jamieson, S. (2004). Likert scales: How to (ab)use them. *Medical Education, 38*, 1212-1218.

Johnson, D. M. (1992). *Approaches to research in second language learning.* New York: Longman.

Kane, M. T. (2006). Validation. In R. Brennan (Ed.), *Educational Measurement* (4th ed.) (pp. 17–64). Westport, CT: Greenwood.

Kehaghan, T., & Greaney, V. (1992). *Using examinations to improve education: A study of fourteen African countries.* Washington, DC: World Bank.

Kim, J. O., & Mueller, C. W. (1978). *Introduction to factor analysis: What it is and how to do it.* Beverly Hills, CA: Sage.

Kirk, R. E. (1968). *Experimental design: Procedures for the behavioral sciences.* Belmont, CA: Brooks/Cole.

Kline, P. (2000). *Handbook of psychological testing* (2nd ed.). New York: Routledge.

Kline, P. (2002). *An easy guide to factor analysis.* London: Routledge.

Kline, R. B. (2005). *Beyond significance testing: Reforming data analysis methods in behavioral research.* Washington, DC: American Psychological Association.

Knapp, T. R. (1990). Treating ordinal scales as interval scales: An attempt to resolve the controversy. *Nursing Research, 39*, 121-123.

Kondo-Brown, K. (2001). Effects of three types of practice in teaching Japanese verbs of giving and receiving. *Acquisition of Japanese as a Second Language, 4*, 82-115.

Kondo-Brown, K., & Fukuda, C. (2008). A separate-track for advanced heritage language students?: Japanese intersentential referencing. In K. Kondo-Brown & J. D. Brown (Eds.), *Teaching Chinese, Japanese, and Korean heritage language students* (pp. 135-156). New York: Lawrence Erlbaum Associates.

Kraemer, H. C., & Thiemann, S. (1987). *How many subjects? Statistical power analysis in research.* Newbury Park, CA: Sage.

Kuder, G. F., & Richardson, M. W. (1937). The theory of estimation of test reliability. *Psychometrika, 2*, 151-160.

Kunnan, A. J. (1992). An investigation of a criterion-referenced test using G-theory, and factor and cluster analyses. *Language Testing, 9*(1), 30-49.

Kuzon, W. M. Jr., Urbanchek, M. G., & McCabe, S. (1996). The seven deadly sins of statistical analysis. *Annals of Plastic Surgery, 37,* 265-272.

Lazaraton, A. (1995). Qualitative research in applied linguistics: A progress report. *TESOL Quarterly, 29,* 455-472.

Lee, J. S., & Kim, H. Y. (2008). Heritage language learners' attitudes, motivations, and instructional needs: The case of postsecondary Korean language learners. In K. Kondo-Brown & J. D. Brown (Eds.), *Teaching Chinese, Japanese, and Korean heritage language students* (pp. 159-185). New York: Lawrence Erlbaum Associates.

Likert, R. (1932). A technique for the measurement of attitudes. *Archives of Psychology, 140,* 1-55.

Linacre, J. M. (2002). Optimizing rating scale category effectiveness. *Journal of Applied Measurement, 3*(1), 85-106.

Lincoln, Y., & Guba, E. (1985). *Naturalistic inquiry.* Beverly Hills, CA: Sage.

Linn, R. L. (1998). Partitioning responsibility for the evaluation of the consequences of assessment programs. *Educational Measurement, 17*(2), 28-30.

Lipsey, M. W. (1990). *Design sensitivity: Statistical power for experimental research.* Newbury Park, CA: Sage.

Liu, J. (2006). *Measuring interlanguage pragmatic knowledge of EFL learners.* Frankfurt am Main: Peter Lang.

Liu, J. (2007). Developing a pragmatic test for Chinese EFL learners. *Language Testing, 24,* 391-415.

Lord, F. (1971). A theoretical study of two-stage testing. *Psychometrika, 36,* 227-242.

Lune, S., Parke, C. S., & Stone, C. A. (1998). A framework for evaluating the consequences of assessment programs. *Educational Measurement, 17*(2), 24-28.

Magnusson, D. (1966). *Test theory.* Reading, MA: Addison-Wesley.

Marshall, C., & Rossman, G. B. (1989). *Designing qualitative research.* Newbury Park, CA: Sage.

Mason, B. (2003). *A study of extensive reading and the development of grammatical accuracy by Japanese university students learning English.* Unpublished doctoral dissertation at Temple University, Philadelphia, PA.

Mason, B. (2004). The effect of adding supplementary writing to an extensive reading program. *The International Journal of Foreign Language Teaching, 1*(1), 2-16. Also retrieved from the World Wide Web at

www.tprstories.com/ijflt/IJFLTWinter041.pdf

Maurer, J., & Pierce, H. R. (1998). A comparison of Likert scale and traditional measures of self-efficacy. *Journal of Applied Psychology, 83*, 324-329.

Maxwell, J. A. (2004). *Qualitative research design: An interactive approach* (2nd ed.). Beverly Hills, CA: Sage.

McDonald, R. P. (1985). *Factor analysis and related methods.* Hillsdale, NJ: Lawrence Erlbaum Associates.

McNemar, Q. (1947). Note on the sampling error of the difference between correlated proportions or percentages. *Psychometrika,* 12(2), 153-157.

Mertens, D. M. (2010). *Research and evaluation in education and psychology: Integrating diversity with quantitative, qualitative, and mixed methods.* Thousand Oaks, CA: Sage.

Messick, S. (1988). The once and future issues of validity: Assessing the meaning and consequences of measurement. In H. Wainer & H. I. Braun (Eds.), *Test validity* (pp. 33-45). Hillsdale, NJ: Lawrence Erlbaum Associates.

Messick, S. (1989). Validity. In R. L. Linn (Ed.), *Educational measurement* (3rd ed.) (pp. 13-103). New York: Macmillan.

Messick, S. (1996). Validity and washback in language testing. *Language Testing, 13*(3), 241-256.

Microsoft [Computer software]. (1996). *Excel®* Redmond, WA: Microsoft Corporation.

Miles, M. B., & Huberman, A. M. (1984). *Qualitative data analysis: A sourcebook of new methods.* Beverly Hills, CA: Sage.

Molloy, H., & Shimura, M. (2005). An examination of situational sensitivity in medium-scale interlanguage pragmatics research. In T. Newfields, Y. Ishida, M. Chapman, & M. Fujioka (Eds.), *Proceedings of the May. 22- 23, 2004 JALT Pan-SIG Conference* (p. 16-32). Tokyo: JALT Pan SIG Committee. Available online at

www.jalt.org/pansig/2004/HTML/ShimMoll.htm.

Moss, P. A. (1998). The role of consequences in validity theory. *Educational Measurement, 17*(2), 6-12.

Murphy, K. R., & Myors, B. (2004). *Statistical power analysis: A simple and general model for traditional hypothesis tests* (2nd ed.). Hillsdale, NJ: Lawrence Erlbaum Associates.

Newman, I., & Benz, C. R. (1998). *Qualitative-quantitative research methodology: Exploring the interactive continuum.* Carbondale, IL: Southern Illinois University.

Nunan, D. (1992). *Research methods in language learning.* Cambridge: Cambridge University.

Onwuegbuzie, A. J., & Johnson, R. B. (2006). The validity issue in mixed research. *Research in the Schools, 13*(1), 48-63.

O'Sullivan, B. (1995). A reaction to Brown and Yamashita "English language entrance exams at Japanese universities: What do we know about them?" *JALT Journal, 17*(2), 255-257.

Park, H. S., Lee, H. E., & Song, J. A. (2005). "I am sorry to send you SPAM": Cross-cultural differences in use of apologies in email advertising in Korea and the U.S. *Human Communication Research, 31*(3), 365-398.

Pearson, E. S. (1947). The choice of statistical tests illustrated on the interpretation of data classed in a 2 x 2 table. *Biometrika, 34,* 139-167.

Pearson, K. (1900). On the criterion that a given system of deviations from the probable in the case of a correlated system of variables is such that it can be reasonably supposed to have arisen from random sampling. *Philosophical Magazine, Series 5, 50*(302), 157-175.

Perneger, T. V. (1998, April 18). What's wrong with Bonferroni adjustments? *British Medical Journal, 316* (7139), 1236-1238. Retrieved from

www.pubmedcentral.nih.gov/articlerender.fcgi?artid=1112991

Plano Clark, V. L., & Creswell, J. W. (Eds.). (2008). *The mixed methods reader.* Thousand Oaks, CA: Sage.

Plonsky, L. (Ed.) (2015). *Advancing quantitative methods in second language* research. New York: Routledge.

Politzer, R. L., & McGroarty, M. (1985). An exploratory study of learning behaviors and their relationship to gains in linguistic and communicative competence. *TESOL Quarterly, 19*(1), 103-123.

Porte, G. K. (2010). *Appraising research in second language learning: A practical guide to critical analysis of quantitative research.* Amsterdam: Benjamins.

Rand, E. (1978). The effects of test length and scoring method on the precision of cloze test scores. *UCLA Workpapers in Teaching English as a Second Language, 12,* 62-71.

Reckase, M. D. (1998). Consequential validity from the test developer's perspective. *Educational Measurement, 17*(2), 13-16.

Robson, G. (1994). *Relationships between personality, anxiety, proficiency, and participation.* Unpublished doctoral dissertation at Temple University, Philadelphia, PA.

Roever, C. (2005). *Testing ESL pragmatics: Development and validation of a web-based assessment battery.* Frankfurt: Peter Lang.

Roever, C. (2006). Validation of a web-based test of ESL pragmalinguistics. *Language Testing, 23,* 229-256.

Roever, C. (2007). DIF in the assessment of second language pragmatics. *Language Assessment Quarterly, 4*(2), 165–189.

Roever, C. (2008). Rater, item, and candidate effects in discourse completion tests: A FACETS approach. In E. Soler & A. Martinez-Flor (Eds.), *Investigating pragmatics in foreign language learning, teaching, and testing* (pp. 249-266). Bristol, UK: Multilingual Matters.

Roever, C. (2013). Testing implicature under operational conditions. In S. J. Ross & G. Kasper (Eds.), *Assessing second language pragmatics* (pp. 43-64). London: Palgrave Macmillan.

Rosenthal, R., Rosnow, R. L., & Rubin, D. B. (2000). *Contrasts and effect sizes in behavioral research: A correlational approach.* Cambridge: Cambridge University.

Rummel, R. J. (1970). *Applied factor analysis.* Evanston, IL: Northwestern University.

Sasaki, C. L. (1996). Teacher preferences of student behavior in Japan. *JALT Journal, 18*(2), 229-239.

Rylander, J., Clark, P., & Derrah, R. (2013). A video-based method of assessing pragmatic awareness. In S. J. Ross & G. Kasper (Eds.), *Assessing second language pragmatics* (pp. 65-97). London: Palgrave Macmillan.

Scholfield, P. (1995). *Quantifying language: A researcher's guide to gathering language data and reducing it to figures.* Clevedon, UK: Multilingual Matters.

Shavelson, R. J. (1981). *Statistical reasoning for the behavioral sciences.* Boston, MA: Allyn & Bacon.

Shavelson, R. J., & Webb, N. M. (1991). *Generalizability theory: A primer.* Newbury Park, CA: Sage.

Sheeler, W. D., & Brown, J. D. (1980a). *Welcome to English placement tests* (including listening comprehension and grammar subtests with user's manual, test booklets, answer sheets, answer keys, and tapes). Los Angeles: ELS Publications.

Sheeler, W. D., & Brown, J. D. (1980b). *Welcome to English progress quizzes tests* (including items sampled from the points taught in the associated textbook series with user's manual, test booklets, and answer keys). Los Angeles: ELS Publications.

Shohamy, E. (1992). Beyond performance testing: A diagnostic feedback testing model for assessing foreign language learning. *Modern Language Journal, 76*(4), 513-521.

Shohamy, E., Donitsa-Schmidt S., & Ferman, I. (1996). Test impact revisited: Washback effect over time. *Language Testing, 13*(3), 298-317.

Sick, J. (2006). *The learner's contribution: Individual differences in language learning in a Japanese high school.* Unpublished doctoral dissertation at Temple University, Philadelphia, PA.

Sick, J. (2009). Rasch measurement in language education part 3: The family of Rasch models. *Shiken: JALT Testing & Evaluation SIG Newsletter, 13*(1), 4-10. Also retrieved from the World Wide Web at

jalt.org/test/sic_3.htm; jalt.org/test/PDF/Sick3.pdf

Siegel, A. F. (1990). Multiple t tests: Some practical considerations. *TESOL Quarterly, 24*(4), 773-775.

Siegel, S. (1956). *Nonparametric statistics for the behavioral sciences.* New York: McGraw-Hill.

Smith, J. K. (2003). Reconsidering reliability in classroom assessment and grading. *Educational Measurement: Issues and practice, 22*(4), 26-33.

Sprent, P., & Smeeton, N. C. (2007). *Applied nonparametric statistical methods* (4th ed.). Boca Raton, FL: Chapman & Hall.

Stansfield, C. W., & Kenyon, D. M. (1992). Research of the comparability of the oral proficiency interview and the simulated oral proficiency interview. *System, 20,* 347-364.

Stapleton, P. (1996). A reaction to J. D. Brown's recent inquiry on the English entrance exam. *The Language Teacher, 20*(3), 29-32.

Tabachnick, B. G., & Fidell, L. S. (1996). *Using multivariate statistics* (3rd ed.). New York: Harper Collin.

Tabachnick, B. G., & Fidell, L. S. (2001). *Using Multivariate Statistics* (5th ed.). Upper Saddle River, NJ: Pearson Allyn & Bacon.

Tabachnick, B. G., & Fidell, L. S. (2012). *Using multivariate statistics* (6th ed.). New York: Pearson.

Tada, M. (2005). *Assessment of ESL pragmatic production and perception using video prompts.* Unpublished doctoral dissertation at Temple University, Philadelphia, PA.

Taleporos, E. (1998). Consequential validity: A practitioner's perspective. *Educational Measurement, 17*(2), 20-23.

Tashakkori, A., & Teddlie, C. (1998). *Mixed methodology: Combining qualitative and quantitative approaches* (Applied Social Research Methods series Number 46). Thousand Oaks, CA: Sage.

Tashakkori, A., & Teddlie, C. (Eds.) (2010). *Sage handbook of mixed methods in social & behavioral research* (2nd ed.). Thousand Oaks, CA: Sage.

Teddlie, C., & Tashakkori, A. (2009). *Foundations of mixed methods research: Integrating quantitative and qualitative approaches to social and behavioral sciences.* Thousand Oaks, CA: Sage.

Thompson, B. (2006). *Foundations of behavioral statistics: An insight-based approach.* New York: Guilford.

Thurstone, L. L. (1947). *Multiple factor analysis: A development and expansion of vectors of the mind.* Chicago: University of Chicago.

Timpe, V. (2013). *Assessing intercultural language learning.* Frankfurt am Main: Peter Lang.

Van Alphen, A., Halfens, R., Hasman, A., & Imbos, T. (1994). Likert or Rasch? Nothing is more applicable than a good theory. *Journal of Advanced Nursing, 20,* 196-201.

Vickers, A. (1999). Comparison of an ordinal and a continuous outcome measure of muscle soreness. *International Journal of Technology Assessment in Health Care, 15,* 709-716.

Vigderhous, G. (1977). The level of measurement and 'permissible' statistical analysis in social research. *Pacific Sociological Review, 20*(1), 61-72.

Vogt, W. P. (1993). *Dictionary of statistics and methodology: A nontechnical guide for the social sciences.* Newbury Park, CA: Sage.

Vogt, W. P., & Johnson, R. B. (2011). *Dictionary of statistics & methodology: A nontechnical guide for the social sciences.* Thousand Oaks, CA: Sage.

Wall, D. (1996). Introducing new tests into traditional systems: Insights from general education and from innovation theory. *Language Testing, 13*(1), 231-354.

Watanabe. Y. (1996). Does grammar translation come from the entrance examination? Preliminary findings from classroom-based research. *Language Testing, 13*(3) 318-333.

Waugh, R. F. (2002). Creating a scale to measure motivation to achieve academically: Linking attitudes and behaviours using Rasch measurement. *British Journal of Educational Psychology, 72,* 65-86

Weaver, C. (2005). Using the Rasch model to develop a measure of second language learners' willingness to communicate within a language classroom. *Journal of Applied Measurement, 6*(4), 396-415.

Weaver, C. (2007). A Rasch-based evaluation of the presence of item bias in a placement examination designed for an EFL reading program. In T. Newfields, I. Gledall, P. Wanner, & M. Kawate-Mierzejewska (Eds.), *Second Language Acquisition—Theory and Pedagogy: Proceedings of the 6th Annual JALT Pan-SIG Conference.* Sendai, Japan: Tohoku Bunka Gakuen University. Retrieved from

jalt.org/pansig/2007/HTML/Weaver.htm

Weaver, C. (2010). *Japanese university students' willingness to use English with different interlocutors.* Unpublished doctoral dissertation at Temple University, Philadelphia, PA.

Wickens, T. D. (1989). *Multiway contingency tables analysis for the social sciences.* Hillsdale, NJ: Lawrence Erlbaum Associates.

Yamashita, S. O. (1996). *Six measures of JSL pragmatics* (Technical Report #14. Second Language Teaching and Curriculum Center). Honolulu, HI: University of Hawai'i.

Yaremko, R. M., Harari, H., Harrison, R. C., & Lynn, E. (1986). *Handbook of research and quantitative methods in psychology: For students and professionals.* Hillsdale, NJ: Lawrence Erlbaum Associates.

Yates F. (1934). Contingency tables involving small numbers and the χ^2 test. *Journal of the Royal Statistical Society Supplement, 1,* 217-235.

Yen, W. M. (1998). Investigating the consequential aspects of validity: Who is responsible and what should they do? *Educational Measurement, 17*(2), 5-6.

Yoshida, K. (1996a). Language testing in Japan: A cultural problem? *The Daily Yomiuri.* (Educational Supplement). January 15, 15.

Yoshida, K. (1996b). Testing the bounds of culture. *The Daily Yomiuri* (Educational Supplement), February 12, 15.

Yoshitake, S. S. (1997). *Measuring interlanguage pragmatic competence of Japanese students of English as a foreign language: A multi-test framework evaluation.* Unpublished doctoral dissertation at Columbia Pacific University, Novata, CA.

Youn, S. J. (2008). *Rater variation in paper vs. web-based KFL pragmatic assessment using FACETS analysis.* Unpublished MA thesis at University of Hawai'i at Mānoa.

Youn, S. J. (2013). *Validating task-based assessment of L2 pragmatics in interaction using mixed methods.* Unpublished doctoral dissertation at University of Hawai'i at Mānoa.

Youn, S. J., & Brown, J. D. (2013). Item difficulty and heritage language learner status in pragmatic tests for Korean as a foreign language. In S. J. Ross & G. Kasper (Eds.), *Assessing second language pragmatics* (pp. 98-123). London: Palgrave Macmillan.

INDEX

A

achievement tests, 20, 22, 34, 57, 67, 201

agreement coefficient, 139–42

alpha. *See* Cronbach alpha

ANOVA, 29, 284

    and Bonferroni adjustment, 225

    and construct validity, 29

    and effect size, 205

    and generalizability theory, 132

    and multiple statistical tests, 177

    and statistical power, 190

B

B-index, 13, 17

Bonferroni adjustment, 177, 221–27, 288, 296

books related to language testing, 7

C

categorical scales. *See* nominal scales

chi-square (χ^2) statistics, 277–85

chi-square test, 214, 277

clarification, in mixed methods research, 169

cloze tests, 111–15, 127, 231, 234, 264

coefficient of determination, 231–35, 265

Cohen's kappa, 21, 101, 139–47

communality, in factor analysis, 240–44, 248, 272–74

complex variables, 248, 258, 261, 266, 275

computer based testing, 3, 36, 38, 42, 43

confidence intervals, 122, 213–20

confidence level, 217

confidence limits, 217

confirmability, in qualitative research, 159

consistency, 15, 21, 29, 107–9, 127, 149–53, 158

construct validity, 27–31, 275

contextual conditions, in pragmatics testing, 38, 42

contingency tables, 277–85

continuous scales. *See* interval scales

convergence, in mixed methods research, 169

correlation, 231–32

    and Likert scales, 101

    and reliability, 104, 107, 128, 151, 162, 174

    and standard error of estimate, 121, 215, 219

    and validity, 27, 29

    assumptions of, 173–79, 201, 203

    item-total, 94

    standard error of, 197

correlation coefficients, 39, 231–35, 75–81, 174–77, 284
    and factor analysis, 238, 240, 265
    point-biserial, 66, 75–81
    Spearman rank-order, 76, 231
credibility, in qualitative research, 158
criterion-referenced tests, 13, 19–25, 91
    and Cronbach alpha, 109
    and dependability, 134, 150
    and generalizability theory, 40, 137
    and skewed distributions, 201
    and washback, 57
    item analysis of, 69–71
Cronbach alpha, 107–9, 111, 120, 162, 215, 274
    and Likert Scales, 101, 104
    and norm-referenced tests, 23
    and questionnaires, 149–52
    and Spearman-Brown prophecy formula, 125–26

D

decisions
    affecting test design, 132, 133, 136
    consequences for students, 13–16, 24, 109, 122, 150, 203
    generalizability and decision studies, 131–37
dependability, 23
    in G Theory, 133, 136
    in qualitative research, 158
difference index, 13–17, 91, 94
discourse completion tasks (DCT), 37
discourse role-play tasks (DRPT), 37
discourse-completion tasks (DCT), 265
discourse-role-play tasks (DCT), 265
distractor analysis, 83–89
distributions, 173–79
    and factor analysis, 265
    and statistical power, 191
    of scores, 266
    of test scores, 20
    skewed and peaked, 199–201
divergence, in mixed methods research, 169

E

effect size, 205–11, 218, 220
eigenvalues, 241, 247–50
eigenvectors, 241, 255, 258
elaboration, in mixed methods research, 169
entrance examinations, xiii, 55–59
equivalent forms reliability, 108, 150, 151
eta^2 (η^2), 205–11
exemplification, in mixed methods research, 169
extraneous variables, 49–53
    environment issues, 49

grouping issues, 49
measurement issues, 50
people issues, 50

F

FACETS. *See* Rasch analysis
factor analysis, 29, 101, 174, 237–44
    choosing which type of rotation, 237–44
    identifying the number of factors, 245–54
Fisher exact test, 284–85
formulaic implicatures. *See* implicature
F-ratio, 214

G

gain scores, 13, 45
generalizability, 164
Generalizability theory (G theory), 39, 129, 131–37

H

halo effect, 49, 50, 163
Hawthorne effect, 49, 50, 163

I

implicature, 38–43
imposition, in pragmatics testing, 38
interaction, in mixed methods research, 170
intercoder agreement, 158, 162
intercultural pragmatics, testing of, 38–43, 131, 265

internal consistency. *See* consistency
interrater agreement, 158, 162
interval (continuous) scales, 75–76, 97, 99–104, 173
item analysis, 13, 21, 81
    criterion-referenced, 69–71
    distractor analysis, 83–89
    item discrimination, 63–67
    norm-referenced, 63–67
    with PCA and EFA, 275
    with weighted items, 91–94
item discrimination, 22, 70, 79, 91, 93
item facility, 22, 63–67, 79, 83, 91
item writing. *See* test development

J

journals related to educational measurement, 5
journals related to language testing, 4

K

Kaiser's stopping rule, 246–47, 252, 254
kappa. *See* Cohen's kappa
K-R20, 23, 108, 115, 131, 152, 162, 215
K-R21, 15, 17, 23, 107, 108, 131, 152
Kuder-Richardson formulas. *See* K-R20 and K-R21
kurtosis, 202–3

L

legitimation, in mixed methods research, 167

Likert scales, 95–98, 99–104
    and principle component analysis, 238
    deciding scale type, 96
    odd versus even number of options, 96
    reliability of, 152, 153, 162

M

Mantel Haenszel Chi-square, 283

Messick, theory of validity, 30, 48, 50

mixed methods research, sound practice of, 167–70

motivation, 239
    for studying Korean, 238
    of test takers, 45–48

N

$N-1$ chi-square test, 285

nominal (categorical) scales, 75, 79, 99

normal distribution, 117, 122, 202

norm-referenced statistics (for questionnaires), 149

norm-referenced tests, 9, 14, 19–25, 34, 63–67, 80, 83, 87, 91
    and Cronbach alpha, 108
    and dependability coefficients, 134

O

open-ended items, 10, 57, 238

ordinal (rank-ordered) scales, 76, 97, 99–104, 173

organizations related to language testing, 6

P

Partial eta^2 ($\eta^2_{partial}$), 209

Pearson product-moment correlation, 75, 128, 197, 231, 284

phi-square statistic (ϕ^2), 280, 285

placement tests, 4, 33–36, 45–48, 66, 114, 203

power difference, in pragmatics testing, 38

power, statistical, 189–93, 195, 205, 206, 211, 264

pragmatics. *See* intercultural pragmatics

pretest-posttest (designs, analyses, and issues), 13, 28, 45–47, 50, 70, 91, 178, 190, 224

principle component analysis (PCA). *See* factor analysis

proficiency tests, 33–36, 66

Q

qualitative research, sound practice of, 157–60

quantitative research, sound practice of, 161–65

questionnaires, 95–98, 99–104
    and extraneous variables, 50
    and factor analysis, 269–76

reliability of, 149–53, 162

R

Rasch analysis, 39
    and Likert scales, 102
    FACETS, 39, 41, 43
ratio (continuous) scales, 99–104, 173
reliability, 107–9, *see also* consistency
    and G Theory, 131
    and statistical power, 190
    in quantitative research, 162
    of cloze tests, 111–15
    of surveys, 149–53
    of test scores, 14
replicability, 163
rotation, in factor analysis, 255–62
    oblimin rotation, 256
    orthogonal vs. oblique rotation, 256
    promax rotation, 256, 261
    varimax rotation, 237, 239, 242, 248, 255, 263, 269

S

scales of measurement, 96, 99–104
scree test, 249–50
skewed distributions, 20, 109, 112, 151, 175, 200, 201
skewness, 199–201, 220
social distance, in pragmatics testing, 38

Spearman-Brown prophecy formula, 125–30, 152
speech acts, 37–41, 49, 133, 135
standard deviation, 15, 97, 117–19, 195, 199
    and Likert scales, 101, 104
    and reliability of cloze tests, 112
standard error of estimate (*see*), 120–22, 214, 218
standard error of measurement (*SEM*), 109, 119–20, 214, 215, 218
standard error of the mean (SE_M), 117–19, 196, 218
standard errors, 213
standardized scores, 20, 33, 34, 36
standardized tests, xiv, 9, 20
statistical power. *See* power
surveys. *See* questionnaires

T

test development, 9–16
test-retest reliability, 23, 107, 108, 150, 151, 162
transferability, in mixed methods research, 168
transferability, in qualitative research, 160
transferability, in quantitative research, 165, 184
t-tests, 175, 178, 214, 284
    and precision, 197
    and skewness, 201

Index   321

and the null hypothesis, 187

problems of multiple *t*-tests, 221–27

two-stage testing, 33–36

V

validation of tests, 13–16, 19–24

validity, 23, 27, 163

    concurrent, 28

    consequential, 48

    construct, 28

    content, 27

    convergent, 270, 275

    criterion-related, 27

    discriminant, 270, 275

    predictive, 28

    threats to, 29

variance

    analysis of variance. *See* ANOVA

    and effect size, 205–11

    cumulative variance, 252

    proportion of common, unique, etc., 240–44, 271–75

    true score variance, 108, 213

    variance components in G Theory, 39, 131–36

W

washback, 49–53, 55–59

websites related to language testing, 3

weighted items, 91–94

Y

Yates' correction, 284–85

---------------------------- **Notes** ----------------------------

Made in the USA
San Bernardino, CA
13 September 2017